RUSSIAN SECURITY AND AIR POWER
1992–2002

CASS SERIES ON SOVIET (RUSSIAN) MILITARY THEORY AND PRACTICE
Series editor: David M. Glantz
ISSN 1462–0936

This series examines in detail the evolution of Soviet (Russian) military science and studies the Soviet method of converting theory into military practice. Separate volumes focus on how successful the Soviets were in applying their theories in combat and on how they structured their forces to suit the requirements of changing times.

1. SOVIET MILITARY DECEPTION IN THE SECOND WORLD WAR
David M. Glantz
(ISBN 07146 3347 X cloth, 0 7146 4063 8 paper)

2. SOVIET MILITARY OPERATIONAL ART: IN PURSUIT OF DEEP BATTLE
David M. Glantz
(ISBN 0 7146 3362 3 cloth, 0 7146 4077 8 paper)

3. SOVIET MILITARY INTELLIGENCE IN WAR
David M. Glantz
(ISBN 0 7146 3374 7 cloth, 0 7146 4076 X paper)

4. THE SOVIET CONDUCT OF TACTICAL MANEUVER
Spearhead of the offensive
David M. Glantz
(ISBN 0 7146 3373 9 cloth, 0 7146 4079 4 paper)

5. THE MILITARY STRATEGY OF THE SOVIET UNION
A history
David M. Glantz
(ISBN 0 7146 3435 2 cloth)

6. THE HISTORY OF SOVIET AIRBORNE FORCES
David M. Glantz
(0 7146 3483 2 cloth, 0 7146 4120 0 paper)

CASS SERIES ON SOVIET (RUSSIAN) MILITARY EXPERIENCE
Series editor: David M. Glantz
ISSN 1462–0944

This series focuses on Soviet military experiences in specific campaigns or operations.

5. RACE FOR THE REICHSTAG
The 1945 battle for Berlin
Tony Le Tissier,
(ISBN 0 7146 4929 5 cloth, 0 7146 4489 7 paper)

6. RUSSO-CHECHEN CONFLICT, 1800–2000
A deadly embrace
Robert Seely
(ISBN 0 7146 4992 9 cloth, 0 7146 8060 5 paper)

RUSSIAN SECURITY AND AIR POWER 1992–2002

The development of Russian security thinking
under Yeltsin and Putin and its consequences for
the air forces

Marcel de Haas

FRANK CASS

LONDON • NEW YORK

First published 2004
by Frank Cass
2 Park Square, Milton Park, Abingdon,
Oxon, OX14 4RN

Simultaneously published in the USA and Canada
by Frank Cass
29 West 35th Street, New York, NY 10001

Frank Cass is an imprint of the Taylor & Francis Group

© 2004 Marcel de Haas

Typeset in Times New Roman by
Newgen Imaging Systems (P) Ltd, Chennai, India
Printed and bound in Great Britain by
Antony Rowe Ltd, Chippenham, Wiltshire

British Library Cataloguing in Publication Data
A catalogue record for this book is available
from the British Library

Library of Congress Cataloging in Publication Data
A catalog record for this book has been requested

ISBN 0–714–65608–9

CONTENTS

CONTENTS

FIGURES

TABLES

SERIES EDITOR'S PREFACE

During the more than 10 years that have passed since the collapse of the Soviet Union and the emergence of the modern Russian Federation during 1991, Western strategists have tended to diminish the potential impact on the world stage of the new nascent Russian democracy in comparison with the superpower stature of its Soviet predecessor. While the Russian Federation's physical territorial limits, as well as its political and economic potential, are certainly far less than those of the Soviet Union, these analysts often overlook the fact that the new Russian state still spans much of the Eurasian land mass and its southern and eastern borders are adjacent to a vast zone of potential instability, which stretches from the Caucasus region across central Asia to the western shores of the Pacific's tributary oceans in the Far East. Its territorial expanse aside, the Russian Federation's geographical location alone places it in contact with some of the most divisive and threatening forces in the world, ranging from the expansionist power of Islamic fundamentalism through the nationalistic demands of peoples subject to crumbling former empires to uncertainties associated with the evolving colossus of China and the unreformed and irrational Stalinist North Korea.

Along with many others, these factors alone should impel the would-be strategists and 'geo-politicians' alike to ponder the future stance and stature of the Russian Federation, militarily as well as politically and economically. Those who do so, however, often note the decline of Russia's military prowess, but without being able to clearly describe either the present state of Russia's military institutions, how they may evolve in the future, or why.

Fortunately, Marcel de Haas' new book helps lift this veil of obscurity shrouding military developments in the Russian Federation; in this case, by examining in detail the evolution of Russian air power. Within the context of evolving Russian security policies, in itself a major contribution, De Haas describes how and why the Russian air force has changed during the 10 years since 1992. In addition to surveying the Russian Federation's official structures and procedures for formulating and implementing national security policy, he also examines how and why that policy has evolved and the military doctrine the Federation has adopted to implement it. He then covers the changing nature of the Russian air force, including the operations it conducted during the first and second Chechen wars and other border conflicts, and ends with an assessment of the role the air force will play in the Russian military establishment in the future. Superbly documented, this detailed analysis is likely to remain the standard work on the subject for years to come, as well as a yardstick by which to measure those changes, if any, made by President Putin as he attempts to increase the Federation's stability, capabilities and, by extension, its prestige as a major actor on the international stage.

David M. Glantz
Carlisle, Pennsylvania

PREFACE

In almost every book a word of appreciation is found for the relatives of the author. This is rightly so. Carrying out book research is a lonely business. Family members play a key role. They provide support for the job and grant you the freedom to fulfil the assignment. Furthermore they act as a 'distraction', making you realize that daily life goes on. Therefore I would like to express my heartfelt gratitude to my wife Edith and my children Martijn and Esther.

I would also like to thank my PhD supervisors, Professor Dr G. Teitler and Dr A.W.M. Gerrits, of the University of Amsterdam, for their support and encouragement for this research project. With Professor Teitler, who in addition to his appointment at Amsterdam also has professorships in Military History and Strategic Studies at the Royal Naval College and at the Royal Netherlands Military Academy (RNLMA), I had the honour to share an office at the military academy as his assistant for lectures on international relations and military strategy. I have benefited a great deal from his insights in these two academic disciplines. The fact that the levels of strategy form the thread of this book is proof of the knowledge which I gained from his lectures and remarks on my thesis.

I also wish to thank Professor Dr W.B. Simons, Director of the Institute of East European Law and Russian Studies at Leiden University. I got to know Professor Simons as an accurate reviewer, who, as a legal expert, compensated for the absence of a military background with sharp-witted remarks, especially on verifying statements and deepening of my thoughts. There are two other former associates of the Institute of East European Law and Russian Studies to whom I am indebted. In the 1980s, Professor Dr F.J.M. Feldbrugge, as predecessor of Professor Simons, introduced me to Soviet law and politics. His lectures encouraged me to write on this subject. The late Dr G.P. van den Berg, who also lectured in Soviet law when I was a student, was known for his unfailing knowledge of legal sources of the USSR and the Russian Federation. During my research he was often kind enough to help me find sources that I was not able to discover.

I also owe a word of acknowledgement to the RNLMA and the Royal Netherlands Air Force (RNLAF), which have afforded me the opportunity of carrying out this research. During the seven years of my posting as lecturer in international relations and international law at RNLMA I published some 40 articles, was interviewed by various mass media agencies and acted as guest speaker for military, political, academic and civic organizations in the Netherlands and abroad. With these activities and the completion of this book I hope to have made a contribution to the academic status of the RNLMA.

At the start of my research I could not have presumed that developments in the international arena would increase the topicality of my subject. In the wake of the war of the United States against terrorism the government of the Netherlands dispatched a number of RNLAF units to the airbase of Manas in Kyrgyzstan, a former Soviet republic and member state of the Commonwealth of Independent States. This connected my research, the employment of air power by the RNLAF and the implementation of Dutch foreign and security policy.

I am most grateful to the Conflict Studies Research Centre (CSRC) of the Defence Academy of the United Kingdom. I visited CSRC in September 2000, March 2001 and December 2002. My colleagues at CSRC have been a tremendous support to me, scientifically as well as socially. The greater part of Russian sources I used for this work were provided by CSRC. Although I have appreciated the kind contact with every member of CSRC, I would like to mention a couple of people especially. At the start of my research, Charles Dick, Director of CSRC, was so kind as to discuss my work with me. Later he introduced me to the *Journal of Slavic Military Studies*, which published my first article abroad. Librarian Pam Bendall has done the bulk of the work for me. Since my first visit, she has provided me with a large amount of the sources requested, which was so huge that it did not fit into my luggage. Pam has continued to give a positive response to my numerous additional (electronic) requests for sources. Sometimes she even presented sources I had not thought of. Anne Hull has been so kind as to copy the sources I wanted to take home. But apart from 'functional' support, she has always been a valuable social contact, on topics such as vacations, royalty or any other subject. She truly is a great ambassador of CSRC. As one of the 'permanent residents' in the premises of CSRC, Dr Steven Main has been pleasant company during my stays at CSRC. Exchanging views with Steven on Russian security developments has been very worthwhile for me both in further exploring and establishing the contents of my work. A number of good ideas, which have arisen from these conversations, are now incorporated here. I am also thankful to him for introducing me as a contributor to *Russian Military Reform 1992–2002*, published by Frank Cass in 2003. Last, but surely not least, is Anne Aldis. During my visits Anne was so kind as to offer me the use of her office, which I greatly appreciated. I value her support in promoting the results of my research, such as in her capacity as co-editor of the Russian military reform book cited above, and by publishing a part of my research as a CSRC paper. Once again, thanks a lot to all members of CSRC for their support and valued relationships.

ACKNOWLEDGEMENTS

Sponsoring

This is an abridged version of a PhD thesis in Dutch, which was sponsored by the Royal Netherlands Air Force and the Royal Netherlands Military Academy.

Cover

Jacket illustration: Colonel-General Anatoly Kornukov, Commander-in-Chief of the Russian Air Forces VVS and Prime Minister Vladimir Putin, during a visit to the Chechen battlefield, November 1999.

Source: Russian Ministry of Defence newspaper *Krasnaya Zvezda*, no. 234 (23015), 3 November 1999, p. 1.

Maps

Map 1: Military Districts of the Russian Federation (1997).

Source: Adapted from the map 'Russian Military Districts and Naval Bases', in V. Baranovsky, SIPRI, *Russia and Europe: The Emerging Security Agenda* (Oxford University Press: Oxford, 1997), p. 162.

Map 2: Russian routes of attack at the beginning of the first Chechen war (1994–96).

Source: www.amina.com/maps/maprus.gif

ABBREVIATIONS

ASV   *Aviatsiya Suchoputnych Voysk* or *Armeyskaya Aviatsiya*. Army aviation
ATG   *Aviatsionnaya Takticheskaya Gruppa*. Tactical formation of
          rotary wing
AWACS   Airborne Warning And Control System
C-   Commander of a military formation or institution
CAP   Combat Air Patrol
CAS   Close Air Support. Air support for ground operations
CFE   Treaty on Conventional Forces in Europe (1990); revised in 1999
          Arms control treaty, which determines the levels of specified
          conventional arms (of ground and air forces) for each member state
CGS   Chief of the General Staff
CIS   Commonwealth of Independent States
CPSU   Communist Party of the USSR
EU   European Union
EW   Electronic warfare
FAC   Forward Air Controller or *avianavodchik*. Forms the link between
          ground and air component
FAPSI   *Federal'noye Agentstvo Pravitel'stvennoy Svyazi i Informatsiyi*
          Federal service for governmental communications. Organizes and
          secures communication among the highest organs of government
          RF signal intelligence service
FSB   *Federal'naya Sluzhba Bezopasnosti*. Federal Security Service.
          Internal security service of the RF
FSK   *Federal'naya Sluzhba Kontrrazvedki*. Predecessor of the FSB
GRU   *Glavnoye Razvedyvatel'noye Upravleniye*
          Military intelligence service of the General Staff
GS   General Staff of the Armed Forces (MoD)
GSA   General Staff Academy
GSh   *General'nyy Shtab*. General Staff of the Armed Forces (MoD)
IMEMO   Institute of the RAS for universal economy and international
          relations

ISK[R]AN	Institute of the RAS for research on the United States and Canada (ISKAN as name for the Soviet institute and ISKRAN for the RF institute)
KGB	*Komitet Gosudarstvennoy Bezopasnosti* Committee for State Security; Security Service of the USSR
LEMD	Military District Leningrad
MD	Military District
MID	*Ministerstvo Inostrannykh Del*. Ministry of Foreign Affairs
MIC	military–industrial complex
Minoborony	Ministry of Defence
MoD	Ministry of Defence
MOMD	Military District Moscow
MVD	*Ministerstvo Vnutrennykh Del*. Ministry of Internal Affairs
NATO	North Atlantic Treaty Organization
NCMD	North Caucasus Military District
NSC	National Security Concept. Political or grand strategy of the RF
OSCE	Organization for Security and Cooperation in Europe
PfP	Partnership for Peace. Bilateral cooperation between NATO and an individual partner state
PGMs	Precision-guided munitions
RAS	Russian Academy of Sciences
RF	Russian Federation
RSFSR	Russian Soviet Federative Socialist Republic
RVSN	*Raketnyye Voyska Strategicheskogo Naznacheniya*. Strategic Missile Forces
SCRF	Security Council of the Russian Federation. Highest state organ for internal and external security affairs
Spetsnaz	*Spetsal'nogo naznacheniya (voyska ~)*. Military units with a special destination; special forces
SU	Soviet Union
SV	*Suchoputnyye Voyska*. Ground Forces
SVOP	*Sovet po Vneshney i Oboronnoy Politiki* or Council on Foreign and Defence Policy. Russian political lobby organization for foreign and security affairs, formed in February 1992
SVR	*Sluzba Vneshney Razvedki*. Foreign Intelligence Service of the RF
TsVSI	*Tsentr Voyenno-Strategicheskich Issledovaniy General'nogo Shtaba*. Centre of the GS for military-strategic research. Contributes to drafting of NSC and military doctrine
UN	United Nations
UNSC	United Nations Security Council
USSR	Union of Soviet Socialist Republics

VMF	*Voyenno-Morskoy Flot*. Naval Forces
VPVO	*Voyska Protivovozdushnoy Oborony*. Air Defence Forces. In 1998 amalgamated with the Air Forces (VVS)
VVS	*Voyenno-Vozdushnyye Sily*. Air Forces

NOTE ON DESIGNATION OF RANKS OF GENERAL OFFICERS AND STRENGTH OF RUSSIAN MILITARY FORMATIONS

Russian rank	*Similar rank in Western armed forces*
Major-General	Brigadier-General
Lieutenant-General	Major-General
Colonel-General	Lieutenant-General
Army General	General

(a) Operational level (Ob''yedineniye)

Front/Army group	>850 aircraft	Front ground forces	>75,000 personnel
Air army	280–410 aircraft	Army ground forces	>35,000 personnel

(b) Tactical level (Soyedineniye, chast', podrazdeleniye)

Air division	90–120 aircraft	Division (infantry) ground forces	13,000 personnel
Not applicable	—	Brigade	3,500 personnel
Air regiment	36–54 aircraft	Regiment	2,500 personnel
Squadron	12–18 aircraft	Battalion	500 personnel
Flight	3–4 aircraft	Company	115 personnel

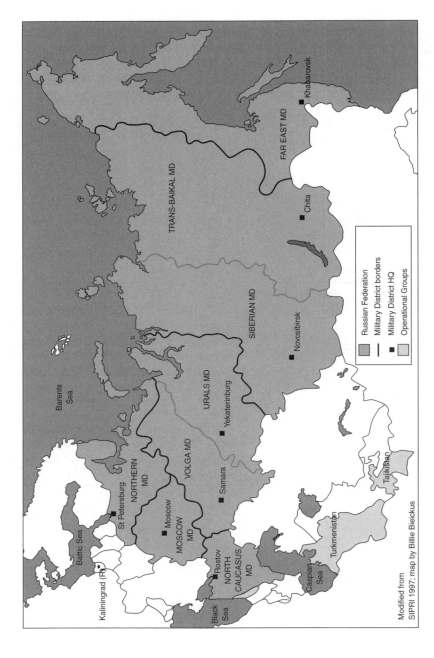

Map 1 Military Districts of the Russian Federation (1997).

	Russian Federation
	Military District borders
	Military District HQ
	Operational Groups

Modified from
SIPRI 1997; map by Billie Bieickus

Barents
Sea

Baltic Sea

Kaliningrad (R)

St Petersburg

NORTHERN
MD

Moscow

MOSCOW
MD

Rostov

NORTH
CAUCASUS
MD

Black
Sea

VOLGA MD

Samara

URALS MD

Yekaterinburg

Caspian
Sea

Turkmenistan

Tajikistan

SIBERIAN MD

Novosibirsk

TRANS-BAIKAL MD

Chita

FAR EAST MD

Khabarovsk

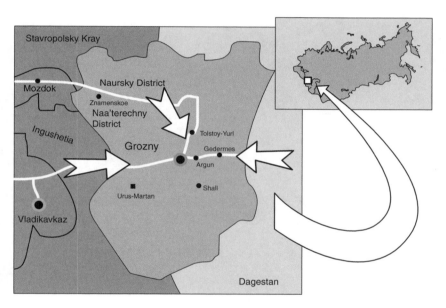

Map 2 Russian attack axes at the beginning of the first Chechen war (1994–96).

INTRODUCTION

In December 1991, with the dissolution of the Soviet Union, the Russian Federation (RF) became its successor state.[1] The establishment of the Russian state was attended by huge political and military changes internally as well as externally. The Soviet configuration of distribution of power among party, security service and army was replaced by an indistinct make-up of institutions, eager to achieve influence. The armed forces were one of these contenders. Externally enormous geostrategic changes had occurred. The buffer zone of the Warsaw Pact in eastern Europe was annulled and the territory of the former USSR was now divided over the member states of the Commonwealth of Independent States (CIS) and over the Baltic States. These developments entailed serious consequences for the order of battle of Russia's Armed Forces. The fact that a number of CIS states disagreed with Russia's intention of forming RF-led CIS forces necessitated the formation of an RF Armed Forces and a Ministry of Defence (MoD). Next, the RF needed to formulate a security policy.

Value of this research

This book focuses on the development of Russian security thinking and its consequences for the air forces from 1992 to 2002. The value of this work is meant to be twofold: a contribution to Western thinking on military doctrine and a furtherance of research on security thinking in the USSR and the RF. US and British military documents tend to be the main sources for the larger part of Western armed forces. However, concentrating attention on the doctrines of these two states means the focus may become too narrow. Therefore, it seems to be a good idea to weigh Western thinking against doctrinal thought from other regions. Russian doctrinal development is qualified to serve such a purpose. In the 1990s, the RF was involved in several armed conflicts in the CIS and has twice fought a conflict in Chechnya. The importance of the contribution of Russian air forces increased during this decade, quantitatively as well as qualitatively, especially when the two conflicts in Chechnya are compared. Thus, the Russian experiences, for instance in conducting irregular warfare, can be useful for the further development of Western doctrinal thought.

1

The value of this work comes to the fore also with regard to scientific research. In the Netherlands P.M.E. Volten and G. Snel have carried out research on developments in security policy in the Soviet Union, in the 1970s and the 1980s respectively.[2] Reviewing Snel's thesis Volten suggested that similar research on Russia's security policy in the 1990s should be performed.[3] To a certain extent my dissertation, on which this book is based, can be regarded as such. However, there is an important difference in the direction of my research compared to that of Volten and Snel. Their emphasis is first on the political decision-making process and, second, on the role of the military in its implementation. The accent in my book tends to be the other way round; it gives prominence to the contribution of the military leadership in the drafting of security policy as well as in implementing it. In the portrayal of the development of Russia's security policy in the 1990s, this book covers an area from the highest political level of decision-making to the lowest level of military action at which this is put into practice. With this objective the levels of strategy are chosen as the thread. Hence, in addition to military–political security policy this thesis will stress military policy at the various levels. Within military policy, air power will be the central point of focus. The ultimate aim is to assess the effect of political-strategic decision-making on the use of air power in irregular warfare. Consequently, this work on Russian security policy can be considered as the consistent continuation of the works of Volten and Snel, in which in my research preference is given to military aspects and the use of air power in particular.

National security policy

The fact that a state lays down the safeguarding of its continuation in a national security policy is a broadly accepted principle. The objective of this policy is to ensure independence, sovereignty, territorial integrity, welfare and stability by taking political, economic, socio-cultural and military measures. Each state has specific interests. The use of armed forces is especially determined by the perception of to which degree these interests are threatened. The conversion of interests into objectives takes place at the highest decision-making level, the political or grand strategy.

Another way of explaining this political strategy is from the perspective of security. Looked at from this point of view, the national security policy encompasses all activities regarding internal and external security. In this case, grand strategy is the product of the opinion of the state concerning the optimal guarantee of its security. Taking into account the anarchistic nature of the international environment the state is confronted with a diverse and considerable set of threats. The aim of grand strategy is to identify these threats and to generate options in repelling them. Because of the fact that the means of the state are scarce, the political strategy is tasked to prioritize threats and their neutralization. As a consequence of limited resources, the military instrument, as one of the security mechanisms of the state, should be employed in the most efficient way in order to meet the objectives of the grand strategy.[4] This is of course a theoretical point of view. Consequently, states may follow a different course. For example, in the case of the Soviet Union, the military apparatus enjoyed a priority status. Hence, the allocation of means was disproportional in favour of the military instrument of the state. In that situation it was doubtful if the military leadership used its resources as efficiently as possible.

The conversion of interests into objectives can be portrayed with the model of the levels of strategy. This model consists of five levels, which influence one another, and the dividing lines of which are not completely determined. At the top level, the conversion of interests is described as the aforementioned political or *grand strategy*. This is the level of the national government, at which economic, diplomatic, psychological, military and other political processes are generated in a coordinated and synchronized way. One level down, *military strategy* is found, at which military authorities, such as a chief of defence staff or commanders-in-chief of the armed forces employ the military means to meet the political-strategic objectives of the state. These authorities command and control military operations from outside the theatre; at this level, which forms an integral component of political strategy, the military doctrine is found. The doctrine provides the guidelines for the use of military power. The next echelon down is the level of *operations*. At this level, armed forces and troops conduct joint military action to fulfil a military-strategic objective in a specific theatre of crisis or conflict. The operational commander has his headquarters within this theatre. This level connects strategy with tactics. At the level of *tactics* military units perform actions to realize an operational objective. The lowest stage of warfare is the *technical level*, which contains actions of small units, sometimes even single servicemen or weapon systems, with the purpose of achieving a tactical objective.[5]

Russian security policy

Levels of strategy

This work analyses Russian security policy in the 1990s along the model of levels of strategy. In the Russian situation at the grand strategy level policy is written down in the National Security Concept (NSC). On the level of military strategy, the Chief of the General Staff and the commanders of forces and troops implement political objectives by using military power. The remaining three levels of strategy will describe air power exclusively. In this book the Chechen conflict is taken as a case study for the operational level. An example at the tactical level in this conflict is the neutralization of the complete Chechen air force by a formation of *Frogfoot* ground attack aircraft on 1 December 1994. A pair of *Hind* combat helicopters conducting a 'free hunt' mission over Chechnya can be regarded as an example of the technical level.[6]

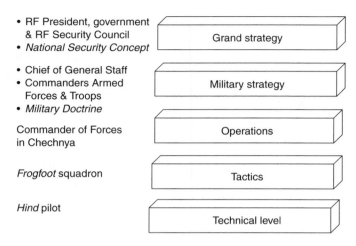

• RF President, government
& RF Security Council
• *National Security Concept*

Grand strategy

• Chief of General Staff
• Commanders Armed
Forces & Troops
• *Military Doctrine*

Military strategy

Commander of Forces
in Chechnya

Operations

Frogfoot squadron

Tactics

Hind pilot

Technical level

Figure I.1 The levels of strategy applied to Russian security policy.

Military conceptual thinking

Russian thought on national security policy corresponds with the aforementioned broadly accepted paradigm. Russia's grand strategy, the NSC, explains that the RF has military, diplomatic, international law, information, economic and other means at its disposal to meet its objectives. The NSC sets out Russia's interests and states measures to be taken against threats which prevent it from meeting its objectives. From the NSC, as the principal security document, doctrines and concepts are drawn. The most important documents for clarifying Russia's security policy are the *Military Doctrine* and the Foreign Policy Concept. At the doctrinal level, security policy is converted into the use of military power. Here the Russian and the common paradigm show a difference. Russian doctrine is more abstract and has more politics in it than other doctrines, which usually concentrate on guidelines for military action. As a result, Russia's doctrine is closely associated with the political-strategic level and therefore rises above the next echelon, military art. *Military art* comprises the preparation and implementation of military action on land, sea, in the air and in space. *Military strategy* comprises the preparation, planning and implementation for war. In other countries military doctrine is generally portrayed at this level. In Russian conceptual thinking *operative art* entails coordinated military operations of various forces and troops of the size of armies and larger. Finally, *tactics* involve military actions from the lowest unit level up to army corps.[7]

4

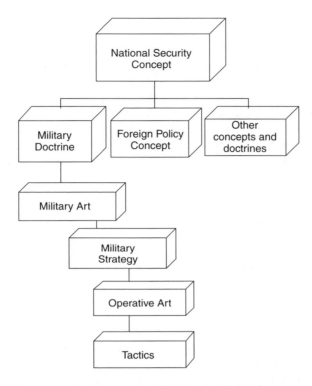

Figure I.2 Military conceptual framework of the Russian Federation.

Research set-up

Objective and ordering principles

The objective of this research on the development of Russia's security policy is: to acquire insight into the development of Russian security policy; subsequently, to determine the realization and the contents of RF security policy; and, finally, to analyse the effects of security policy on the use of air power, especially in irregular conflicts. In this book, these objectives are organized into four ordering principles: (1) What was the thought process of the Russian political–military leadership in formulating a security policy and establishing armed forces? (2) Was the Russian security policy characterized by a structural development or by opportunistic decisions? (3) What were the consequences of the security policy for the build-up, tasks and status of the air forces? (4) What was the interaction between doctrinal thought and experience of the use of air power in and around Chechnya?

Structure

This book is divided into two parts. The first part comprises Russia's national security policy. The second part depicts the consequences of this security policy for air power. This work is ordered in an alternation of descriptive and analytic chapters. Chapter 1, 'Structure of security policy' is descriptive and is intended to explain the institutions and individuals involved in making security policy. Chapter 2 on 'Implementation of security policy' provides an analytic approach to the decision-making process on security policy as well as on the development and contents of the leading security documents. Chapter 3 on 'Structure of air power' is again descriptive, clarifying the development, organization and status of Russia's military aviation as well as the thought processes involved in using air power. In chapter 4, 'Implementation of air power', using an analytical method, the practice of employing air power is elaborated, and the conflicts in Chechnya are utilized as a case study. The concluding chapter, Chapter 5, employs a combination of descriptive and analytical methods, presents answers to the above-mentioned basic questions and also discusses the validity of this work. Furthermore, this final part provides a description of recent developments in international and Russian security and also offers an outlook on the future development of RF security policy.

Methodology

The research was based exclusively upon analysis of the literature. I made use of predominantly Russian sources, official as well as independent ones. I have applied three methods of research: Analysis of the development of and relationship amongst security actors (institutions as well as individuals); textual comparison of the three leading security documents (NSC, Military Doctrine and Foreign Policy Concept), thematically as well as chronologically; case study: the conflicts in and around Chechnya.

Demarcation

The research was delimited in the following ways. Although obviously this work began with the foundation of the RF in 1992, developments in the USSR were looked at, since Russia's security cannot be analysed properly without incorporating its Soviet heritage. The greater part finishes in 2000, when a solid and comprehensive structure of security documents was completed. As security policy did not stop in this year (inter-)national developments since then have also been included. The rather broad scope of the subject was narrowed down mostly by excluding internal political and economic factors as well as developments within the CIS. Furthermore, the work concentrated on security actors, the leading security documents and the practice of air power. Regarding the latter, the fact that the RF in the 1990s was confronted increasingly with internal, irregular warfare allowed me to concentrate the analysis on conventional forces, since nuclear

Table I.1 Developments in Russian and in the international arena, 1991–2002

Developments in the Russian Federation	*International developments*
1991	
December	*July*
Annulment of the USSR; Formation of CIS and RF	Disbandment of the Warsaw Pact Treaty Organization
1992	
February	*January*
Proposal for a CIS Military Doctrine	Formation of a unified CIS Command of Armed Forces
May	Tensions between the RF in Ukraine in the Crimea, Black Sea Fleet and nuclear arms
Formation of SCRF and RF Armed Forces *Draft* Military Doctrine RF 1992	
	May
	CIS Collective Security Treaty signed
1993	
April	*June*
Foreign Policy Concept 1993	Unified CIS Command of Armed Forces cancelled
October	
Military action against the Supreme Soviet	*September*
	Withdrawal of RF forces from Poland completed
November	
Military Doctrine 1993	*December*
	NATO introduces Partnership for Peace
1994	
December	*February*
Start of first Chechen conflict	Yeltsin objects against intention to enlarging NATO
1995	
RF confrontation with the West: statements against NATO action in Bosnia, NATO expansion and international interference regarding Chechnya	*August*
	NATO conducts an air and artillery offensive against the Bosnian Serbs
	December
	Dayton Peace Agreement and deployment of IFOR peacekeeping force
1996	
August	*March*
End of first Chechen conflict	Formation of the GUAM grouping within the CIS
1997	
December	*May/July*
National Security Concept 1997	Founding Act signed between NATO and Russia; Poland, Hungary and Czech Republic invited by NATO to join the alliance
1998	
P.M.	P.M.

(Table I.1 continued)

Table I.1 Continued

Developments in the Russian Federation	International developments
1999	
August Vladimir Putin Premier	*March/June* NATO air offensive on Kosovo
September *Draft* Military Doctrine 1999	*April* New Strategic Concept NATO
October Start of second Chechen conflict; *Draft* National Security Concept 1999	*June* NATO deploys KFOR peacekeeping force in Kosovo; RF enforces participation
December Putin wins parliamentary elections Putin succeeds Yeltsin as President	*November* OSCE-Summit: RF agrees with phased withdrawal of forces from Moldova and Georgia *December* Union Treaty between RF and Belarus
2000 *January* National Security Concept 2000	*January* CIS Anti-Terror Centre formed
March Putin elected as President	*October* CIS-Summit calls for formation of a collective rapid deployment force against aggression and terrorism
April Military Doctrine 2000	
June Foreign Policy Concept 2000	
2001 *Autumn* Wide-spread opposition in the RF military and political security establishment against Western 'invasion' in the CIS and Putin's endorsement of this military action in Russia's backyard	*Autumn* US-led coalition forces enter Afghanistan and set up bases in Central Asian CIS states to fight international terrorism *December* US unilaterally cancels ABM Treaty and continues its National Missile Defence program
2002 *October* RF threatens to invade Georgia's Pankisi Valley for alleged presence of Chechen terrorists; 'Nord-Ost' hostage-taking in Moscow by Chechen fighters	*February* Georgia accepts US military support and shows an interest in joining NATO *May* Cooperation between NATO and Russia revised and deepened

forces were not applicable. The next restriction is the focus on air power, mainly excluding the remaining services of the RF Armed Forces (MoD) as well as the Other Troops of the so-called 'power ministries'. The consequences of RF security policy for the most part have been similar for all forces and troops. To avoid duplication, I have decided to concentrate therefore on the analysis of development, reforms, combat readiness and employment of air power. With regard to the case study of Chechnya, the following can be said – in the 1990s Russia's main threat became internal, irregular warfare. Western armed forces are also more and more confronted with irregular warfare, for instance in Afghanistan and Iraq. Hence, my choice for the analysis of irregular warfare in Chechnya is justified by the fact that it forms the most important military challenge for Russia's security policy and is a worthwhile military experience for Western doctrinal thinking.

Notes

1 *Mezhdunarodnoye Pravo, sbornik dokumentov* (Moscow: Yuridicheskaya Literatura, 2000).
2 P.M.E. Volten, *Brezhnev's Peace Program: A Study of Soviet Domestic Political Process and Power* (Boulder, CO: Westview Press, 1982); G. Snel, G. *From the Atlantic to the Urals, the Reorientation of Soviet Military Strategy, 1981–1990* (Amsterdam: VU University Press, 1996).
3 P.M.E. Volten, 'Burgers in het offensief: het debat over het defensief in de militaire strategie van de Sovjet-Unie', *Transaktie*, 26, 1 (1997), p. 146.
4 *KLu Airpower Doctrine* (The Hague: Commander-in-Chief Royal Netherlands Air Force, 1996), pp. I–4 and I–5; B.R. Posen, *The Sources of Military Doctrine – France, Britain, and Germany between the world wars* (Ithaca, NY: Cornell University Press, 1984), p. 13.
5 *KLu Airpower Doctrine*, pp. I–4 and I–5; E.N. Luttwak, *Strategy, the logic of war and peace* (Cambridge, MA, and London: The Belknap Press of Harvard University Press, 1987), pp. 69–71; G. Teitler, J.M.J. Bosch, W. Klinkert, *et al. Militaire Strategie* (Amsterdam: Mets & Schilt, 2002), pp. 28–9; *Militaire Doctrine, LDP-I* (The Hague: Royal Netherlands Army, 1996), pp. 12–15.
6 'Rossiya gotova otstaivat' svoi interesy', *Krasnaya Zvezda*, 27 Dec. 1997, p. 1; Yavorskiy, A. 'Lëtchikam ne dali razvernut'sya', *Nezavisimoye Voyennoye Obozreniye*, 48 (171), 10 Dec. 1999, p. 5.
7 A.F. Klimenko, 'Osobennosti novoy Voyennoy doktriny', *Voyennaya Mysl'*, 5 (May 2000), pp. 24–5; V.L. Manilov, *Voyennaya Bezopasnost' Rossii* (Moscow: Probel, 2000), pp. 165 and 321; V.D. Zabolotin, *Slovar' voyennykh terminov* (Moscow: Kosmo, 2000), pp. 53, 74 and 230.

1

STRUCTURE OF SECURITY POLICY

Institutions, persons and their influence on policy

Introduction

After the break-up of the Soviet Union in December 1991, the Russian Federation (RF) became its legal successor state. Initially the Russian military and political leadership was convinced that the Commonwealth of Independent States (CIS) would develop into an organization similar to that of the former Soviet Union, naturally under Russian supervision. This would allow the CIS to have combined armed forces at its disposal. However it was not long before a number of CIS states decided differently. After creating their own armed forces they subsequently developed independent security policies. In response to this, Russia too formed the RF Armed Forces and a Ministry of Defence (MoD) in spring 1992.

A discussion on the implementation and nature of RF security policy (see Chapter 2), cannot take place without a proper insight into the people and organizations responsible for it. Therefore I will describe the actors involved. In this description of the structure of Russian security policy the expression 'actors' refers to institutions (organizations, organs, bodies) as well as to persons. I will enumerate the primary organs of RF national security: components of the presidential apparatus, the government, as well as a formally independent lobby organization. Following that, prominent individual actors in security policy are listed. Next, as the cornerstone of the implementation of security policy, the build-up of Russia's military power will be discussed: the RF Armed Forces of the MoD and the so-called 'Other Troops' of the power ministries, departments and services which also had military formations at their disposal. I will conclude by discussing the influence of institutions and persons on security policy.

Organs of national security

Western and Russian sources agree that security power in Russia are determined by three centres: the presidential administration, the Security Council of the Russian Federation (SCRF) and the Council of Ministers (government). This division of power was laid down in the RF Law on Security of 1992 (*Zakon Bezopasnosti*).[1] Article 11 of this law states that control over the state organs of

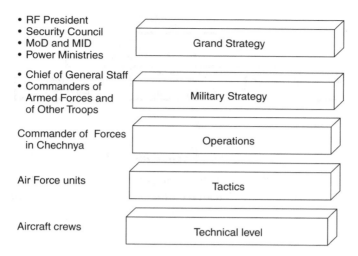

- RF President
- Security Council
- MoD and MID
- Power Ministries

Grand Strategy

- Chief of General Staff
- Commanders of
  Armed Forces and
  of Other Troops

Military Strategy

Commander of Forces
in Chechnya

Operations

Air Force units

Tactics

Aircraft crews

Technical level

Figure 1.1 Position of RF security actors in relation to the levels of strategy.

security was lodged in the President, who is head of the SCRF, and in the government and the corresponding departments and state committees. The analysis of leading security documents, as described in Chapter 2, will testify that a limited number of institutes, belonging to the three above-mentioned centres of power, had a decisive influence on security policy: the President and his apparatus, the SCRF, the MoD and the Ministry of Foreign Affairs. Naturally, this raises the question of the contribution of the government in policy-making, since the listed departments were elements of this centre of power. The presidential apparatus and the SCRF took care of consultation on and formulation of policy matters, whereas the government, just like its predecessor in the Soviet era, in general, was restricted to implementating policy. The Prime Minister and his Council of Ministers were charged mainly with internal and economic affairs. However, the members of the government dealing with foreign and security matters were not responsible to the Prime Minister, but directly to the President. Consequently, the government can not be considered as one of the defining institutions of security policy. In addition to the aforementioned government agencies, the Council on Foreign and Defence Policy, a non-governmental organization, also made a vital contribution to the realization of Russian national security policy.

The power ministries mentioned in Figure 1.2, were of minor importance in formulating security policy but, because of their military assets, they did contribute to the implementation of security policy. Therefore, because of the smaller significance of other institutions on security policy, the description of security organs and their influence on security policy will be limited to the aforementioned five organs: President, SCRF, MoD, Ministry of Foreign Affairs and Council on Foreign and Defence Policy.

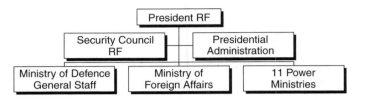

Figure 1.2 RF organs of national security.

The President and his staff

The Constitution of 1993 granted the President far-reaching powers in the field of security. According to the Constitution the powers of the RF President are as follows:

Appointment of high officials

- The RF President appoints the Chairperson of the RF government, makes decisions on dismissal of the RF government, and appoints and removes from office the Deputies of the Chairperson of the RF government and federal ministers (article 83.a, c, e);
- nominates the Security Council of the RF (article 83.g).

Foreign affairs

- The RF President determines the basic directions of the state's foreign policy (article 80.3);
- the RF President exercises guidance over the foreign policy of the RF.

Military affairs

- The President approves the military doctrine of the RF (article 83.h);
- appoints and removes the high command of the RF Armed Forces (article 83.k);
- the RF President is the Supreme Commander in Chief of the RF Armed Forces (article 87.1).

Security policy

- The RF President heads the Security Council of the RF (article 83.g);
- the RF President determines the basic directions of the state's domestic policy (article 80.3);
- in case of aggression against the RF, or a direct threat of aggression, the RF President introduces martial law on the territory of the RF or in individual localities of its territory (article 87.2);

- under the circumstances and in the procedure laid down by a federal constitutional law, the RF President declares a state of emergency on the territory of the RF or in individual localities of its territory (article 88);
- The RF President issues edicts and resolutions, which are mandatory for execution throughout the territory of the RF (articles 90.2). For instance, the three leading security documents, which will be discussed later, were all ratified by presidential decree.

The RF presidential apparatus is comparable to that of the US President. It is the personal staff of the RF President, consisting of a number of departments on different policy areas. This institution not only ensures that presidential decisions are executed, but was involved often also in the policy-making itself, by formulating presidential decrees. In some cases this apparatus even duplicated the activities of federal departments and committees. In 1996, Vladimir Putin joined the presidential administration of Boris Yeltsin. Until 1998, Putin had served in a number of posts in this apparatus, which might have resulted in his nomination for the presidency.

As mentioned earlier, the departmental chiefs of foreign and security policy had to report to the President instead of to the Council of Ministers. All security organs and all 12 departments (MoD and power ministries) with armed formations were under the direct control of the President. Thus, it was not the government, but the President who was in charge of foreign and security policy, as well as of all armed forces and troops.[2] Not long after his appointment as President, Putin started using his extensive powers to intensify central control over the state and over the security organs; for instance, by appointing his 'own people', the former SVR (Foreign Intelligence Service) Generals Sergey Ivanov and Mikhail Dmitriyev, to senior positions in the MoD. Additionally, he transferred authority over military reforms from the military to the SCRF. Furthermore, Putin created a special management organ for arms export, to increase his grip on the military–industrial complex (MIC). These decisions prove the range of the powers of the RF President and show that Putin, more than Yeltsin, was eager to use them.

Security Council

On 5 March 1992 Yeltsin signed the Law on Security (*Zakon RF o Bezopasnosti*), which among other items included the formation of the Security Council of the RF (SCRF or *Sovet Bezopasnosti RF*). According to this law, the SCRF drafts presidential decisions on security affairs. Also, the SCRF analysed aspects of internal and external security, as well as strategic problems concerning economic, social, military, information, ecological and other forms of security. In June 1992 a presidential decree further defined the range of tasks the SCRF could carry out to support the President in setting up domestic, foreign and military policy, ensuring state sovereignty and socio-economic stability. Thus, the remit of the SCRF covered all aspects of Russia's grand strategy. Apart from the Law on Security, the foundations of the SCRF were also rooted in the Constitution of 1993.[3]

Composition

During Yeltsin–Putin's regime up to 2001, the SCRF consisted of 15–25 members. Formally the President chaired the SCRF but daily management was entrusted to the Secretary of the SCRF. Under Putin the Secretary of the SCRF usually had a background in the armed forces or the intelligence services. The SCRF comprised permanent and normal members. Under Yeltsin as well as under Putin the following functionaries were installed as permanent members: the President, the Prime Minister, the Secretary of the SCRF, the Ministers of Defence and of Foreign Affairs and the Director of the Intelligence and Security Service, FSB (*Federal'naya Sluzhba Bezopasnosti*). Among the remaining members were the Chairmen of both Houses of the Federal Assembly, as well as the heads of a number of power ministries and intelligence services. On 10 June 2000 the Chief of the General Staff, Army-General Anatoly Kvashnin, was appointed a member of the SCRF. The SCRF was supported by an administrative body. This body was in fact a main directorate of the above-mentioned presidential apparatus. However, in practice, the SCRF turned out to act as an independent organ. In 1999 President Yeltsin decided that the personnel strength of the administrative body of the SCRF should total 175 persons.

The SCRF apparatus consisted of interdepartmental commissions and a scientific council. The 12 interdepartmental commissions drafted policy proposals for the SCRF and contributed to coordinating activities of federal and regional executive organs in implementing federal programmes and decisions of the SCRF. Amongst them were thematically organized commissions on topics such as the CIS, military security, the fight against corruption and crime, the MIC, the economy, international security, public health and preparations for mobilization. The scientific council carried out research on security-related aspects in support of the activities of the SCRF. In 1999 the scientific council included around 60 members, 30 of whom came from academic circles, over 10 from (power) ministries, and the remainder from intelligence services and private enterprises.[4]

To the membership of the scientific council of the SCRF also belonged a number of individuals who were frequently mentioned in the Russian media as influential actors on the subject of security policy. These individuals were Garayev (Academy of Military Sciences), Karaganov (Europe Institute, Academy of Sciences), Klimenko (General Staff), Kokoshin (Academy of Sciences, RAS) and Rogov (Institute of the RAS for research on the United States and Canada, ISKRAN). Because of its structure of interdepartmental commissions and the presence of prominent security experts in its scientific council, the SCRF was able to cover the full spectrum of internal and external security. Hence, in principle, the SCRF possessed the potential to influence strongly national security policy.

Position

With its interdepartmental commissions the SCRF had copied practically all other security organs, since they covered the policy areas of the departments, the security services and the military. Thus, the SCRF could easily bypass the government as well as Parliament. Furthermore, the SCRF coordinated and gathered together the activities of key functionaries in the various areas of security. The fact that the SCRF drafted policy proposals which were subsequently ratified by presidential decrees, provided evidence of its decisive role in policy-making. All principal security documents were at least discussed, but often also formulated and after that approved by the SCRF, before being ratified by the President. Among the topics on the agenda of the SCRF were the development of the MIC, military reforms, the Chechen conflicts, socio-economic problems, refugees and displaced persons, trade in narcotics, cooperation within the CIS and international terrorism.

Future status

This influential position of the SCRF was not acceptable to all other parties involved in national security. The military have done everything in their power to damage the position of the SCRF. In particular, in autumn 1999 this was demonstrated when the military purposely presented their new military doctrine prior to the revised RF grand strategy and without the consent of the SCRF. From March to August 1999 Putin filled the position of Secretary of the SCRF. Probably as a result of this experience Putin recognized the importance of this organ and its potential as overarching security institution, and subsequently he followed a course of strengthening the SCRF to reach this status. Evidence of this assumption might be found in Putin's policy of repelling the autonomy of the regional governors (of the constituent entities), which allegedly was initiated by the SCRF. Furthermore, to bring to a close disputing views on military reforms within the military leadership, Putin reinforced the position of the SCRF on military reforms, military build-up and other security-related topics at the expense of the General Staff and the MoD. Circles within the SCRF revealed their aim of transforming this security organ into an executive organ of the President, as his plenipotentiary responsible for ensuring the implementation of presidential decisions on military and security affairs. Hence, the SCRF could develop into the principal decision-making organ of the RF.[5] Whether this will be accomplished depends to a great extent on the President. Instead of using the SCRF as his primary security organ, he could also choose to employ the aforementioned key functionaries, who report directly to him and his presidential apparatus, for the purpose of personally controlling security policy. Another option for the President is to exercise control over security affairs in his capacity as Chairman of the SCRF, and delegate matters to the Secretary of the SCRF and the administrative apparatus of the SCRF. In comparison with the presidential apparatus, the SCRF seemed to be better equipped for a role as primary security organ, because of its larger structure of thematically organized interdepartmental commissions. In view of the former options and with the proviso that the relationship between President and Secretary of the SCRF will continue to be cooperative, I expect that the SCRF will develop into Russia's supreme security organ. If so, Putin will most

Table 1.1 Secretaries of the Security Council (SCRF) 1992–2001

Name	Period in function
Skokov, Yuri	May 1992–May 1993
Shaposhnikov, Yevgeni	June–September 1993
Lobov, Oleg	September 1993–June 1996
Lebed, Aleksandr	June–October 1996
Rybkin, Ivan	October 1996–March 1998
Kokoshin, Andrei	March–September 1998
Bordyuzha, Nikolai	September 1998–March 1999
Putin, Vladimir	March–August 1999
Ivanov, Sergey	November 1999–March 2001
Rushalo, Vladimir	As of March 2001

Sources: M.A. Smith, *The Security Council*, C94 (Camberley: Conflict Studies Research Centre, January 1997); www.scrf.gov.ru/personnels (website SCRF).

likely have two objectives: to accomplish a more efficient and unified security policy, and to enhance his grip on disputing security organs.

Ministry of Defence and General Staff

In the Soviet Union power was divided among three institutions: the Communist Party of the USSR, the (CPSU), the security service of the USSR, the KGB (*Komitet Gosudarstvennoy Bezopasnosti*, the Committee for State Security) and the Armed Forces of the USSR. In this triad of power, the armed forces, because of their potential for violence which could be a threat to the other two actors, were politically subject to the CPSU and KGB. In general, supervising the armed forces was not really necessary, since the leadership belonged to the same elite as the political leadership. Consequently, there were no differences in military–political objectives between the military and the party. With the collapse of the USSR this triad of powers also vanished. After the failed *coup-d'état* of August 1991, Gorbachev ordered the KGB to be split into separate parts, to prevent a possible concentration of power against the political leadership. Initially the CPSU was banned, but later on was allowed to return and to participate in the multiparty system of the RF. Thus the structure of a one-party system, which controlled all political and state functions, had gone on the blink. However, the Soviet Armed Forces, although reduced in size, continued to exist as RF Armed Forces. Now the supervision of the two other centres of power, the party and security service, was no longer present. Furthermore, with the fall of Marxism–Leninism, the ideological primacy of the party (CPSU) over the army, encompassing the psychological barrier which prevented the military from exercising influence on security policy, had also disappeared. Hence, the military had more opportunities than in the Soviet era to defend or reinforce its interests as well as to influence foreign and security policy. After the disintegration of the Soviet Union and during the subsequent political chaos, initially only the armed forces were capable of ensuring the survival of the central political authorities in their fight against regionalism and other appearances of internal threat. Externally, towards the CIS, the military leadership envisaged its interests as the reinstatement of a common military-strategic theatre, naturally under Russian rule. The military considered this aspect of foreign policy as an exclusive internal military affair. Consequently, interference by the Ministry of Foreign Affairs (MID) in this area was not appreciated. This was not the only aspect of foreign and security policy in which the military leadership felt entitled to have some say. Examples of military intervention are the transfer of authority from the Ministry of Foreign Affairs to the MoD, regarding Russia's response to the Kosovo conflict in spring 1999, and ignoring the SCRF in presenting a new military doctrine, in autumn 1999.

Origin and legal foundation

In mid-March 1992 Yeltsin appointed himself as Minister of Defence, with Army-General Pavel Grachev and the civil defence expert Andrei Kokoshin as First and Second Deputy Ministers respectively. Subsequently, on 7 May, Russia's Armed Forces and an MoD were installed. Next, Grachev was appointed as Minister of Defence with Kokoshin as his First Deputy. On 24 September 1992, the Law on Defence came into force, which, among other aspects, dealt with the powers of President, Parliament and government in the military area, determined the organizational structure of the armed forces as well as the set of tasks of the MoD and General Staff.[6] Thus in 1992 the legal basis of the defence organization was laid down in two laws and one decree:

- The Law on Security, of 5 March 1992
- The Decree on establishing the RF Armed Forces, 7 May 1992
- The Law on Defence, 24 September 1992.

Organizational structure

Control over the armed forces was lodged in the MoD. The General Staff (GS) was part of this ministry. The staffs of the services of the armed forces, together with the corresponding departmental directorates, were responsible for build-up, recruitment, equipment, training and provisioning. Following the example of the Soviet Armed Forces, at the outset the RF Armed Forces embraced a structure of five services and independent Airborne Troops, under direct command of the GS. Also subordinated to the MoD were the Military Districts. These districts were in fact regional 'duplicates' of the federal MoD, with their own departments and main staffs. Their peacetime tasks, dealing with the implementation of conscription, provisioning and training, were derived also from those of the MoD. Every district organized security and defence for its own territory. In wartime the

Military Districts were to be transformed into operational-strategic territorial units of combined arms. Then they would have military units of the various services, training institutes and local logistic elements under their command. In wartime the districts would carry out tasks in the area of mobilization, deployment of forces and preparation of reserve troops. The number of Military Districts was reduced from eight in 1992 to six in 2001. The peacetime personnel strength of the districts varied between 30,000 and 100,000 servicemen. The latter number applied to the North Caucasus Military District (NCMD), which had to cope with the conflict areas of Dagestan and Chechnya. The Military Districts were to be renamed as Operational-Strategic Commands.[7]

Assignment of duties between the MoD and GS

According to official Russian sources the primary task of the MoD was to lead the defence of the state. The department was charged with leading the armed forces and coordinating the activities of federal and regional executive organs in the field of defence. Furthermore, the Ministry drafted federal programmes on development, production and procurement of arms and equipment for the armed forces, the composition of the defence budget, scientific research on defence and ensured the implementation of conscription and preparation for mobilization. The highest consultative body of the MoD was the Collegium, which discussed topics such as build-up, combat readiness and training. The Collegium was chaired by the Minister of Defence and its membership consisted of senior officials of the department.[8]

The GS of the RF Armed Forces was the highest body for operational-strategic command of the forces. As the central organ of military command and control, the GS was tasked to analyse and assess the geostrategic situation, drafting proposals for the military doctrine, as well as with planning and organizational preparation for mobilization and deployment of forces. Specifically, this meant the drafting of war and exercise plans and exercising control over training and combat readiness. In implementing defence assignments the GS also coordinated the activities of organs and troops of the Federal Border Guard Service, the Ministry of Internal Affairs (MVD) (*Ministerstvo Vnutrennykh Del*), the Federal Service of Railway Troops, the Federal Communications Service (FAPSI) (*Federal'noye Agentstvo Pravitel'stvennoy Svyazi i Informatsiyi*), the Ministry of Emergencies, the Foreign Intelligence Service (SVR) (*Sluzba Vneshney Razvedki*), the Federal Security Service (FSB), military engineering and construction units, and the federal institutions of state security. The principal main directorates of the GS were those of operations, intelligence and organization and mobilization. The Chief of the General Staff (CGS) was subordinated to the Minister of Defence and held the position of First Deputy Minister.

One of the most prominent bodies of the GS was its centre for military-strategic research (TsVSI) (*Tsentr Voyenno-Strategicheskich Issledovaniy General'nogo Shtaba*). In January 1985 the TsVSI had been established at the instigation of the

CGS at that time, Marshal Sergey Akhromeyev, and his deputy, Army-General Makhmut Garayev. After Kvashnin had obtained the post of CGS in 1997, the set of tasks of this research centre was enlarged which increased its influence in the decision-making process of leading security documents. TsVSI developed into the primary research institute of the GS on ensuring the military security of the state and the build-up as well as the use of forces. Its set of task consisted of:

- analysing current military–political developments and assessing the sources of military threat;
- predicting the nature and contents of wars and armed conflicts and proposing ways to prevent them;
- clarifying the basic direction of RF military policy and build-up, and of the methods of safeguarding universal and regional military security, including strategic stability and strategic deterrence;
- developing a methodology to determine principles of military doctrine.

Based upon this set of tasks the TsVSI has been involved in drafting (parts of) principal security documents such as the National Security Concept (NSC) and the military doctrine, as well as instructions on the use of conventional forces and warfare in Chechnya.[9]

Relations between the MoD and GS

The relationship between the Minister of Defence and the CGS has not always been good, because of personal differences. For instance, from 1998 to 1999 there was a serious dispute between Minister of Defence Marshal Sergeyev and CGS Army-General Kvashnin, on the subject of prioritizing nuclear (Sergeyev) or conventional (Kvashnin) forces. At that time Sergeyev tried to persuade Yeltsin to reinforce nuclear capabilities, whereas in 2000 Kvashnin endeavoured to convince Putin to enhance the status and power of the GS, at the expense of the MoD. Kvashnin was of the opinion that the MoD should be transformed into a political body, led by a civilian. Furthermore, his intention was that the GS should carry out all military tasks and be placed under the direct command of the President. Under the pretence of budgetary reasons, Kvashnin also aimed at transferring the Border Troops as well as the Internal Troops from their respective departments, and resubordinating them to the GS. Obviously Kvashnin had taken a course which would reinforce his own position and that of the GS. This was demonstrated by fact, that in spring 1999 he allegedly received permission from Yeltsin to redeploy troops from Bosnia to Kosovo, without informing Sergeyev. Next, in autumn 1999, Kvashnin was supposed to have taken the initiative in reoccupying the southern part of Chechnya. Furthermore, in 2000 he became a member of the SCRF, which until that moment had been the privilege of the Minister of Defence. In March 2001 President Putin appointed Sergey Ivanov, then Secretary of SCRF, to succeed Sergeyev to the office of Minister of Defence. Putin's objective with

Table 1.2 Ministers of Defence (*Minoborony*) 1992–2001

Name	Period in function
Yeltsin, Boris	March–May 1992
Grachëv, Pavel	May 1992–June 1996
Rodionov, Igor	June 1996–May 1997
Sergeyev, Igor	May 1997–March 2001
Ivanov, Sergey	As of March 2001

Source: www.mil.ru (website RF MoD).

this appointment was probably to strengthen his grip on the military. Repeatedly, Russian independent sources revealed evidence of Kvashnin's attempts to use the inexperience of former SVR Intelligence General Ivanov for the benefit of his own position or even to promote himself in the eyes of Putin with the intention of obtaining the post of minister. However, Ivanov compensated for his inexperience by exercising effective and efficient management of the ministry, which earned him respect in military circles as well as with the President.[10] Reviewing the development of relations between the minister and the CGS, the fact is that the influence of the Russian CGS on military–political decision-making is much larger than that of a chief of defence staff, his counterpart in Western armed forces, who is unambiguously subject to the (civil) leadership of the MoD.

Ministry of Foreign Affairs

In 1992, the RF inherited from the USSR a Ministry of Foreign Affairs (MID) (*Ministerstvo Inostrannykh Del*), with a properly trained and very experienced staff. However, low pay and the attraction of commercial enterprises caused an unintended outflow of personnel and complicated the recruitment of new staff. In mid-1993, 1,000 of the 4,000 staff members of the MID in Moscow had left the department and the number of staff members abroad had dropped from 9,500 to 7,500. The MID was the federal executive organ in charge of maintaining relations between the RF and other states as well as with international organizations. With diplomatic means this ministry ensured national security, sovereignty, territorial integrity and other interests of the RF in the international arena. For carrying out this set of tasks the MID had a Secretariat at its disposal, which encompassed the office of the Minister, a coordinating and analysis group of experienced diplomats, and a consultative group. The Deputy Ministers were responsible for one of the geographically or functionally organized directorates. Just like the MoD, the MID also had a Collegium, which in 1994 consisted of 11 deputy ministers, 9 chiefs of directorates, the Private Secretary of the Minister and his principal advisor. The various directorates specialized in topics such as CIS, information, Europe, other continents, security and cooperation in Europe, non-proliferation of weapons of mass destruction, disarmament and military

Table 1.3 Ministers of Foreign Affairs (MID) 1992–2000

Name	Period in function
Kozyrev, Andrei	1992–December 1995
Primakov, Yevgeni	January 1996–September 1998
Ivanov, Igor	As of September 1998

Source: www.gov.ru (website RF Government).

technology, the arms trade and conversion, international organizations, global problems, international humanitarian and cultural cooperation, and international scientific and economic relations. The MID was involved in a large number of consultative and coordinating agencies, on topics such as participation in UN bodies, peace-keeping operations, international military–technological cooperation and border security.[11]

Council on Foreign and Defence Policy

The Council on Foreign and Defence Policy (SVOP) (*Sovet po Vneshney i Oboronnoy Politiki*) was formally a private organization, founded in February 1992. In 1998, SVOP included some 100 members from decision-making circles: representatives of the presidential apparatus, government, Parliament, ambassadors, media, scientific institutes, the military, intelligence services, banks and other essential branches of trade and industry. This background of the larger part of the membership, by and large from government agencies, was detrimental to the claim of this organization to possess a non-governmental and independent position. In 1998, some of the prominent members were: Duma defence-expert Aleksey Arbatov, the then Secretary of the SCRF, Andrei Kokoshin, former First Deputy Minister of Foreign Affairs Anatoly Adamishin, and the First Deputy CGS of the time, Valery Manilov. Considering the composition of its membership this body must have had a substantial influence on the contents of major RF documents on foreign and security policy. After the first edition of the SVOP's 'Russian strategy for the twenty-first century' in 1992, another three revised versions were made public in 1994, 1998 and 2000. This policy document was one of the foundations of the RF Foreign Policy Concept of 1993 and the RF National Security Concept of 1997.[12]

Persons involved in national security

Having explained the role of institutions, from examples of prominent persons the involvement of individuals on decision-making will now be clarified. These persons will be discussed separately from institutions, because, sometimes independently and sometimes as representatives of various organs, they expressed their opinion on foreign and security policy. The following enumeration of influential individuals

21

does not pretend to be complete; in addition to this list the Russian media have mentioned other actors involved in security and foreign policy.[13] This selection of individuals is based upon two arguments. First, these persons were time and again mentioned in Russian sources for their participation in the political debate in the aforementioned areas. Because of their frequent appearances in connection with these subjects they must have made an essential contribution to the contents of security policy. Second, these actors were active in more than one institution, and therefore covered a wide range of institutes, all of which were engaged in the decision-making process of security policy. The selection of persons involved in national security will be divided into three categories, defined by Kassianova:[14] the intellectual elite, the political elite and the state.

The intellectual elite

This group of public speakers regarded foreign policy as an academic question, for example from the viewpoint of Russia's (historical) position in the world. The members of this elite were found in the circles of the mass media and in the academic world. In particular, representatives of the Russian Academy of Sciences (RAS) regularly participated in the discourse on national security policy. Prominent spokesmen of RAS were Karaganov, Rogov, Arbatov, Kokoshin, Primakov and Klimenko. Because of the fact that their professional careers were in areas other than the academic field, Arbatov will be discussed under 'Political elite' and Kokoshin, Primakov and Klimenko under 'State'.

Sergey Karaganov was Deputy Director of the Europe Institute of RAS. At the same time he fulfilled functions such as Chairman of the SVOP, member of the scientific council of the SCRF, and member of the foreign policy council of the MID. With this combination of occupations Karaganov had influence on related scientific research as well as on the founding of Russia's foreign and security policy.

Sergey Rogov was Director of the Institute on research into the United States and Canada (ISKRAN) of RAS. It was Rogov who in March 1992 had stressed the necessity of drafting a national security strategy. Furthermore, he contributed to the first issue of 'Russia's strategy for the twenty-first century' of the SVOP, even though he was not associated with this organization. In addition to this, he also participated in the debate on military doctrine. Rogov was a member of a large number of consultative councils of the RF executive and legislature, such as those of SCRF, MID and of both Houses of Parliament.

The political elite

This social group pursued a pragmatic, realistic approach, resulting in straight recommendations for decision-making. To the political elite belonged the political parties, members of Parliament, the political media and lobby organizations. From this group in particular, members of Parliament and of the SVOP came to the fore in the discourse on security policy. Representatives of Parliament were Arbatov, Kokoshin, Primakov, Manilov and Nikolayev. Just like Kokoshin and Primakov, Manilov and Nikolayev will be examined under 'State'.

Aleksey Arbatov became a member of the Duma in 1994, for the moderate liberal party *Yabloko*. He obtained the post of Deputy Chairman of the defence committee of the Duma, which was led by Nikolayev. As a member of the SVOP, Arbatov had contributed to its 'Russia's strategy for the 21st century'. Because of his large number of publications and lectures abroad Arbatov gained an international reputation as defence expert. In the 'post-Kosovo' debate he presented a balanced view on this event, on the one hand severely criticizing NATO's military action, but on the other hand emphasizing cooperation with the West. As Director of the Institute on Global Economy and International Relations of RAS (IMEMO) and former member of ISKAN, Arbatov should also be recorded among the intellectual elite.

The state

The individuals in this group, that is, the highest governmental institutions, included functionaries of the SCRF and of departments. The state laid down its strategic objectives for foreign and security policy in principal documents, such as the aforementioned NSC, Foreign Policy Concept and Military Doctrine. Prominent members of state institutions were the civilians Kokoshin and Primakov and the general officers Rodionov, Garayev, Klimenko, Manilov, Kvashnin and Nikolayev.

Andrei Kokoshin served from 1992 to 1998 under Yeltsin as Deputy Minister of Defence and Secretary of the SCRF. A proponent of military reforms in his publications, he played an active role in the security debate. His other affiliations were member of the Duma, Deputy Director of ISKAN and member of RAS.

Yevgeni Primakov participated in all three categories of persons involved in national security. After fulfilling the post of Director of IMEMO, Primakov served from 1992 to 1999 under Yeltsin, respectively as Chief of the SVR, Minister of Foreign Affairs and Prime Minister. Following this he became Chairman of the Duma faction 'Fatherland is entire Russia'. Considering his wide-ranging career, Primakov must have made an essential contribution to the content of foreign and security policy. Evidence of this can be found in his memoirs, in which, for instance, he outlined his involvement, as director of the SVR and Minister of Foreign Affairs, in the negotiations between the RF and NATO on the enlargement plans of the latter and on the achievement of the NATO–Russia Founding Act of May 1997. Also, a number of policy proposals described by Primakov, such as awarding the OSCE the status of primary European security agency to counter 'NATO centrism', were adopted in RF security documents.[15]

Colonel-General Igor Rodionov, in his capacity as head of the General Staff Academy, attempted to incorporate RF national security policy into the contents of the military doctrine. Although this endeavour was not a success, his influence, as an exponent of conservative military thinking, was substantial. Internationally conservatively orientated, Rodionov, as Minister of Defence, proved to be a modern thinker in the field of military reforms. After his retirement from the military, he joined the Duma as a member of the Communist Party. Army-General Makhmut Gareyev, President of the Academy of Military Sciences, was already in the Soviet era well known for his military-strategic expertise. Subsequently, he made an essential contribution in the drafting of Russia's security policy. His influential position continued as late as 1999, when his thoughts on the future of national security policy were adopted in the revised versions of the NSC and the military doctrine.

Lieutenant-General Anatoly Klimenko as head of the TsVSI was intensively involved in the 2000 edition of the NSC and the military doctrine. Klimenko's reputation as an expert on doctrinal thinking was longstanding. As early as February 1992 he published a draft military doctrine for the CIS. Although this doctrine, because of changes in political circumstances, was not approved as the formal CIS concept, it did form the foundation of the first draft RF Military Doctrine, which was published three months later. Other positions held by Klimenko were as a member of the scientific council of the SCRF and, after his retirement from the military in mid-2001, member of the Far East Institute of RAS. Therefore the know-how of this officer was broadly recognized, in military as well as in academic circles.

Colonel-General Valery Manilov chaired the VRRF as well as MoD commissions, which generated the NSC of 1997 and the (draft) Military Doctrine of 1999. In addition to this, Manilov was a member of the SVOP and, after his retirement, from the military became a member of the Federation Council, the Upper House of Parliament. Because of his successive functions in SCRF (Deputy Secretary) and GS (First Deputy CGS), as well as his leading role in commissions charged with drafting the principal security documents, without any reservation it can be stated that this general officer made a vital contribution to the realization of RF security policy.

Army-General Anatoly Kvashnin from the start of his posting as CGS in 1997 delivered a substantial input into RF security policy, in its content as well as in its implementation. In relation to its content he made his views public on military reforms, where his efforts were focused at improving the combat readiness of conventional forces and strengthening the position of the GS, at the cost of the MoD and the power ministries. Concerning the implementation of security policy, Kvashnin in 1999 came to the fore as advocate of military intervention by the RF Armed Forces in Kosovo and in Chechnya. In view of his positions as CGS and as a member of the SCRF he ought to have been involved in the drafting of the 1999 (draft) Military Doctrine. The fact that the Russian media did not connect his name to this document leads one to the conclusion that Kvashnin rather concentrated his efforts on the use of military force and left the content of its theoretical background to his deputy Manilov.

Army-General Andrei Nikolayev was Chairman of the defence committee of the Duma, with Aleksey Arbatov as his deputy. After his last posting in the RF

Armed Forces, as First Deputy CGS, Nikolayev was in charge of the Border Troops. Next, he became a member of the Duma. As Chairman of the defence committee he actively participated in the security discourse, on topics ranging from the dispute between Sergeyev and Kvashin on the primacy of nuclear or conventional forces, the improvement of living and working conditions of servicemen and their families, military reforms, and civil control over the MoD.

In practice, the three categories of intellectual elite, political elite and state were hard to separate. Analyses of the careers of the above-mentioned actors demonstrate

Table 1.4 Affiliation with institutes of influential actors of security policy

Name	SCRF	MoD/GS	Parliament	SVOP	RAS
Arbatov, Aleksey	—	—	Duma	Member	IMEMO ISKRAN
Gareyev, Makhmut	Scientific Council	Dep. CGS / GSA	—	—	—
Karaganov, Sergey	Scientific Council	—	—	Chairman	Europe Institute
Klimenko, Anatoly	Scientific Council	TsVSI GS	—	—	Far East Institute
Kokoshin, Andrei	Secretary SCRF, Scientific Council	First Deputy Defence Minister	Duma	Member	ISKRAN
Kvashnin, Anatoly	Member	CGS	—	—	—
Manilov, Valery	Dep. Secretary SCRF	First Dep. CGS	Federation Council	Member	—
Nikolayev, Andrei	Member as Director Federal Border Service	First Dep. CGS	Duma	—	—
Primakov, Jevgeni	Member as Chief SVR, Foreign Affairs and Prime Minister	—	Duma	Member	IMEMO
Rodionov, Igor	Member as Defence Minister	Defence Minister/ C-GSA	Duma	—	—
Rogov, Sergey	Scientific Council	—	Member of advisory councils	Advisor	ISKRAN

Sources: www.mil.ru; www.days.peoples.ru; www.nns.ru/ssi/persons.cgi; www.whoiswho.ru; www.ras.ru; www.svop.ru; www.duma.gov.ru; www.council.gov.ru; www.mil.ru; www.mn.ru; www.atlcom.nl; www.ng.ru; www.nvo.ng.ru; www.rian.ru; www.president.kremlin.ru; www.gov.ru; www.scrf.gov.ru.

that many of them moved frequently from one post to another in all three groupings, or at the same time fulfilled functions in more than one category. Table 1.4 gives details of the affiliation of actors with various institutions involved in foreign and security policy. The interaction between persons and institutions dealing with the aforementioned policy can certainly be described as intensive.

Military power

Russia's military organization consisted of two categories: the RF Armed Forces of the MoD and the Other Troops of the power ministries. In the 1990s, including the MoD, in total 12 departments and services had military formations at their disposal.[16] Dating back to the Soviet era, the armed forces of the MoD traditionally carried out *external* security – the defence of the state against foreign aggression. The troops of the power ministries were tasked for *internal* security, to protect the state against domestic threats. During the 1990s, the RF, in particular as a consequence of the Chechen conflicts, was confronted with an increasingly violent internal opposition. This made the military and political leadership conclude that assigning internal security tasks to MoD forces had become inevitable. I will now explain the organization and development of the Armed Forces and Other Troops.[17]

Build-up of RF Armed Forces

Organization and size

In 1992, when the MoD forces, or formally RF Armed Forces, were formed they consisted of five services: Ground, Air, Air Defence, Naval and Strategic Missile Forces. As a result of unremitting military reforms and reductions in the defence budget the number of services was reduced to three in 2001. The Air Defence Forces (VPVO) (*Voyska Protivovozdushnoy Oborony*) had merged with the Air Forces (VVS) (*Voyenno-Vozdushnyye Sily*), and the status of the Strategic Missile Forces (RVSN) (*Raketnyye Voyska Strategicheskogo Naznacheniya*) was lowered to that of an independent arm under direct command of the GS. The size of the MoD forces has been reduced from 1993 to 2000. Probably due to his background in the RSVN of Minister of Defence Sergeyev, the nuclear component, the Strategic Missile Forces, survived the reductions without much damage. However, the conventional forces and in particular the Ground Forces (SV) (*Suchoputnyye Voyska*), which were cut by two-thirds, as well as VVS, VPVO and Naval Forces (VMF) (*Voyenno-Morskoy Flot*), which were reduced by half, suffered severely from the cuts. As the successor state of the USSR, the RF had taken over the obligation of removing troops of the former Soviet Groups of Forces from Eastern Europe. From 1990 (USSR) to 1995 (RF) around 600,000 servicemen were pulled out of Czechoslovakia, Hungary, Poland, East Germany and the Baltic States.[18]

Working and living conditions

Apart from specific military problems, among them the relocation of units and the storage or demolition of arms and equipment, the withdrawals from Eastern Europe had serious socio-economic consequences. It brought about the resignation of professional servicemen, a lack of living accommodation as well as shortcomings in educational and medical facilities for the military families that had returned to the homeland. These problems occurred when the economic situation in Russia was increasingly difficult. Many of the problems described had not been solved by the beginning of the twenty-first century. Insufficient living and working conditions, the reduced status of the military profession and the appalling state of arms and equipment led to an exodus of professional servicemen. According to the GS, from 1991 to 2002, 400,000 officers left the forces. In 2002, one out of ten positions for middle management officers was vacant as well as one out of three positions for non-commissioned officers.[19] The conscript component of the Armed Forces also had to cope with the harsh socio-economic situation. In the 1990s exemption from conscription, which took two years, was only possible on medical grounds or because of studies. The GS publicly recognized that the actual turn-out of conscripts increasingly continued to drop. In 1994, 27 per cent of the potential recruits actually answered their conscription call, in 1998 this number had fallen to 17 per cent and in 2002 only 11 per cent put on a uniform. The large number of absentees was caused by postponement for studies but also by evasion, medical rejection, family affairs, imprisonment and the demographic aspect that Russia's population

Table 1.5 Development in personnel strength of Armed Forces (MoD) of USSR and RF 1990–2000

Year (state)	Total strength MoD forces	Strategic Missile Forces	Ground Forces	Air Forces (VVS)	Air Defence Forces (VPVO)	Navy
1990 (USSR)	3,988,000	376,000	1,473,000	420,000	500,000	410,000
1991 (USSR)	3,400,000	280,000	1,400,000	420,000	475,000	450,000
1992 (RF)	2,720,000	181,000	1,400,000	300,000	356,000	320,000
1993	2,030,000	194,000	1,000,000	170,000	230,000	300,000
1994	1,714,000	167,000	780,000	170,000	205,000	295,000
1995	1,520,000	149,000	670,000	130,000	200,000	200,000
1996	1,270,000	149,000	460,000	145,000	175,000	190,000
1997	1,240,000	149,000	420,000	130,000	170,000	220,000
1998	1,159,000	149,000	420,000	210,000		180,000
1999	1,004,000	149,000	348,000	184,600		171,500
2000	1,004,000	149,000	348,000	184,600		171,500

Sources: Military Balance (London, Brassey's, and Oxford, Oxford University Press: the International Institute for Strategic Studies, 1990–2001); CFE (Treaty on Conventional Forces in Europe) *Dogovor ob obychnykh vooruzhënnykh silakh v Yevrope: informachiya ob obychnykh vooruzhënnykh silakh Rossiyskoy Federatsii* (Moscow: MoD, 1992–2000).

was in a state of decline. In the short term, none of these problems in the conscript component was likely to be solved.[20]

The combination of dreadful social conditions, low morale, conscripts with a low level of education and poor health, many vacancies in military posts and lack of means (fuel, spare parts and maintenance) severely damaged the level of professionalism of Russia's military. On top of this, shortcomings in finance for training and exercises and the obsolete status of arms and equipment lowered the combat-readiness of the RF Armed Forces to a level that, according to CGS Kvashnin, was so low as to be irreversible if radical emergency measures were not taken.[21]

Build-up of Other Troops of the Power Ministries

Organization

The so-called 'power ministries' were 11 departments and services, other than the MoD, which had troops at their disposal. Just like the MoD, all 11 power ministries reported not to the government but directly to the RF President. The term 'other troops, military units and entities', which was regularly used in the military doctrine, referred to military formations of the power ministries, since MoD forces were referred to as the RF Armed Forces. Although the Other Troops of the power ministries were not as heavily armoured as the MoD forces, with personnel strength between 400,000 and 500,000 servicemen in the 1990s they represented a considerable military force.

According to an official RF military handbook, the Other Troops encompassed five elements: Internal Troops, Border Troops, Railway Troops, Civil Defence Troops and FAPSI Troops. Western sources added FSB Troops and Protection Troops to this list. In addition to these seven components independent Russian sources mentioned another four state institutions which had troops at their disposal: the Foreign Intelligence Service (SVR), the State Commission on Technology, the Federal Service for Special Construction and the Main Directorate for Special Programmes. During the Soviet era six of these power ministries, the Federal Border Guard Service, the Federal Protection Service, FAPSI, SVR, FSB as well as the Main Directorate for Special Programmes, had been elements of the KGB.[22] Next, organization and tasks of the various power ministries will be clarified.

Internal Troops

These troops of the MVD were assigned to ensure law and order and security, as well as, in case this had been declared, martial law. In addition to this they secured vital objects of the state, participated in territorial defence and provided support for the Border Troops in securing the state borders. The Internal Troops had armoured vehicles as well as a military aviation section at their disposal. Besides conventional forces the following special units also formed part of these troops: *Vithaz, Rus, Rosich, Skif, Bars*, OMON and SOBR, with a total strength of several thousand servicemen.[23]

Border Troops

The troops of the Federal Border Guard Service were destined for the protection of Russia's water and land borders as well as for defending the state against aggression, together with MoD forces and the remaining components of the Other Troops. In addition to ground troops the Border Troops also had maritime units, and a military aviation section was available, equipped with helicopters and transport aircraft.[24]

Railway Troops

The units of the Federal Service of Railway Troops were tasked with maintaining or repairing railway infrastructure. In peacetime they carried out reconstruction work on existing railways as well as the construction of new railway lines.[25]

Civil Defence Troops

The Ministry of Emergencies had troops at its disposal for humanitarian, rescue, disaster relief and other emergency operations. The Civil Defence Troops conducted these missions in order to indicate, localize and fight against the effects of natural and human calamities, and of military action, as well as to provide relief work for the population. These troops were equipped with armoured and amphibious vehicles, helicopters and transport aircraft.[26]

FAPSI Troops

The troops of the Federal Communications Service took care of the upkeep and protection of communications among the highest state organs and also performed duties as the signal intelligence service of the RF.[27]

FSB Troops

The Federal Security Service had troops at its disposal for a set of tasks, defined as safeguarding the constitutional system of the state against threats such as (counter-) espionage, terrorism and crime. Just like the Internal Troops the FSB Troops also contained special forces alongside its conventional forces. The special formations of the FSB comprised the *Alfa, Beta, Zenit* and *Vympel* units, with estimated personnel strength of some 2,500 servicemen.[28]

Protection Troops

The troops of the Federal Protection Service were installed in July 1996 with the merger of the former Presidential Security Service and the Main Directorate of Protection. The latter had been responsible for law and order and security in Moscow and other principal cities.[29]

29

Remaining elements

The SVR troops, founded in 1998, were special units by the name of *Zaslon*. The units of the Federal Service for Special Construction were involved in road construction and were also connected to the Federal Ministries for Communications and for Nuclear Energy. The troops of the Main Directorate for Special Programmes had an extensive set of tasks, ranging from the preparation of security organs for mobilization to the upkeep of specific state objects. There were no details on the tasking of the State Commission on Technology.[30]

Developments in size and position

Although at the end of the 1990s the total personnel strength of the Other Troops showed a decline, the overall development in size in that decade clearly expressed considerable growth. However, a thorough analysis of this development is complicated because far from all data needed are available for public use. Still, two trends can be discerned from the development in personnel strength. First, the gradual enlargement of the Other Troops is probably related to the growing attention in the Kremlin to internal threats. Yeltsin, for example, was faced with fierce internal political opposition and with two conflicts in and around Chechnya. Since the MoD forces were tasked for external defence, the rise in domestic threats logically entailed an increase in Other Troops. Consequently, the expansion of Border Troops could have been related to the outbreak of internal conflicts in CIS states bordering Russia, and also to the intensification of the border crossing trade in arms and narcotics. A second tendency seems to have been that troops whose performance turned out to be a failure had to cope with cuts in the forces. This was most likely the case with the Internal Troops which clearly fell short in the first Chechen conflict and were significantly reduced at the end of the 1990s.

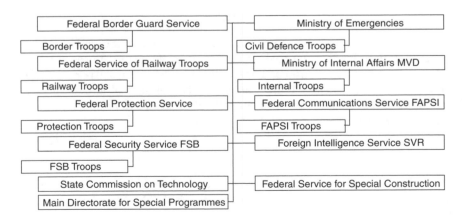

Figure 1.3 Eleven power ministries and corresponding Other Troops.

Table 1.6 Development in personnel strength of Other Troops (power ministries) of USSR and RF 1990–2000

Year (state)	Total strength Other Troops	Internal Troops	KGB Troops/ Border Troops	FSB Troops	SVR	Protection Troops	FAPSI Troops	Special Programmes Service	Railway Troops	Civil defence Troops	Special Construction Service	Technology Commission
1990 (USSR)	580,000	350,000	230,000	n.a. (KGB)	n.a. (KGB)	n.a. (KGB)	n.a. (KGB)	n.a. (KGB)	—	—	—	—
1991 (USSR)	580,000	350,000	230,000	n.a. (KGB)	n.a. (KGB)	n.a. (KGB)	n.a. (KGB)	n.a. (KGB)	—	—	—	—
1992 (RF)	>390,000	170,000	220,000	—	—	—	—	—	—	—	—	—
1993	>270,000	170,000	100,000	—	—	—	—	—	—	—	—	—
1994	>280,000	180,000	100,000	—	—	—	—	—	—	—	—	—
1995	>300,000	180,000	100,000	—	—	20,000	—	—	—	—	—	—
1996	>352,000	232,000	100,000	—	—	20,000	—	—	—	—	—	—
1997	>583,000	329,000	220,000	9,000	—	25,000	—	—	—	—	—	—
1998	>525,000	237,000	200,000	9,000	—	25,000	54,000	—	—	—	—	—
1999	>478,000	140,000	196,000	4,000	—	25,000	54,000	—	59,000	—	—	—
2000	>477,500	140,000	140,000	4,000	300–500	25,000	54,000	20,000	50,000	30,000	14,000	—

Sources: Military Balance (London, Brassey's, and Oxford, Oxford University Press: the International Institute for Strategic Studies, 1990–2001); CFE (Treaty on Conventional Forces in Europe) Dogovor ob obychnykh vooruzhënnykh silakh v Yevrope: informachiya ob obychnykh vooruzhënnykh silakh Rossiyskoy Federatsii (Moscow: MoD, 1992–2000); V. Saranov, 'Critical mass: there are too many armed formations in Russia', Versiya, 47, 11 December 2001.

Note

n.a. = not available.

This failure also resulted in the set of tasks of the MoD forces expanding to include domestic duties and efforts to improve coordinated and unified employment of the RF Armed Forces and the Other Troops.

Influence of actors on security policy

Weight on security documents

Regarding the realization of a national security policy, the first years after the formation of the Russian Federation were characterized by a lack of clarity. For instance, there was ambiguity about powers between President and Parliament. Furthermore, after the cancellation of the leading role of the communist party and Marxist–Leninist ideology as consistent pillars of the state, there was vagueness concerning competences and responsibilities among the various decision-making institutions of security policy. Apparently only a power struggle at different levels could clarity this situation. Thus, in October 1993, President Yeltsin violently dissolved Parliament and introduced a new Constitution in December of that year, which concentrated powers with the President at the expense of Parliament. With regard to relations among federal decision-making organs, a struggle of competence made available a clear definition of tasks. The outcome was a valid assignment of duties, based upon the competences of the corresponding institutions. Hence, the SCRF was granted a leading role in the realization of the NSC, the

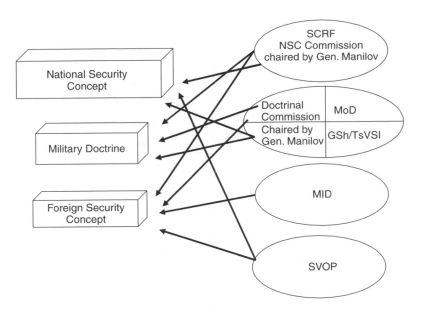

Figure 1.4 Institutes involved in drafting RF security documents.

32

MoD with regard to the military doctrine, and the MID concerning the foreign policy concept. However, prior to this assignment of duties but also in spite of it, the military unmistakeably played first fiddle in the realization of security policy in the 1990s. For example, already in 1992 the first Military Doctrine was made public, whereas the other leading security documents came into being in 1993 (Foreign Policy Concept) and 1997 (NSC). In addition to this, the military made a substantial contribution in drafting the NSC and the military doctrine. Evidence of this assumption can be found in the fact that General Manilov was in charge of the drafting commissions of NSC (SCRF) as well as of military doctrine (MoD). Also, from the analysis of persons involved in national security, it became clear that the views of military representatives on security affairs played a decisive role in the Russian media and thus in the security debate. Therefore, the conclusion seems to be justified that in the 1990s, at least until Putin came to power, the military were able to position themselves as the most influential institution with regard to security policy. Only after President Putin implemented a tighter control over security institutions, was the demarcation of the tasks of the various security organs refined into a more steadfast security policy, which still did not fully exclude the possibility of a power struggle among them.

Impact on decision-making

In the 1990s, the influence of the mass media in Russia had grown, certainly in comparison with the USSR before Gorbachev came into power. In relation to this, consequently, in theory, opportunities for participating in the national security discourse were also greater. However, in practice, the situation was that only a small number of institutions and a restricted group of decision-making individuals decided upon security policy, behind closed doors and without the approval or even involvement of Parliament. In spite of the democratization process in Russian society, decision-making on RF security policy had to do without democratic supervision. Even though open discussion on security matters did take place in the media, this did not generate openness or external civic influence on the decision-making process and was seemingly only meant to give the impression of open decision-making.

Russia sought cooperation with the West, above all for economic reasons. However, if this cooperation was to be successful, structural and intensive, then the consequence was that the Russian decision-making process would have to be adapted according to the current principles, values and standards of a democratic, constitutional state. That is, the West expected, in exchange for cooperation, transparency in security policy. This was, for instance, demanded by NATO from the countries that entered into cooperation with this alliance within the framework of the Partnership for Peace.[31] In practice, for the RF this had to entail the decision-making process being removed from behind closed doors and Parliament being able to discuss and to approve policy proposals on security. However, the Constitution of 1993 had provided the President with exclusive powers on foreign and security policy. Taking into account Putin's perception on the centralization of powers, it was not likely that a corresponding revision of the Constitution would take place. Thus, a reform of the decision-making process according to Western standards, including the principles of civic and parliamentary supervision on defence as well as openness on defence plans and budgets, was doubtful. A prolongation of lack of transparency with regard to its security policy might prevent Russia realizing its desire for further deepening of cooperation with the West in this field.

Notes

1 M.A. Smith, *Putin's Power Bases*, E109 (Camberley: Conflict Studies Research Centre, 2001), p. 1; N. Malcolm, A. Pravda *et al.*, *Internal Factors in Russian Foreign Policy* (Oxford: Clarendon Press, 1996), p. 107; 'Zakon Rossiyskoy Federatsii o Bezopasnosti', *Vedomosti RF*, 15 (9 April 1992), item 769, *Rossiyskaya Gazeta*, 103, 6 May 1992; www.scrf.gov.ru/Documents/2646-1.html#sb

2 'Konstitutsiya Rossiyskoy Federatsii', *Rossiyskaya Gazeta*, 25 Dec. 1993; www.gov.ru:8104/main/konst/konst0.html; Smith, *Putin's Power Bases*, p. 2; 'Struktura federal'nykh organov ispolnitel'noy vlasti', *Sobraniye Zakonodatel'stva RF*, 39, item 4886, 1998.

3 M. Khodarenok, 'Vremya sobirat' kamni', *Nezavisimoye Voyennoye Obozreniye*, 2 (224), 19 Jan. 2001, p. 1; 'Zakon Rossiyskoy Federatsii o Bezopasnosti', article 13; 'Konstitutsiya Rossiyskoy Federatsii', article 83.g.

4 M.A. Smith, *The Security Council*, C94 (Camberley: Conflict Studies Research Centre, 1997), p. 25; Smith, *Putin's Power Bases*, pp. 3-5; *Rukovodstvo apparata Soveta Bezopasnosti Rossiyskoy Federatsiya*, 2001, www.scrf.gov.ru/Personnels/Staff.htm; *Polozheniye ob apparate Soveta Bezopasnosti Rossiyskoy Federatsiya*, 1998, www.scrf.gov.ru/Documents/Decree/1998/294-1.html; *Sovet Bezopasnosti Rossiyskoy Federatsii, istoriya, sozdaniya, pravovoy status, struktura i osnovnyye napravleneyiya deyatel'nosti*, 2002, www.scrf.gov.ru/Documents/History.html; *Mezhvedomstvennyye komissii Sovet Bezopasnosti Rossiyskoy Federatsii*, 2002, www.scrf.gov.ru/Documents/ Commissions.html; *Sostav nauchnogo soveta pri Soveta Bezopasnosti Rossiyskoy Federatsiya*, 1999, www.scrf.gov.ru/Documents/Decree/1999/1317-2.html

5 Khodarenok, 'Vremya sobirat' kamni', p. 4; *Sovet Bezopasnosti Rossiyskoy Federatsii, istoriya, sozdaniya, pravovoy status, struktura i osnovnyye napravleneyiya deyatel'nosti*, 2002; Smith, *Putin's Power Bases*, p. 4; M. Khodarenok, 'Zadumano radikal'noye usileniye Sovet Bezopasnosti', *Nezavisimaya Gazeta*, 28 Sept. 2000, p. 3.

6 V. Suvorov, *Inside the Soviet Army* (London: Hamish Hamilton, 1982), p. 23; W.E. Odom, *The Collapse of the Soviet Military* (New Haven, CT, and London: Yale University Press, 1998), pp. 17, 36, 385, 412; 'Ukaz Prezidenta Rossiyskoy Federatsii o sozdanii Vooruzhёnnykh sil Rossiyskoy Federatsii', *Armiya*, 11-12 (June 1992), p. 2; *Vedomosti RF* (1992), item 1077, p. 1401; 'Zakon Rossiyskoy Federatsii ob Oborone', *Vedomosti RF* (1992), item 2331, p. 3026; or 'Law of the Russian Federation on Defence', *Military News Bulletin*, 10, Oct. 1992, pp. 1-7.

7 V.L. Manilov, *Voyennaya Bezopasnost' Rossii* (Moscow: Probel, 2000), p. 54; V.D. Zabolotin, *Slovar' voyennykh terminov* (Moscow: Kosmo, 2000), p. 130; *Military Balance* (London: Brassey's, and Oxford: Oxford University Press: International Institute for Strategic Studies), 1992-93: p. 100 and 2001-2002: p. 106; CFE (Treaty on Conventional Forces in Europe) *Dogovor ob obychnykh vooruzhёnnykh silakh v Yevrope: informachiya ob obychnykh vooruzhёnnykh silakh Rossiyskoy Federatsii* (Moscow: MoD, 1999-2001).

8 Manilov, *Voyennaya Bezopasnost' Rossii*, pp. 176–7; Zabolotin, *Slovar' voyennykh terminov*, pp. 80, 97.

9 Odom, *The Collapse of the Soviet Military*, p. 25; Manilov, *Voyennaya Bezopasnost' Rossii*, pp. 70–1; A.F. Klimenko, 'TsVSI issleduyet, prognoziruyet, rekomenduyet…', *Krasnaya Zvezda*, 10 Aug. 2000, p. 2.

10 P. Fel'gengauer, 'Kakov mozg, takova i armiya', *Moskovskiye Novosti*, 3, 16 Jan. 2001, p. 14; A. Korbut, 'Genshtab berët upravleniye na sebya', *Nezavisimaya Gazeta*, 17 Nov. 2000, p. 1; V. Solovyev, 'Voyenachal'niki usilivayut davleniye na Kreml'', *Nezavisimoye Voyennoye Obozreniye*, 42, 16 Nov. 2001, p. 1; V. Solovyev, 'V Minoborony gryadet chistka', *Nezavisimoye Voyennoye Obozreniye*, 7, 1 March 2002, p. 1; I. Korotchenko, 'Novyy pretendent na post ministra oborony', *Nezavisimoye Voyennoye Obozreniye*, 9, 22 March 2002, p. 1; V. Mukhin, 'The Army: One Year with Sergei Ivanov', *Former Soviet Union Fifteen Nations: Policy and Security*, 3 (March 2002), pp. 1–2.
   Preceding the appointment of Sergey Ivanov as Minister of Defence, civil defence experts such as Fradkov (arms export), Klebanov (MIC) and Kokoshin (former First Deputy Minister of Defence) were nominated for this post. In addition to this appointment Putin made further changes in the leadership of the MoD. On 28 March 2001 besides Ivanov, financial expert Kudelina, former SVR General Dmitriyev, as well as the Colonel-Generals Puzanov and Moskovsky were appointed Deputy Ministers of Defence. Next, in July 2001, Colonel-General Baluyevsky succeeded Colonel-General Manilov as First Deputy CGS and Lieutenant-General Mazurkevich replaced Colonel-General Ivashov as Chief Main Directorate International Military Cooperation. For further details see Appendix I: Biographies of Security Policy Actors.

11 Malcolm, *Internal Factors in Russian Foreign Policy*, pp. 118, 120, 122–3; Manilov, *Voyennaya Bezopasnost' Rossii*, p. 176.

12 Council on Foreign and Defence Policy (CFDP or Russian acronym SVOP), list of members, provided at Wilton Park Conference, Steyning, June 1998. For a current list of members see www.svop.ru; V. Mukhin, 'Voyennaya strategiya dlya novogo prezidenta', *Nezavisimoye Voyennoye Obozreniye*, 8 (181), 3 March 2000, p. 3.

13 For additional prominent security actors, see Appendix I: Biographies of Actors of Security Policy.

14 A. Kassianova, 'Russia: Still Open to the West? Evolution of the State Identity in the Foreign Policy and Security Discourse', *Europe–Asia Studies*, 53, 6 (2001), pp. 821–39.

15 'Kontseptsiya natsional'noy bezopasnosti Rossiyskoy Federatsii', *Krasnaya Zvezda*, 27 Dec. 1997, pp. 1, 3–4; *Sobraniye Zakonodatel'stva RF* (1997), item 5909, p. 10418; J.B.K. Lough, *Years in Big Politics – Ye.M. Primakov*, F70 (Camberley: Conflict Studies Research Centre, 2000), pp. 7, 15.

16 P. Fel'gengauer, 'Armii obeshchayut perestroyku', *Moskovskiye Novosti*, 45, 14 Nov. 2000, p. 3; Khodarenok, 'Vremya sobirat' kamni', p. 1.

17 *Military Balance, 1990–2002*; CFE.

18 Manilov, *Voyennaya Bezopasnost' Rossii*, pp. 65–6; *Military Balance*, 1993–1994, p. 99; *Military Balance*, 1991–1992, p. 31; Malcolm, *Internal Factors in Russian Foreign Policy*, pp. 266, 320, 326; *Military Balance*, 1992–1993, pp. 90–1, 98.

19 N. Kamalov, 'Komandiry otdeleniy bezgramotnoy armii', *Nezavisimoye Voyennoye Obozreniye*, 24, 19 July 2002, p. 3; 'U ofitserov net deneg i zhil'ya', *Nezavisimoye Voyennoye Obozreniye*, 11 (233), 30 March 2001, p. 1; S.M. Powell, 'Russia's Military Retrenchment', *Air Force Magazine*, Aug. 2001, pp. 71–4; 'Russian Army Suffers from Mass Exodus of Officers', *Radio Free Europe/Radio Liberty Security Watch*, 3, 6, 15 Feb. 2002.

20 V. Rukavishnikov, 'The Military and Society in Post-communist Russia at the Threshold of the 21st Century', in J. Kuhlmann and J. Callaghan, *Military and Society*

in 21st Century Europe (Garmisch-Partenkirchen, Germany: George C. Marshall European Center for Security Studies, 2000), p. 163.

In July 2002 a law on conscientious objection was passed which would come into force in 2004. See S. Suleymanov, '23-ya otsrochka ot prisyva', *Nezavisimoye Voyennoye Obozreniye*, 27, 9 Aug. 2002, p. 4.

For specifics on the situation of conscription, see S. Suleymanov, 'Sluzhba – delo desyatoye', *Nezavisimoye Voyennoye Obozreniye*, 11, 5 April 2002, p. 3; Rukavishnikov, 'The Military and Society in Post-communist Russia', p. 165; M.J. Orr, *Manpower Problems of the Russian Armed Forces*, D62 (Camberley: Conflict Studies Research Centre, 2002), pp. 1, 3.

21 'Military Chief says Army in Critical Condition', *Radio Free Europe/Radio Liberty Security and Terrorism Watch*, 3, 20, 4 June 2002; C.J. Dick, 'Down, but not out', *Jane's Defence Weekly*, 2 August 2000, p. 19.

22 'Voyennaya doktrina Rossiyskoy Federatsii', *Nezavisimoye Voyennoye Obozreniye*, No. 15, 28 April 2000, pp. 1, 4–5; *Sobraniye Zakonodatel'stva RF* (2000), item 1852, p. 3843; Zabolotin, *Slovar' voyennykh terminov*, p. 30; *Military Balance*, 1995–2001; Khodarenok, 'Vremya sobirat' kamni', pp. 1, 4; V. Saranov, 'Critical Mass: There Are Too Many Armed Formations in Russia', *Versiya*, 47, 11 Dec. 2001; 'Intelligence Community Celebrates its Soviet Origins', *Radio Free Europe/Radio Liberty Security Watch*, 3, 45, 24 Dec. 2002.

On 11 March 2003 President Putin decided to abolish the independent status of the Federal Border Guard Service and of FAPSI, and to incorporate these services into the FSB. See 'President Consolidates Security Agencies', *Radio Free Europe/Radio Liberty Security Watch*, 4, 10, 11 March 2003.

23 Zabolotin, *Slovar' voyennykh terminov*, p. 29; Saranov, 'Critical mass'; 'The Special Forces Are More than Special Forces in Russia', *Vek*, 9 Aug. 2002, p. 5.

24 Zabolotin, *Slovar' voyennykh terminov*, p. 31; Saranov, 'Critical Mass'.

25 Zabolotin, *Slovar' voyennykh terminov*, p. 30.

26 Ibid.; Manilov, *Voyennaya Bezopasnost' Rossii*, p. 177; Saranov, 'Critical mass'.

27 Zabolotin, *Slovar' voyennykh terminov*, p. 30; Manilov, *Voyennaya Bezopasnost' Rossii*, p. 177.

28 Manilov, *Voyennaya Bezopasnost' Rossii*, pp. 340; Saranov, 'Critical mass'; 'Special Forces'.

29 C.J. Dick, *If Democracy Fails in Russia*, Occasional Brief 49 (Camberley: Conflict Studies Research Centre, 1996), p. 4.

30 Saranov, 'Critical mass'.

31 *NATO Handbook* (Brussels: NATO Office of Information and Press, 2001), pp. 68–9.

2

IMPLEMENTATION OF SECURITY POLICY

Generating Major Security Documents – National Security Concept, Foreign Policy Concept and Military Doctrine

Introduction

In spring 1992, after the Russian intention of creating combined CIS Armed Forces had failed, Russia subsequently formed its own armed forces and a Ministry of Defence. With the abandonment of the Marxist–Leninist ideology the RF was now in need of basic documents for its security policy.

Russian military conceptual thought

Current Russian thinking on *national security policy* is that the state has military, diplomatic, legal (both national and international), information, economic and other means at its disposal for achieving its objectives.[1] These means are joined in the National Security Concept (NSC), Russia's grand strategy. From the NSC separate concepts and doctrines are derived to guarantee security in, amongst others, international, military, economic, social, environmental and information areas. Two of these doctrines are the Foreign Policy Concept and the Military Doctrine.

The differences between Russian security, foreign and military policies are as follows. The security policy (NSC) is aimed at safeguarding national interests against external and internal threats. The foreign policy (Foreign Policy Concept) deals with maintaining relations with actors in the international arena, such as states and international organizations.[2] The military policy (Military Doctrine) consist of views and measures concerning war, conflicts, crises and their prevention, deterrence and the suppression of aggression, force generation and preparation of armed forces, population and economy, in securing the vital interests of the state.[3]

National Security Concept

Russia's security policy is defined as actions by *organs of state power* (lower) government agencies, social and other organizations directed at safeguarding

Table 2.1 Chronology of leading security policy documents of RF

Date	Policy document
May 1992	Draft RF Military Doctrine published
April 1993	Foreign Policy Concept ratified by Presidential Decree
2 November 1993	Military Doctrine ratified by Presidential Decree
17 December 1997	National Security Concept ratified by Presidential Decree
29 September 1999	Draft Military Doctrine accepted by the Collegium of the Ministry of Defence
5 October 1999	Draft National Security Concept accepted by the RF Security Council
10 January 2000	National Security Concept ratified by Presidential Decree
21 April 2000	Military Doctrine ratified by Presidential Decree
28 June 2000	Foreign Policy Concept ratified by Presidential Decree

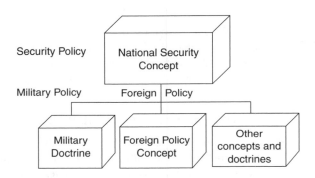

Figure 2.1 Military conceptual framework of the Russian Federation.

national interests against foreign and domestic threats. These actions consist of predicting and identifying threats; determining tasks to secure national interests; improving *forces*, *means* and the system of guaranteeing *national security*, and finally, mobilizing resources and determining the order of using them.

I shall try to clarify this rather cryptic definition. The *organs of state power* are the President and the executive, legislative and judicial powers. Contrary to what is common in the West, where the President belongs to the executive, the President in the RF is listed separately. This is probably a result of the review of the Constitution in 1993, which led to a more powerful role for the President at the expense of the legislature. The national security policy is aimed at guaranteeing national security against external (foreign) as well as internal (domestic) threats. The forces that guarantee national security are the Armed Forces of the Ministry of Defence (MoD), the (paramilitary) forces of the other Power Ministries and the units of the security services. The means of guaranteeing national security consist of the package of all political, legal, diplomatic, economic, scientific, military and other measures of the state and its apparatus which can take these measures.

As I mentioned earlier, the national security policy of the RF is laid down in the NSC. The NSC is the basic document for formulating and accomplishing a clear-cut and comprehensive policy that determines and accordingly secures Russia's national interests.[4]

Chronological development of the National Security Concept (NSC)

After the demise of Marxist–Leninist ideology in 1991 the non-communist Russian state had to determine a basis for its national security policy. Since the first edition of the Military Doctrine, in May 1992, the RF has consistently described the NSC as the highest security document, from which military doctrine is derived.[5] Still it was to be another five and a half years before the first NSC was published.

Initially, neither President Yeltsin nor his government had a clear view of the direction of Russia's security policy. Would the RF proceed as the unchallenged leader of the CIS or would it choose to take an independent course, with an exclusively Russian security policy and national armed forces? Probably because of this lack of clarity and the atmosphere of indecision, no effort was made at that point to develop a security concept (at national or at CIS level), although such a concept had already been mentioned in a draft Military Doctrine for the CIS in February 1992.[6] The following month, however, on 5 March 1992, a decree 'On National Security' was issued, establishing the Security Council of the RF (SCRF), an organ tasked to deal with problems of internal and external security.[7] At the same time a strong appeal to form a national security policy was published by Sergey Rogov, Deputy Director of the Institute for American and Russian Studies of the Russian Academy of Sciences (ISKRAN RAS). Rogov warned of possible conflicts with other former Soviet republics; in particular, with Ukraine, where differences on nuclear arms, the Crimea and energy deliveries, meant relations were quite tense at that moment. Because of this threat, according to Rogov, fundamental decisions on security could no longer be delayed. Apparently, there was an urgent need to establish a mechanism for military–political decision-making. Therefore, a national security council was to be formed in order to develop a security strategy.[8] In May, the decision for an independent Russian security policy was made more explicit, Yeltsin ratified a decree which proposed that Russia would have its own Ministry of Defence and RF Armed Forces.[9]

It did not take long for the military to enter the debate on security. In May 1992 Colonel-General Igor Rodionov, Head of the General Staff Academy, presented a conservative alternative to the official Military Doctrine that had been published earlier that month. Rodionov regarded his document as the leading security document. His view on the national security documents, however, was not shared by all members of the military leadership. For instance, Marshal of Aviation Yevgeny Shaposhnikov, who, until recently, had served as Secretary of the SCRF, spoke out after the publication of the Military Doctrine of November 1993, saying that this doctrine was premature. First a national security concept should be developed, which would include national interests and threats against national security. Only then, could other subordinated documents such as military and foreign policy doctrines be drafted.[10] Clearly, the military were divided on which course to take on security policy and the hierarchy of the different security documents.

In 1992 Yuri Skokov, Secretary of the SCRF, made a start in drafting the NSC. At its first session in the summer of 1992, the SCRF assigned a high priority to the production of the NSC.[11] However, no earlier than July 1994 the SCRF installed a commission on drafting the NSC.[12] The purpose of the NSC was to fill the gap in the political vacuum that was the result of the demise of the communist ideology. A basis of political consensus was supposed to be raised, based upon national interests.[13] These rather democratic principles sounded attractive, but disguised reality. Since the Constitution of 1993, national security policy was the President's responsibility. No longer did Parliament have the power to approve documents on security policy, as it did under the previous constitution. Now the President, who could decide upon security policy without the consent of Parliament, filled the gap. Consensus was no longer necessary. However, it lasted until December 1997 when the President signed the first NSC. The most likely reasons for the long delay (1992–97) in drafting the NSC are as follows:

- during the first few years after the RF succeeded the Soviet Union, the Russian security elite seriously debated which course to follow in foreign and security policies;
- the security organs were engaged in a power struggle. For instance, in 1992 the General Staff Academy launched an unofficial military doctrine which was supposed to become the leading security document and, as I shall explain later, the SCRF overrode the Ministry of Foreign Affairs in presenting the first Foreign Policy Concept in 1993.
- the period 1992–97 was characterized by instability, both internal (e.g. the fight between the President and the legislature in 1993; the first Chechen conflict in 1994–96) as well as external (e.g. civil wars in neighbouring CIS states such as Moldova, Georgia and Tajikistan; hotspots in the Balkans). The Russian executive (President and government) was forced to pay a lot of attention to these internal and external incidents, which held up the further development of RF security policy into a national security concept.

Following the Kosovo conflict, which took place in the first half of 1999, a radical change occurred in Russian security policy. Army-General Makhmut Gareyev, President of the Academy of Military Sciences, expressed this change in policy in an interview on geopolitics, national security and other security-related topics.[14] Gareyev stated that NATO's strategy, following the security policy of the United States, was no longer directed at defensive but at pre-emptive use of force, including possibly deploying forces outside the territory of the alliance's treaty. The emphasis was more on the use of military force rather than on diplomatic or other non-violent policies. The United States and other influential Western countries were aiming at a unipolar system of international relations at global level under their authority. According to Gareyev, the aggression of NATO against the former Yugoslavia was a clear example of its policy to ignore the United Nations (UN) and the standards of international law.

Gareyev's statements were an unambiguous example of Russian feelings with regard to NATO's new Strategic Concept of April 1999 and towards the military intervention of this alliance in Kosovo of March–July of that year.[15] Western security policy was now considered to be a threat and resulted in statements in Russian security policy expressing these anti-Western sentiments. Gareyev claimed that not only external developments but also internal threats, such as the conflict in Chechnya, demanded adjustments to the current security concepts. The statement in the 1997 issue of the NSC, that direct threats against the RF no longer existed, was declared out of date. Most of the amendments to the security policy that Gareyev proposed were to be implemented in the new (draft) editions of the NSC and the Military Doctrine in Autumn 1999. By ratifying the final draft of the new NSC on 10 January 2000, President Putin authorized the revised Russian security policy.

Development of the contents of the National Security Concept

The major *destabilizing factors*, pointed out in one or more of the different versions of the NSC, are the following: international dominance by Western states under US authority; a weakening of Russia's international position; ignoring Russian national interests; and the danger of (international) terrorism. In comparison with the 1997 edition, in the NSC of 1999 the number of destabilizing factors had increased. This was probably due to the conflicts in the former Yugoslavia and in Chechnya and because of the enlarged influence of NATO on international politics.

Russia's *national interests* as stated in the NSC were a reflection of the internal and external developments of the 1990s. Internal developments, such as the (critical) social-economic situation and the conflict in Chechnya, manifested themselves in policy objectives on removing the causes for internal conflict and on guaranteeing state power and sovereignty. External developments, such as NATO's security policy (in the Balkans), were reflected in the policy objectives on strengthening ties within the CIS and with other allies. However, *internal* national interests, such as security against terrorism, disasters and acts of war, were considered paramount.

With respect to *threats*, the 1997 NSC expressed a generally positive view on international developments and perceived the internal social-economic circumstances as the most important threat to Russia's national security. Within two years this perspective had changed radically. In the 1999 NSC a rise in military threats, both in number and in strength, and related especially to NATO, is described. The 1999/2000 editions of the NSC clearly illustrated a turning point in threat perception. Although formally internal threats were still seen as the most important, the extensive description of external threats points out that these now have priority. This inconsistency was possibly related to clashes between military and civil experts in drafting the NSC, in which the former consider external and the latter perceive internal threats to be the most significant.

For the purpose of *guaranteeing national security* the following objectives are presented in the NSC. Externally, the RF has changed its objectives from stress on international cooperation at global level, as declared in the 1997 NSC, to an emphasis on economic, political and military cooperation and integration within the CIS. It is likely that this review in policy was the result of disappointment with the lack of cooperation from the West, but was also driven by the growing desire to regain Russia's superpower status, which could best be achieved starting from the CIS. Internal political objectives were directed at strengthening (central) authority. With regard to military objectives, the two Chechen conflicts convinced the military and political leadership that the RF Armed Forces (of the MoD) could also now be deployed in internal conflicts and that cooperation between these forces and the troops of the other so-called Power Ministries had to be improved. The chain of command of the decision-making organs of national security in the NSC unmistakably revealed that the President has the overall deciding factor in guaranteeing national security.

Foreign policy

Earlier I explained the difference between security policy and foreign policy. Security policy is involved in providing security for national interests against external and internal threats. Foreign policy, as an instrument of security policy, deals with maintaining relations with actors in the international arena. According to the formal definition of foreign policy, in the RF, the organs of state power as well as institutes and state structures on international affairs carry out the foreign policy by maintaining relations with other states and regional and global international organizations.[16] In a continuation of the Soviet tradition, the RF Prime Minister and the government are responsible for economic and internal affairs; these functionaries therefore have a subordinated position in foreign policy. Nowadays the President of the RF possesses overall responsibility on security policy, i.e. including foreign policy, that at the time of the USSR was in the hands of the Secretary-General of the Communist Party and the Politburo.[17] I mentioned earlier that the position of the President was strengthened in the 1993 Constitution. Not surprisingly, the following account of the development of foreign policy illustrates that it is the President rather than the Minister of Foreign Affairs or the institutes and state structures involved in international affairs, who plays first fiddle in RF foreign policy.

Development of the Foreign Policy Concept

Initially, the MID was the logical organ to draft the Foreign Policy Concept. In February 1992 this department tried to implement a Foreign Policy Concept. However, the Supreme Soviet prevented this, claiming that the concept was too abstract. Yeltsin, who at the time was involved in a struggle for power with the Legislative Power, in the course of 1992 adopted a more assertive foreign policy. With this change of course Yeltsin almost certainly tried to gain support in his fight with the legislature. Remarkably, the final version of the Foreign Policy Concept was not under the auspices of the Minister of Foreign Affairs but under Yuri Skokov, Secretary of the SCRF.[18] Skokov happened to be the Chairman of the SCRF's interdepartmental commission on foreign policy that was to draft the Foreign Policy Concept. After approval of the Foreign Policy Concept by the SCRF and confirmation by the President, on 29 April 1993, an apparently officially approved summary of the concept was published by Vladislav Chernov, Deputy Head of the Department on Strategic Security of the SCRF.[19]

More than seven years later, on 28 June 2000, President Putin signed a revised version of the Foreign Policy Concept, which replaced the 1993 edition. In the introduction to the new document it states that certain tendencies in international politics have compelled the RF to review its foreign and security policies. These negative tendencies were in contrast to the expectation, listed in the 1993 concept, that multilateral cooperation would further intensify. The 2000 edition of the Foreign Policy Concept mentions the following basic principles of RF foreign policy:

- the RF is a great power;
- Russia's influence in international politics should be strengthened;
- political, military and economic cooperation and integration within the CIS has a high priority;
- an aversion to Western security policies.

Russian foreign policy manifests in two different approaches. On the one hand, it maintains great power status, which results in a striving for more influence within the CIS and an emphasis on military and geopolitical aspects. On the other hand, the policy is characterized by an acceptance of its lower post Cold War status, with emphasis on integration into the international system, which is dominated by the West. The danger of the first approach is confrontation with the West, which could lead to isolation and a diminished international position. The danger of the second approach is that this could result in a position dependent on the West.[20] This dilemma, of two sometimes contrasting approaches, leads to Russia's foreign policy appearing to be somewhat ambiguous.

Continuing on this duality in foreign policy, the following may be said regarding Putin's policy upto the terrorist attacks against the United States on 11 September 2001. With regard to the first approach, it can be concluded that

Russia's fixation on its influence within the CIS was prolonged. In order to stress the great power status and the independent course of RF foreign policy, Putin followed an active line to intensify relations with a number of countries. He displayed interest in relations with so-called 'pariah' states such as North Korea and Cuba and strengthened political, economic and military ties with China, India and Iran.[21] He thus demonstrated that his foreign policy was not dictated by the West. However, Putin realized quite well that rapprochement with dubious states might cause resistance in the West and weaken Russia's international position.

With reference to the second approach in foreign policy, Putin has regularly admitted that nowadays influence on international politics is determined by economic rather than military power. Taking into account the fact that internal and external policies are so closely connected, as is also stated in the Foreign Policy Concept, Putin has given a high priority to economic cooperation and integration in the global economy. In view of Russia's geographic position, this leads to the conclusion that closer ties with Europe are in the interest of the RF. Not surprisingly, Minister of Foreign Affairs Igor Ivanov has stated that Russia's primary external interests lie in Europe. Therefore, the RF aims at structural and balanced relations with the European Union (EU). Trade relations between the RF and the EU are strong; in 2000, 40 per cent of Russia's trade was conducted with the EU.[22] Former Deputy Minister of Foreign Affairs and foreign policy expert Anatoli Adamishin confirmed the importance of economic cooperation with Europe and the EU in particular. In his opinion, Russia's entry into the EU could be realized within 10–20 years.[23] Hence, international (economic) cooperation, especially with the EU, must be considered a central point of Russian foreign policy.

Military Doctrine

After the break-up of the Soviet Union, it did not take long for it to become clear that the other CIS states refused to be under Russia's military 'umbrella'. They created their own armed forces, independent of Moscow's expectations. The effect of these developments was that Russia felt itself forced to form the RF Armed Forces and an RF Ministry of Defence. Subsequently the RF was in need of a national military doctrine. In May 1992, the RF General Staff published a draft military doctrine. According to Colonel-General Manilov, the Military Doctrine, which received the force of law in April 2000, formed the culmination of Russian doctrinal development, which started with the creation of the RF Armed Forces in Spring 1992.[24]

When assessing Russian military policy of the last decade, it is obvious that the development of its military doctrine commands an important role. Military doctrine forms part of the national security policy and is a reflection of past and possibly future policy. Therefore, in order to gain a good knowledge of Russian security policy, a thorough analysis of doctrinal development is inevitable. Since the RF political and military leadership was educated in the Soviet political and military establishment, it would be logical that the military policy of the RF would, to a certain extent, be based upon its Soviet heritage. Therefore, I will provide a thematic analysis of six military doctrines, including the last Soviet draft doctrine of 1990 and a proposal for a CIS doctrine of 1992.

Russian military doctrine: definition and categories

A definition of most of the analysed doctrines usually starts as follows: '[The doctrine] represents a set of officially approved state views concerning war and its prevention, force generation, preparation of the country and the Armed Forces for suppression of aggression and methods of warfare to defend its sovereignty and territorial integrity.' In a current military dictionary, military doctrine is described in a similar way, stressing the fact that the doctrine is subject to and forms a part of the national security concept.[25] The doctrines provide guidelines in two directions. First, they deal with the needs of the armed forces in the field of organization, personnel and equipment. Second, the doctrines provide guidelines in waging wars and armed conflict.

Military doctrines can be divided into three categories. The most detailed are service doctrines. On a national level we find the armed forces doctrine, which includes all the services. And finally there are multinational or alliance doctrines. Russia does have one service doctrine, a naval doctrine, which was adopted in March 2000. However I will concentrate on the comparison of the armed forces doctrines and therefore not deal with this naval doctrine. At the time of the USSR, the Warsaw Pact doctrine was the alliance doctrine. This doctrine was, not surprisingly due to the dominating position of the USSR, identical to the doctrine of the Soviet Union.[26] After the collapse of the USSR a proposed CIS doctrine was supposed to be the new alliance doctrine. The development of the proposed CIS doctrine shows a similar pattern to the relationship between the doctrines of the Warsaw Pact and the USSR. When it became clear that most of the CIS states did not support the formulation of a CIS doctrine, a draft military doctrine for the Russian Federation was published a few months later. This doctrine was very similar to the proposed CIS doctrine; the tables were almost identical copies of those in the CIS doctrine. The doctrines that I shall analyse are, with the exception of the proposed CIS doctrine, armed forces doctrines. They deal with the action of all armed forces and troops, in this case the Armed Forces of the Ministry of Defence, as well as the Other Troops of the power ministries, such as FSB and MVD.

Chronological development of RF Military Doctrine

The draft Military Doctrine of May 1992 seemed to be the beginning of a movement towards a more assertive, confrontational Russian security policy. For example, by adopting the mission of conflict solution within the CIS, Russia claimed a leading role in this region and in the joint military effort. Another example was an entry in the doctrine stating that Russia granted itself the right to protect Russian minorities in other CIS states, using violence, if necessary. Mobile forces, yet to be formed, could be used to carry out this objective. The 1991 war in the Gulf had shown the weakness of a static (Iraqi) defence. The doctrine illustrated that this lesson had been learned by introducing the concept of a mobile defence with high-tech weapons in all azimuths. Apart from defensive use, the offensive use of force was reintroduced as an acceptable concept of operation. The deplorable economic situation made these costly aspirations quite unattainable.

In March 1993, the draft Doctrine of 1992 was submitted to the Supreme Soviet. After approval by Parliament the doctrine was to be ratified by the President. As I described earlier, at that time Yeltsin was involved in a struggle for power with the legislature and as a result there was no parliamentary debate on the doctrine. This struggle for power culminated in the use of military force by Yeltsin to end the rebellious occupation by the Supreme Soviet of its 'White House' on 4 October 1993. With the legislature eliminated the SCRF approved a revised version of the doctrine on 2 November. The same day Yeltsin signed the 1993 Military Doctrine.[27] In December 1993 a new constitution was adopted, which formalized the exclusion of the Legislative Power from decision-making in security (and other fields of) policy and thus strengthened the position of the President. From now on, only the President endorsed military doctrine. Judging from the importance attached to the role of MoD forces in security matters, it is likely that the military supported Yeltsin in his battle against the Legislative Power in exchange for their strong influence on the contents of the doctrine.

In this doctrine for the first time attention is given to internal conflicts, probably as a result of internal conflicts in some of the CIS states. Another new development is the fact that MoD forces now could be deployed in internal conflicts; until then this had been the prerogative of the (paramilitary) Internal Troops. The intention to acquire a dominant position within the CIS is further developed by an entry on the possibility of stationing RF troops outside its territory.

In 1996 the Defence Council, a competing security organ of the SCRF, announced the need for a new doctrine.[28] Since 1993 a number of negative military–political developments have demanded a revised doctrine:

- attempts to diminish Russia's influence in the Caucasus;
- enlargement of NATO;
- new military threats and regional conflicts;
- the worsened socio-economic circumstances in the RF.

First Deputy Chief of the General Staff at the time, Colonel-General Valeri Manilov, became the acting chairman of the working group on the new doctrine, which was supposed to be interdepartmental but was dominated by the military. As former Deputy Secretary of the SCRF, Manilov had also played a decisive role in drafting the first NSC. On 29 September, the 1999 Draft Military Doctrine was approved by the highest organ of the MoD, the Collegium. This doctrine was published before the revised NSC, thereby by passing this theoretically leading

46

security document as well as the SCRF, the highest state organ on security matters.[29] The military personnel dominating the working group, publication of the draft doctrine before the revised NSC, exclusion of the SCRF in the paragraph on the chain of command and the emphasis on the MoD forces in the draft doctrine, all indicate that the military exploited the 1999 Draft Doctrine to strengthen their own position at the expense of other security organs and the paramilitary troops. As with the drafting of the 1993 Doctrine the military had again 'used' the by now physically feeble Yeltsin to strengthen their own position.

New doctrinal developments included increased attention to internal conflicts, irregular warfare and joint operations by MoD and other forces, coming from the experiences of the first Chechen War. Nuclear weapons became more important, because of the weakness of the conventional forces but also in order to regain the status of superpower. In the analysis of the military–political situation and threat perception the draft clearly displayed a strong anti-Western point of view. 'Kosovo' apparently stirred up existing negative sentiment against Western security policy within the military. The draft unmistakably stated that both internal (the Chechens) and external 'aggressors' (the West) had to realize that Russia was no longer to be trifled with.

The 2000 Doctrine, signed by President Putin in April 2000, maintained the standpoints of the 1999 draft but also introduced some new ones. Opposition to the West and the consequences of the second Chechen conflict were worked out in more detail. New entries regarding the President and Belarus were included. Taking into account his policy of centralization of power, it is not surprising that the position of the President in the chain of command was strengthened. As a result of the Union Treaty of December 1999, Russia and Belarus had intensified their cooperation. The military aspects of strengthened relations were stated in the doctrine. The new positions were to a great extent the result of Putin's personal ideas and are not yet to be seen as structural.

Development of the contents of RF Military Doctrine

Six military doctrines of the USSR, CIS and RF will now be analysed thematically. The themes of comparison are derived from questions which the political and military leadership have to answer when a military doctrine is being shaped.[30]

- Does the state consider war acceptable as a means of implementing its policy or does it reject war?
- Does a military danger exist, and what are its dimensions and sources?
- What are the nature and objectives of a possible war in which the state and its armed forces will have to take part, and what are their missions?
- What armed forces are needed to wage war successfully and in what direction is their force generation to be carried out?
- What is the procedure for preparing the country and armed forces for a possible war and what are the methods of waging it?

Originating from these questions, themes such as the definition of the doctrine, the military–political situation, threats, command and control over the forces, objectives and tasks of military employment and international military cooperation, will be dealt with in the following analysis.

Division, size and definition of doctrines

Initially the military doctrines were divided into two: a military–political and a military–technical (since 1999 listed as military-strategic) aspect. The political aspect deals with the international situation, the threat of war and the position of the state towards warfare. The military–technical aspect deals with the nature of wars and with the structure, organization and tasks of the Armed Forces. In the 1993 Doctrine a third aspect was added: the economic fundamentals of security policy. The main goal of these fundamentals was described as to 'Timely provide the Armed Forces and the Other Troops of the RF with effective weapon systems to an extent that the vital interests of society and state are ensured'.[31] The mention of an economic basis was not entirely new; in the 1992 draft doctrine it was included in the military–technical aspect. The content of the economic aspect has remained the same throughout the different doctrines. In fact it is nothing more than a 'shopping list' of the military leadership in order to realize their needs for equipment and personnel strength. The RF has to cope with a situation in which military–economic cooperation, both among CIS countries but also between the Russian military–industrial complex and the Armed Forces, is no longer self-evident, as it was at the time of the ideologically led USSR. In the USSR the Armed Forces and military industries both served the aims of the socialist state. In order to establish collective (CIS) security and to maintain common military production, it was necessary for the RF to insert an economic aspect into the doctrine. However, this military 'shopping list' cannot be considered as realistic, considering the difficult situation of the Russian economy.

The size of the doctrine documents has increased over the years. The previous Soviet (draft) Doctrine of 1990 consisted of only five pages, whereas the present RF Doctrine of 2000 consists of 25 pages. The expansion in volume of the doctrine might be explained as follows. At the time of the USSR, before Gorbachev came to power, the number of people involved in writing a doctrine was limited to a few high-ranking party and military officials. This contrasted with Gorbachev's policy of transparency and increase in freedom of the press, which made it possible not only for officials but also for civilian experts to participate in the doctrinal debate. Even so, many officers felt that they were being excluded from the debate. This was stated openly in an article on a proposed CIS doctrine, in February 1992.[32] They demanded openness on and consultation in the contents of the doctrine. In spite of the increase of transparency under Gorbachev, restrictions on openness concerning the doctrine remained in force until the 1999 version. For example, in 1993, the Deputy Secretary of the RF Security Council of the time, Colonel-General Manilov, declared that the final version of the doctrine would be only released for publication in part. In contrast to the situation in 1993, in 1999 the draft Military Doctrine was developed by a working group consisting of representatives of different ministries, institutions, academics and others. As well as the change in Russian politics, Russian society has also changed rapidly. Nowadays there is more room for discussion on security matters, by military and civilian participants, both in official and in independent publications. The military leadership is aware of how to use the possibilities of the mass media for its own benefit. The same Colonel-General Manilov, when fulfilling the function of first Deputy Chief of the General Staff, declared himself in favour of complete publication of the 1999 draft Doctrine and of involving the public in the doctrinal debate.[33] The use of the media by the General Staff and the MoD will be included in the detailed discussion on command and control over the Armed Forces and the Other Troops.

The increase in size of the doctrines therefore has to do with the increased possibilities for open debate on security matters. This apparently is also related to the desire of the political leadership to involve a broad number of representatives of different affiliations in discussion on the doctrine, which results in a doctrine with a wider spectrum of subjects. Both the political–military leadership and society in general have gone through a development of more openness, which was demanded by officers in an article on the CIS doctrine, proposed in 1992.

When discussing comparison of doctrines, I stated the more or less standard definition of the military doctrines. The definitions of the doctrines provide guidelines in two directions. First, they deal with the needs of the armed forces in the fields of organization, personnel and equipment. Second, the doctrines provide guidelines in waging wars and armed conflicts. This standard definition is absent from the 2000 Doctrine; in the 2000 Doctrine the definition is limited to the enumeration of the three fundamentals. There is no clear explanation for this change; possibly the standard definition is now considered to be archaic. Another reason could be that the political–military leadership does not want the doctrine to be confined to a certain, defined structure.

Analysing the definition of the doctrine, a certain development can be determined in the relation of the doctrine to other security documents, as well as in the development concerning the object of protection. First, the relation to other documents on security policies will be described. The 1990 draft considers the doctrine to be subject to the foreign policy of the USSR. Starting with the 1992 proposed CIS doctrine, the doctrines have been derived from the (all) national security concept, which is the political or grand strategy. In the 2000 NSC it is stated that both doctrine and foreign policy are subject to the NSC. Security policy at the time of the USSR was dictated by the Marxist–Leninist ideology, therefore an NSC, being a capitalist invention, did not exist. Ideology shaped foreign policy, which in turn created the military doctrine.

Second, we observe the development of the object of protection. Corresponding to political developments, the object of protection has changed from 'the socialist fatherland' (1990) to CIS and RF. Since 1993 'vital interests' have been added to the list of objects to be protected. From 1993 on, 'allies' have been mentioned as objects of protection. However, the doctrines fail to mention Russia's allies specifically. In the 2000 Doctrine 'allies' are left out of the text. Russia has considered Serbia to be more or less its ally. Possibly the Kosovo air campaign of the North Atlantic Treaty Organization (NATO) in 1999 was the reason 'allies' were left out, in order to avoid giving unconditional support for Serbia or any other ally in the future.

In general, the definition of the term 'military doctrine' demonstrates consistency, in which the relation of the doctrine to other security documents and the objects of protection are a clear reflection of (inter-)national developments.

Preamble of the doctrines

The Introduction to the Soviet doctrine of 1990 expresses the desire for transparency in (international) security policy, to which the publication of this doctrine apparently had to make a contribution. At the end of the Cold War and even before the agreement on major arms control treaties, this reference to conflict prevention is understandable.

In the (proposed) CIS doctrine of 1992 the creation is announced of unified, combined armed forces, which would serve the interests of all CIS states.[34] In the Russian doctrine of 1992 we find references to a common CIS execution of defence tasks. This doctrine was going to be related to documents of the CIS Defence Council. The emphasis on military cooperation within the CIS fits in with the developments of 1991–93. In February 1992, at a CIS summit in Minsk, unified CIS Armed Forces were created under the command of the Russian Marshal Shaposhnikov. In May 1992, at a summit in Tashkent, Russia, Armenia, Kazakhstan, Kyrgyzstan, Tajikistan and Uzbekistan signed a Collective Security Treaty. Notwithstanding these developments towards enhanced military cooperation, the new independent CIS states apparently preferred national armed forces. Clearly as a result of this development, the CIS Joint Military Command was abolished in June 1993.[35] This change of policy is visible in the next document, the final version of the RF doctrine, which was published in November 1993. Proposals for a common security policy within the CIS are still present in this document, but not explicitly.

Now and then the preamble of the discussed doctrines refers to declarations or documents of the legislature or the executive. Both in 1992 and 2000, RF Doctrines, Parliament and President are mentioned. The reason for referring to these bodies might be found in the fact that the military doctrine, by presidential decree, is laid down in law. In order to adapt it if necessary, reference is made to the bodies that are entitled to make changes when they are required. In the Introduction to the doctrines the National Security Concept has consistently been declared to be the point of reference since 1992.

The importance of the CIS as a guideline of security policy has diminished, probably due to the preference of most CIS states for a national security policy.

The reduced prominence of the CIS is reflected in the text of the doctrines from 1993 on. The hierarchical position of the doctrine is clear; it is a document subject to the National Security Concept, Russia's grand strategy.

Destabilizing factors of the military–political situation

From 1990 on, the doctrines clearly reflect the fact that the threat of a global war has been greatly reduced. Conversely, increasingly destabilizing factors were found in regional and internal developments: political, economic, territorial, religious and ethnic differences. The 1992 RF doctrine for the first time brings up the term 'civil war'. In the 1993 doctrine 'aggressive nationalism' and 'religious intolerance' are stated explicitly as destabilizing factors. The increase in crime also becomes an important factor. In the 2000 doctrine organized crime, terrorism, the illegal arms trade and narcotics are added. These factors were already visible at the time of the break-up of the USSR. Within the CIS armed conflicts broke out in, for instance, Georgia, Nagorno-Karabakh, Moldova and Tajikistan. Within its territory the RF was faced immediately with a rebellious Chechnya, which declared itself independent from Russia. This resulted in two Russian invasions and armed conflicts in Chechnya, in 1994–96 and from October 1999. It is not surprising, therefore, when comparing the doctrines, to see that regional and internal destabilizing factors have grown in importance.

Since 1999 the RF point of view on destabilizing factors has changed. The 1999 and 2000 doctrines focus more on international developments, that is, outside the CIS. The weakening of the mechanism of international security is now considered to be a major destabilizing factor. More explicitly, the use of military force, without the sanction of the UN, is denounced. In 2000, 'The use of force for humanitarian intervention' was inserted into the text. This addition clearly points at NATO's air campaign in Kosovo, March–June 1999.

The description of destabilizing factors gives a clear picture of the Russian perspective on the development of (inter)national security. Again we see the change of emphasis from the CIS towards the wider international security situation.

External threats

In the 1992 and 1993 RF doctrines a distinction is made between military dangers and military threats. In the case of a military danger, the potential for an outbreak of war exists, whereas in a situation of military threat an immediate danger of the outbreak of war is present.[36]

External threats are partly the result of *ad hoc* thoughts, i.e. recent developments are cited as dangers or threats. In this way the 1990 Soviet doctrine clearly expresses the mindset of 'bloc thinking': the presence of opposing military blocs and the US inclination towards a leading role in world politics. Leaning towards a dominating position is another *ad hoc* argument in itself, when in the 1992 CIS doctrine it is mentioned in relation to Iraq and the 1991 Gulf War.[37] In the 1992

RF doctrine, political and economic blackmail of the RF appears as a danger. Possibly the disputes with Ukraine, concerning the Black Sea Fleet, the possession of nuclear arms and the status of the Crimea, gave cause for this *ad hoc* argument. All of these temporary arguments were listed only once in a doctrine as a military danger or threat.

On the other hand, other dangers or threats are inserted in the text at a certain point and are repeated in following doctrines. These long-term dangers or threats are as follows.

Interference in internal Russian affairs (since the 1993 doctrine). The armed conflicts of the RF in Chechnya are the main item of Western criticism on Russian policies. The RF, and especially the President, consider this as interference in internal Russian affairs.

Expansion of military blocs and alliances (since 1993). Already during the early debates on NATO enlargement, President Yeltsin protested against this intention. This point was introduced as a threat in the 1993 doctrine. A first enlargement has taken place with the acceptance of Hungary, Poland and the Chech Republic. A second round of enlargement will definitely be again rejected.

Attempts to ignore (or infringe on) RF interests in resolving international security problems (since 1999); attempts to oppose strengthening of the RF as one of the influential centres (since 1999); and the introduction of foreign troops (without UN Security Council sanction) to the territory of contiguous states friendly with the RF (since 1999). From 1994 on, Yeltsin made clear to the West that Russia demanded consultation in NATO's use of force in the Balkans. Repeatedly the RF was not informed prior to the use of force; neither at the time of the 1994 and 1995 air strikes in Bosnia, nor the 1999 air campaign on Kosovo. This denial of Russia's influence resulted in the rapid and unannounced deployment of Russian ground forces in Kosovo. Also, NATO's new Strategic Concept (1999), which can decide on the use of force in the Euro-Atlantic region, is a problem for the RF. The RF has been invited often to participate in the settlement of security affairs. However, this was generally after NATO had already taken action. This is unacceptable to Russia; it insists on being one of the deciding actors at the beginning. Developments such as Western security policy, Western criticism Russia's actions in Chechnya, neglecting the RF in its Balkan policy, as well as NATO's enlargement and new Strategic Concept, have resulted in a deterioration in relations between the West and the RF. From the Russian point of view the post Cold War security policy of the West is felt as threatening and consequently this impression is also laid down in its military doctrine.

Two dangers or threats are consistently mentioned in the doctrines. These structural threats are the impression of encirclement by enemies and the protection of Russian minorities outside of Russian territory.

The feeling of being surrounded by enemies, which can be found in Soviet, CIS and RF doctrines, is stated as the danger of the build-up of troops near Russia's borders. This argument can probably be traced back to the different invasions by foreign powers (for instance Mongols, French, Germans) that Russia has suffered in the past.

In all of the RF doctrines, the violation of the rights of Russian citizens abroad is mentioned as a danger or threat. However, in the various doctrines the definition changes. In 1992 not only Russian citizens but also ethnic and culturally likeminded people are to be protected. From the 1993 doctrine on, protection is limited to Russian citizens. Another variable is the region where these Russian citizens are located – from the former Soviet republics (1992), via the 'near abroad' (1993 and 1999) to abroad in general (2000). These changes could be regarded as an indication of expansionism. However, in none of the doctrines is it explained how the protection of Russian minorities in some CIS countries can be guaranteed. The application of Russian military force for this purpose in other CIS states is unlikely and on a worldwide level unthinkable. Offering protection to Russian minorities provides the RF with a foundation to continue its influence on the other CIS states. The change of wording to *inostrannykh* in the 2000 doctrine, with the connotation of 'abroad in general', without the previous emotional undertone of an (former) intimate relationship, could be explained as the reduced interest of the MoD/GS in using force to protect compatriots. Formally the protection of Russians living elsewhere is maintained in the text of the doctrine, but the very general description offers little hope of living up to this promise. Thus the external threats in the military doctrine can be divided into three categories:

1   *ad hoc threats*. These are usually in response to recent developments, such as the Gulf War of 1991 and tensions within the CIS. These threats are mentioned only once;
2   *long-term threats*. Threats which are the result of international developments, such as the deterioration of relations with NATO. Once inserted in the text, these threats are continued in the following doctrines;
3   *threats with a structural nature*. The feeling of being surrounded by enemies and the protection of Russian minorities outside of Russian territory. These threats have been part of the text since the first doctrine.

Internal threats

Internal threats were not listed in the doctrines of 1990 and 1992. Since 1993, internal threats, such as attempts to disrupt the unity and territorial integrity of the state and to destabilize the internal situation by national-ethnic, religious, separatist and terrorist movements, organizations and structures, form a consistent part of the doctrines. Up to 1993 armed conflicts within the CIS were recognized as a threat, but as an external one. The military doctrine was purely externally focused. Internal developments, within the borders of the RF, were not taken into account. Already before the break-up of the USSR, Chechnya had declared itself independent. The RF at first neglected this internal thorny heritage, but in December 1994, the RF responded with military force. The military leadership, responsible for the wording of the doctrine, had already recognized this looming up of internal threats by inserting this item in the 1993 doctrine.

Another internal threat is mentioned in the 1993 doctrine – attempts to overthrow the constitutional system. This must be a reference to the battle for power between President Yeltsin and Parliament. In early October 1993 this conflict resulted in the use of military force, ordered by Yeltsin, to clear the occupied Parliament building, thus ending the powers of the legislature. Following the disbandment of Parliament, the new constitution clearly stated that the military doctrine was the prerogative of the executive. So, since 1993 the legislature has had no formal role in the content of the doctrine. The reference to 'Attempts to overthrow the constitutional system' as an internal threat, is kept consistently in new doctrines. With this argument the executive justifies its right, if necessary, to forcefully defend its position.

As has been said earlier, in the first doctrines internal threats were not inserted. Inclusion of internal threats are the result of experience. Apparently Yeltsin's conflict with Parliament and Chechen secessionism have lead to the conclusion that internal threats can no longer be excluded from Russian security policy. In contrast to the build-up of external threats, structural items are missing in the paragraph on internal threats. This difference could be explained as follows. The Soviet Union, according to its Marxist–Leninist ideology, formed a unity, a closed front, against the capitalist enemy. This ideology automatically included a unified state, without internal divisions. The threat came from abroad. The Soviet military doctrine was of course a reflection of this way of thinking. Although with the break-up of the USSR the ideology officially also came to an end, one should be aware of the fact that the present political and military leadership were raised with these ideas. Therefore one cannot but think that this mindset still plays a role in the minds of the current policy-makers. Assuming this, it is not very peculiar that in the doctrine structural external threats are still stressed, but that at the same time some of the recently established internal threats are expanding.

Principles for ensuring military security

Analysing developments and conditions that influence military security, all six analysed doctrines express *ad hoc* points of view, arguments that do not reoccur in following doctrines. Examples of *ad hoc* policies are:

- the disbandment of NATO and the Warsaw Pact (1990 Soviet doctrine);
- the creation of unified CIS Armed Forces (1992 CIS doctrine);
- military cooperation with countries in central and eastern Europe (1993 RF doctrine);
- military cooperation with Belarus (2000 RF doctrine; since this is the first listing, this item might be continued in future doctrines).

As I mentioned earlier (p. 44), doctrines are a reflection of the security situation in a time frame. As a result of this we can also find the evolution of certain important security issues. This especially applies to the development of 'no-first-use' statements concerning both conventional and nuclear weapons. The 1990 Soviet doctrine expressed both a conventional and nuclear 'no-first-use' statement; the USSR rejected the first use of military means as a solution for differences. The conventional 'no-first-use' statement was to be repeated in both doctrines of 1992. The 1993 doctrine referred only to a nuclear 'no-first-use' statement. Subsequently so many conditions were added to this statement that the RF could very well end up being the first to use nuclear weapons in a specific conflict. The 1999 doctrine showed a number of inconsistencies. On the one hand, it rejected the first initiation of military operations, but on the other hand, it claimed the right to use nuclear weapons against large-scale conventional aggression, i.e. the first use of nuclear arms. This contradiction is continued in the 2000 doctrine.

Concerning 'no-first-use' statements a certain development can be observed. Until 1993 both a conventional and nuclear 'no-first-use' statements were listed. A moderate position towards warfare was taken. In the 1993 doctrine the nuclear 'no-first-use' statement was subject to conditions. Apparently this was a transitional phase. From 1999 on the nuclear 'no-first-use' statement was abandoned as well as the declaration that the RF would not have any opponents. Clearly a more assertive course was then begun. This assertive approach might possibly be connected to the following developments:

- *the abandonment of the conventional and nuclear 'no-first-use' statements.* As a result of the conflicts in Chechnya the conventional threat for the RF has increased. This has forced the RF to keep all military options open;
- *lowering of the nuclear threshold.* The present weakness of the conventional forces of the RF could accelerate the use of nuclear arms;
- *opponents.* Deteriorating relations with the West might result in a return of Russian thinking in terms of opponents/enemies.

Consistent in the doctrines of 1992 onwards, is the comment on the necessity of possessing nuclear arms for reasons of deterrence. The principles for ensuring military security show a combination of *ad hoc* and developed thoughts. The right to retain nuclear power status must therefore be regarded as a permanent factor of importance in the Russian doctrines.

Command and control of the Armed Forces and the Other Troops

In order to give guidance to the troops in fulfilling assigned missions, a military doctrine should provide clarity on leadership over the security apparatus. As was described earlier, the Russian security apparatus consists of the Armed Forces of the MoD and Other Troops of the power ministries.

The Soviet and CIS doctrines do not include a paragraph on the command and control of forces. In contrast to the Soviet and CIS doctrines, in RF doctrines from

1992 onwards this item has been mentioned in the text. A number of actors are listed as being involved in the leadership of the security apparatus:

- the Security Council of the RF (SCRF);
- the President;
- the Council of Ministers/government of the RF;
- the Ministry of Defence;
- the General Staff of the RF Armed Forces.

These actors are to be found in more than one doctrine. Others, such as the Commander-in-Chief of the RF Armed Forces, the Staff of the CIS Armed Forces and the Staffs of the branches and arms, are listed only once. Because of their minor importance, the latter actors will not be discussed in detail.

The Security Council of the RF consists of, among others, the President, the Prime Minister, the Secretary of the SCRF, the Ministers of Defence and of the 'power ministries' and the heads of the security services.[38] In the 1992 RF doctrine the SCRF was mentioned as the principal military–political agency, exercising over-all direction of the security apparatus and policy, with the President as its chief. In 1993 the importance of the SCRF was lowered down to an agency responsible for drafting presidential decisions on security matters. The SCRF was not listed in the chain of command and control any more, but was mentioned in a different part of the doctrine. In the 1999 and 2000 doctrines the SCRF was left out completely, which is remarkable for an institution that in 1993 was mentioned as the principal agency for the security apparatus. The reason for this development could be the fol-lowing. The General Staff had an enormous influence on the content of the 1999 and 2000 doctrines. It appears that both the General Staff and the Ministry of Defence have used their leading role in the composition of these doctrines to diminish the influence of other actors, such as the SCRF, upon the security policy.

The President of the RF is Supreme Commander of the RF Armed Forces. Only once, in 1993, has he had the general guidance of the Other Troops as well. In the 2000 doctrine the position of the President in the chain of command is further strengthened. As opposed to the 1999 doctrine, he is now in charge of the direc-tion of the structure, preparation and application of the military organization. The reason for this increase in responsibilities of the President probably is of a per-sonal nature. President Putin's career in the security services and his private inter-est in security matters are most likely the reason for the emphasis on the role of the President in command and control of the forces.

The Council of Ministers/government of the RF has been mentioned since 1993 as one of the elements of the chain of command. The responsibilities of the government vary from the assurance of military security in general to the outfitting and preparation of the Armed Forces and the Other Troops. However the position of the government sticks to responsibilities of a general nature. There are no specific, important tasks assigned to the government.

The positions of the *Ministry of Defence and the General Staff* evolve over time. The responsibilities of the Ministry of Defence vary from development and implementation of military policy (1992), direct control of the RF Armed Forces (1993), structure, development and procurement of the military organization (1999) to the inclusion of the described responsibilities for the Other Troops as well (2000). The evolution of the responsibilities of the General Staff shows a similar pattern: the C-in-C Armed Forces exercises direction of the Russian Armed Forces through the General Staff (1992), the operational control of the Armed Forces (1993), operational control and the strategic planning for the employment of the Armed Forces and the Other Troops (1999) and coordination of the activities of and cooperation of the Armed Forces with the Other Troops (2000). The inclusion of the latter is most likely a direct result of the experiences of the first Chechen War (1994–96), in which the lack of coordination between defence and other forces was one of the major causes of the Russian defeat. The failure of the Other Troops, who played a major part in the Chechen conflict, was probably used by the Ministry of Defence and the General Staff to plea for a reinforcement of their own troops and strengthening of their position in the overall chain of command. As mentioned earlier, the MoD and the General Staff probably had a strong influence by important contributions to the doctrines of 1999 and 2000 in diminishing the position of other actors in the chain of command, such as the SCRF and the Other Troops. The troops of the 'power ministries' are listed at different levels of the command and control chain. However, in the 1999 doctrine it is explicitly stated that the RF Armed Forces of the MoD form the nucleus of the military organization. This is even more apparent in the 2000 doctrine in which it is explicitly stated that the Other Troops are directed by the MoD and the General Staff.

According to the analysed doctrines, the leadership of the security apparatus, as laid down in the command and control chain, is in the hands of the following institutions: the SCRF, the President, the Council of Ministers/government of the RF, the MoD and the General Staff of the RF Armed Forces. Compared to the other actors in the chain of command of the security apparatus, the position of the government seems to be of minor importance, judging from its responsibilities. The government apparently only fulfils a formal but certainly not an influential role in the command and control.

Focusing on the text itself, the President, the MoD and the General Staff are the major institutions. However, in the course of 2000 Putin made it clear that he intends to strengthen the position of the SCRF at the expense of the MoD and the General Staff.[39] Until 2000 the latter were in charge of military reforms. The lack of results of these reforms and also the internal disputes, made Putin decide to give the SCRF the lead. It is likely that the reinforced position of the SCRF will result in amendments to current security documents, such as the military doctrine. It is to be expected that the position of the SCRF in the chain of command will be included in future documents.

Types of conflict

Usually in the doctrine the chapter on military-strategic principles describes different kinds of conflicts. This enumeration of conflicts is missing in the 1992 CIS doctrine. A comparison of the different doctrines shows the following differences in the order of conflicts mentioned. In the doctrines of 1990 and 1992 (RF) the first conflict to be described is a nuclear global war, followed by (large-scale) conventional wars, local wars and local armed conflicts. In the 1993 doctrine the order is reversed: from local wars and armed conflicts, via internal armed conflicts to world war (both conventional and nuclear). In 1999 the previous sequence is restored but in the 2000 doctrine the order of 1993, starting with local armed conflicts and ending with large-scale war, is continued.

If value can be attached to the differences in which these conflicts are ordered, the following remarks might be made. Until 1993 the focus of the RF, and the military leadership especially, was directed at a large-scale or global war, both conventional and nuclear. From 1993 on a change of view can be established. Local wars and internal armed conflicts gain in importance; they are top of the priority list. This development demonstrates a realistic view. During the nineties the threat of a global war diminished. Russia was confronted with a number of armed conflicts within CIS states and later on with the Chechen conflicts within its own state borders. It appears that these conflicts made the Russian military–political leadership realize that the security apparatus increasingly would be faced with local and internal armed conflicts in the future. This particular order of conflicts, with local and internal armed conflicts listed first as the most important conflicts, is in line with the earlier conclusion that the significance of internal threats has increased.

Deployment, methods and tasks of the Armed Forces and the Other Troops

In most of the doctrines the objectives for the use of the Armed Forces are described as:

- prevention of war;
- deterrence of opponents;
- suppression of aggression;
- execution of a defensive strategy.

At the time of the Soviet Union the Armed Forces of the MoD were tasked exclusively for external conflicts, whereas the Other Troops of the power ministries could be employed for internal problems, such as insurrections. In the 1992 RF doctrine it is stressed that the Armed Forces are not to be used to conduct internal political missions.

In addition to the objectives for the use of military force, as mentioned above, in some doctrines other opportunistic objectives are stated under the heading of

'Ways of employing forces'. In the 1990 Soviet doctrine a lot of value was still attached to nuclear warfare. The 1992 RF doctrine considers common defence policy and conflict resolution within the CIS as important aspects. In the latest (2000) doctrine, for the first time new concepts of military action such as joint special operations in internal armed conflicts and anti-terror operations are mentioned. No doubt the inclusion of the latter is based on both Chechen Wars, which showed a demand for well-coordinated joint operations of the RF Armed Forces together with the Other Troops. More specific 'Missions of the forces' follow the format of 'objectives' and 'ways':

- peace support operations;
- internal armed conflicts;
- disaster relief.

In 1993 the perception of missions changed. Internal conflicts, peace support operations as well as joint operations, were now put on the agenda. The term 'peace support operations' does not specifically refer to UN peace operations, but it is more likely that it points at peace operations within the CIS. Since the early 1990s the CIS, dominated by the RF, has conducted a number of peace support operations in Georgia, Moldova and Tajikistan.

Looking at the development of the perception of the use of military force, 1993 clearly is a turning point. Until 1993 stress was laid on external defence and operations within the CIS. Conversely, starting in 1993 internal conflicts and joint operations are also emphasized. The development of the objectives, use and missions of the forces is similar to the development of the threat perception and the priority list of conflicts. They too show evidence of a change of view around 1993 from emphasis on external conflicts to internal conflicts.

Deployment of RF Armed Forces and Other Troops abroad

In the 1990 Soviet doctrine the deployment of military bases and/or forces abroad was condemned. At that time both the Soviet Union and the Warsaw Pact were still intact, although the state as well as the alliance already showed cracks in cohesion. Military cooperation, including the deployment of Soviet Forces in Eastern Europe, was routine. Therefore the disapproval of the deployment of military force abroad must have been directed at NATO, and especially the United States with its worldwide network of military bases.

When the buffer zones of both the Warsaw Pact and the Soviet Union had fallen to pieces, in 1991, the geostrategic position of the RF was suddenly completely different. Russia was now in the 'frontline'. In order to acquire early warning and deterrence of potential opponents, forward deployment of Russian forces became a necessity for the RF. For this reason it is not surprising that in April 1994 Yeltsin's staff presented a report that pleaded for the deployment of RF military bases on the territory of other CIS states.[40] Since 1993 this geostrategic policy choice has been incorporated in the respective doctrines.

International military cooperation

All six analysed doctrines pay attention to international military cooperation. With the introduction of the chapter on military–economic principles in 1993, this issue is part of this chapter. Whereas the 1990 Soviet doctrine deals only with international military cooperation in general terms, from 1992 onwards the doctrines specifically state with which actors and in which order cooperation is to be carried out. Consistently, the CIS receives the highest priority when it comes to this cooperation. As a result of international developments, the other 'most-favoured-nations' for military cooperation vary. In the 1992 CIS doctrine NATO is in second position but already in the RF doctrine of a couple months later, the Western alliance has been replaced by the OSCE as the second organization of priority. From 1993 on, NATO is no longer included in the list of military cooperation. The RF aim for military cooperation is quite interesting. In the 1993 and 1999 doctrines this is expressed as strengthening the RF military–political position across the world.

The development of the Russian concept of international military cooperation could be regarded as a reflection of the deterioration of the relations between East and West. Of course this is influenced by the objective of this cooperation, the strengthening of RF military–political positions. Intensive cooperation with NATO is not likely to support this objective. Within the CIS, and taking into account the economic and military dependence on Russia of a number of CIS members, this objective is more feasible. It is not surprising, therefore, in spite of the decreased status of this alliance, that cooperation with CIS states has constantly received the highest priority.

Summary

I have analysed six military doctrines thematically. The themes of the comparison were derived from questions that the political and military leadership has to answer when a military doctrine is being shaped. Starting from these questions, themes such as the perception of the military–political situation, threats, command and control over the forces, objectives and tasks of military employment and international military cooperation were dealt with. In general, three kinds of perspectives can be drawn from the description of the different themes, and the arguments divided into *ad hoc*, matured and consistent statements:

* *Ad-hoc* A mindset of 'block-thinking', reference made to the 1991 Gulf War, political and economic blackmail, the cancellation of military alliances and the protection of allies.

- *Matured* The reduced importance of the CIS, the deterioration of the relations with the West, higher priority for internal conflicts and cooperation between the RF Armed Forces and the Other Troops, the abandonment of 'no-first-use' declarations, the change in priority listing in the command chain of the security apparatus and the necessity of forward deployment of forces.
- *Consistent* The national security concept as the leading security document, the defensive nature of the doctrine, the feeling of being surrounded by enemies, the protection of Russians abroad and nuclear deterrence.

Mainly this discussion of standpoints on the different themes is a reflection of matured views. *Ad hoc* and consistent standpoints play, in comparison with matured standpoints, only a minor part in the arguments used in the doctrines. It seems that the contexts of the doctrines are based primarily on (inter)national developments, such as internal conflicts within the CIS and the RF, NATO's policies towards the former Yugoslavia, the relationship between the RF and other CIS states, the battle for power inside Russia's security apparatus and the economic situation of the RF.

It is risky to make firm statements on future doctrinal developments for a country such as Russia. However, reviewing a decade of doctrinal maturity, we can establish patterns of development in the areas of internal politics, foreign politics and military concepts. With regard to *internal politics*, we can see that the President will determine major decisions in the field of security. This is the consequence of the battle between the Executive and the Legislative powers, i.e. President Yeltsin and the Supreme Soviet of October 1993. The new constitution of 1993 gave the President exclusive power in formulating the military doctrine. Especially in the case of President Putin, with his interest in security matters, further intensive involvement in security matters and in the content of documents such as the doctrine can be expected. To enforce a breakthrough in the stagnated military reforms, Putin has already strengthened the SCRF at the expense of the MoD and the General Staff. By this decision, Putin has cleared the way to replace the traditional concentration of the military leadership on large-scale warfare by focusing on internal and irregular conflicts.

Concerning *foreign policy*, two aspects can be seen: an anti-Western pattern and an assertive pattern, especially towards the CIS. Developments such as the West criticizing Russia's actions in Chechnya, ignoring the RF in its Balkan policy and NATO's enlargement and new Strategic Concept, have resulted in a deterioration of relations between the West and the RF. If these Russian sensitivities are not taken into account in NATO's security policy, Russian resentment towards the West is likely to increase. Adaptations of the RF military doctrine will reflect this bitterness, as was declared by a military official to members of NATO's Parliamentary Assembly in April 2001.[41] The other as of foreign policy is an assertive approach. This approach is reflected in statements in the doctrines on the protection of the rights of Russian minorities abroad, the abandonment of

Table 2.2 Comparison of Soviet, CIS and Russian Military Doctrines 1990–2000[a]

Doctrinal themes	Draft Military Doctrine of the USSR, December 1990[b]	Proposed Military Doctrine of the CIS February 1992	Draft Military Doctrine of the RF May 1992	Military Doctrine of the RF November 1993	Draft Military Doctrine of the RF October 1999	Military Doctrine of the RF April 2000
Division of the doctrine	1. Political aspect 2. Military–technical aspect	1. Political aspect 2. Military–technical aspect	1. Political *fundamentals* 2. Military–technical fundamentals	1. Political fundamentals 2. *Military fundamentals* 3. Military–technical and *economic* fundamentals	1. Military–political fundamentals 2. Military-*strategic* fundamentals 3. Military–economic fundamentals	1. Military–political fundamentals 2. Military–strategic fundamentals 3. Military–economic fundamentals
Number of pages	5	11	10	10	23	25
Definition of military doctrine	Represents a system of fundamental views officially accepted by the Soviet state concerning the prevention of war, force generation, preparation of the country and the Armed Forces for suppression of aggression and methods of warfare to defend the socialist *Fatherland*. The doctrine is derived from the *foreign policy of the state*	Represents a system of fundamental views officially accepted by all CIS members concerning the prevention of war and the Armed Forces for suppression of aggression and methods of warfare to defend the sovereignty the *general (all-)* and the territorial integrity of the CIS and *is a part of national security concept*	Russia's military doctrine is a component part of the *concept of national security* and represents a set of officially approved state views concerning war and its prevention, *defensive* force generation, preparation of the country and the Armed Forces for suppression of aggression and methods of warfare to defend its sovereignty and territorial integrity	The *main provisions* of the military doctrine of the RF are a component part of the *Security Concept* and represent a system of officially approved state views on averting wars and armed conflicts, force generation, preparation of the country of defence and using the Armed Forces *and the Other Troops* to protect the *vital interests* of the RF	Represents a systemized aggregate of fundamental official views (guidelines) on preventing wars and armed conflicts, on the nature and methods of waging them, and on organizing the activities of the state, society and citizen to ensure the military security of the RF *and its allies*	*Represents a systemized aggregate of fundamental official views (guidelines) on military–political, military-strategic and military– economic fundamentals for ensuring the military security of the RF*

Preamble/ Introduction	• In the present international situation the correct interpretation of the intentions and plans of each state in the military–political field is of decisive importance • For this reason the Soviet Union considers it necessary to publish the fundamental guidelines of its military doctrine • The Soviet military doctrine has a defensive direction	• The doctrine must be integrated into the *general national security concept* • The doctrine should have the force of law • The doctrine is defensive	• The doctrine is a component part of the concept of *national security* • The doctrine assumes *cooperation in the CIS on joint defence tasks* • The doctrine is based upon documents by the President, the Supreme Soviet of the RF and the CIS Council on Defence • Prevention of war and readiness to deter an aggressor are the essential tasks of the doctrine	• The doctrine is a component part of the security concept • The doctrine is implemented by coordinated political, economic, legal and military measures	• The doctrine elaborates on the 1993 military doctrine and specifies the guidelines of the RF National Security Concept • The doctrine is defensive	• The doctrine elaborates on the 1993 military doctrine and, as applied to the military sphere, specifies the guidelines of the RF National Security Concept • The doctrine is strictly defensive • *As a result of changing factors, the doctrine can be adjusted by the annual speech of the RF President to the Federal Congregation and by policy documents*
1. Military–Political Principles *Destabilizing factors of the military–political situation*	The USSR believes that the immediate threat of a global war has been considerably reduced, however there are as yet no guarantees that the positive changes are irreversible	• The threat of a global war and especially of a nuclear one has been considerably reduced • Economic, political, territorial, ethnic, religious and other disputes are not entirely ruled out	• The threat of a global nuclear or a large-scale conventional war has been considerably reduced • Economic, political, territorial, ethnic, religious and other disputes might lead to local (*civil*) wars and military conflicts	• The direct threat of open aggression against the RF has diminished considerably • *Social, political, economic, territorial, religious, national-ethnic and other disputes are the main reasons for armed conflicts and wars*	• Extremist national-ethnic, religious separatist and terrorist movements, organizations and structures • *Diminished effectiveness of existing mechanism for ensuring international security, above all the United Nations and OSCE*	• Extremist national-ethnic, religious separatist and terrorist movements, organizations and structures • Attempts to weaken (ignore) existing mechanism for ensuring international

(Table 2.2 continued)

Table 2.2 Continued

Doctrinal themes	Draft Military Doctrine of the USSR, December 1990[b]	Proposed Military Doctrine of the CIS February 1992	Draft Military Doctrine of the RF May 1992	Military Doctrine of the RF November 1993 October 1999	Draft Military Doctrine of the RF	Military Doctrine of the RF April 2000
				• *Aggressive nationalism and religious intolerance are particularly dangerous*	• *Applying military force in circumvention of international law without UN Security Council sanction*	security, above all the United Nations and OSCE • Applying military force as a means of 'humanitarian intervention' without UN Security Council sanction, in circumvention of international law • *Expansion of the scale of organized crime, terrorism and illegal trade of arms and narcotics*
External threats	Main military *threats*: • The high level of military opposition, especially in Europe and the Asian-Pacific region	• The presence in peacetime of strong groups of armed forces	Military *dangers*[d] • The presence of powerful troop concentrations near Russia's borders	Military dangers: • The build-up of troops on the borders of the RF to an amount that upsets the balance of forces	• Interference in RF internal affairs • *Attempts to ignore (or infringe on) RF*	• Interference in RF internal affairs • Attempts to ignore (or infringe on) RF

				Military threats:		
	• Politics 'by force', executed by the United States and other states dedicated to this principle • The presence of an enormous number of foreign military bases on the borders of the USSR	• The aim of *certain states to hold a dominating position* on global or regional level by all means including military	• The striving of states or coalitions to dominate the global community • The build-up of military potential by some states • *Attempts of political and economic pressure or military blackmail against Russia* • *Violation of the rights of Russian citizens* and of likeminded persons in former USSR republics The stationing on the territory of neighbouring states of foreign troops as well as a build-up of army and naval forces at its borders will be considered as a direct military threat[e]	• Attacks on the borders of the RF or on the borders of its allies • The deployment of foreign troops in states adjacent to the RF *Military threats:* • Local wars and armed conflicts close to the RF • Interference in internal Russian affairs • Suppression of the rights of Russian citizens in the 'near abroad' (*zarubezhnykh*) • Attacks on RF forces stationed abroad • *Expansion of military blocs and alliances*	*interests in resolving international security problems* • *Attempts to oppose the increase of influence of the RF on a global level* • *The expansion of military blocs and alliances* • *The introduction of foreign troops (without UN Security Council sanction) to the territory of contiguous states friendly with the RF* • *Suppression of the rights of RF citizens in the 'near abroad' (zarubezhnykh)*	interests in resolving international security problems • Attempts to oppose the increase of influence of the RF on a global level • The expansion of military blocs and alliances • The introduction of foreign troops (without UN Security Council sanction) to the territory of contiguous states friendly with the RF • Suppression of the rights of RF citizens abroad (*inostrannykh*)
Internal threats	(This paragraph is absent in this military doctrine)	(This paragraph is absent in this military doctrine)	(This paragraph is absent in this military doctrine)	• The unlawful activity of nationalist, secessionist and other organizations to	• The unlawful activities of extremist nationalist-ethnic,	• The unlawful activities of extremist nationalist-ethnic,

(Table 2.2 continued)

Table 2.2 Continued

Doctrinal themes	Draft Military Doctrine of the USSR, December 1990[b]	Proposed Military Doctrine of the CIS, February 1992	Draft Military Doctrine of the RF May 1992	Military Doctrine of the RF November	Draft Military Doctrine of the RF October 1999	Military Doctrine of the RF April 2000
				destabilize the internal situation in Russia • *Attempts to overthrow the constitutional regime* • *The creation of illegal armed formations*	religious and separatist and terrorist movements, organizations and structures in order to disrupt *the unity and territorial integrity of the state and to* destabilize the internal situation • Attempts to overthrow the constitutional system	religious and separatist and terrorist movements, organizations and structures in order to disrupt the unity and territorial integrity of the state and to destabilize the internal situation • Attempts to overthrow the constitutional system
Principles for ensuring military security	• The USSR renounces the use of military means as a solution for contradictions • *Conventional no-first-use:* the SU rejects the first initiation of military action against any state • *Nuclear no-first-use:* the SU rejects the first use of nuclear weapons	• The main task of the doctrine is to provide security against *external threat* • *No nation or alliance is considered to be an opponent* • Non-intervention principle and recognition of inviolability of existing borders	• The military-political goal is to ensure the state's security against external threat • Non-intervention in other states and recognition of inviolability of existing borders • Conventional-no-first use: rejection of first initiation of military action against any state	• *No state is considered to be an opponent* • *Limited nuclear no-first-use:* first use of nuclear weapons is possible in certain circumstances • Strengthening of arms control regimes of weapons of mass destruction and of conventional weapons	• The RF adheres to the system of generally recognized principles and rules of international law (UN Charter, Helsinki Agreements, Paris Charter) • *The RF will not be first to begin military operations against a state or a coalition*	• *The RF adheres to the fundamental principles and rules of international law* • *The RF executes a common defence policy with Belarus in the field of military organization and the development of the Armed Forces of the member states of the Union*

	• No nation is considered to be an enemy • Disbandment of both alliances, Warsaw Pact and NATO and their consequent reorganization into instruments of political cooperation and systems of international security	• Nuclear deterrence is an element of strategic stability • Conventional no-first-use: rejection of first initiation of military action against any state • Nuclear no-first-use: rejection of first use of nuclear weapons • The CIS should have unified armed forces at its disposal	• Nuclear no-first-use: rejection of first use of nuclear weapons • Nuclear weapons remain a realistic means for preventing nuclear attack • *Unity and indivisibility of joint (CIS) defence*: an attack on one CIS member is considered as an attack on all	• To develop *military cooperation* with foreign states, especially with CIS member states and countries of Central and Eastern Europe	• The RF retains nuclear power status for deterring aggression against the RF *or its allies* • The RF retains the right *to use nuclear weapons* in response to weapons of mass-destruction *and in response to wide scale aggression using conventional weapons* against the RF *and its allies* (stated in § 'state military organisation)	• The RF retains nuclear power status for deterring aggression against the RF *and (or)* its allies • The RF retains the right to use nuclear weapons in response to weapons of mass destruction and in response to wide-scale aggression using conventional weapons in situations critical *for the RF*
State military organization	(This paragraph is absent in this military doctrine)	(This paragraph is absent in this military doctrine)	(This paragraph is absent in this military doctrine)	(This paragraph is absent in this military doctrine)	The *RF Armed Forces* are the *nucleus* of the military organization of the state	The state's military organization includes the RF Armed Forces, which are its nucleus, *and the Other Troops, military units and entities*[f], earmarked for fulfilling tasks of military security
Command and control of the Armed Forces, the Other Troops, military units and entities	(This paragraph is absent in this military doctrine)	(This paragraph is absent in this military doctrine)	• The *Security Council of the RF (SCRF)*, chaired by the President, is the principal military–political agency, exercising overall direction of the security apparatus	• The RF President, Supreme Commander-in-Chief of the RF Armed Forces, has the general guidance of the RF Armed Forces *and the Other Troops*	• The RF President, Supreme Commander of the RF Armed Forces, leads the activities of ensuring military security	• The RF President, Supreme Commander of the RF Armed Forces, *directs the organization, preparation and the use of the military organization*

(Table 2.2 continued)

Table 2.2 Continued

Doctrinal themes	Draft Military Doctrine of the USSR, December 1990[b]	Proposed Military Doctrine of the CIS February 1992	Draft Military Doctrine of the RF May 1992	Military Doctrine of the RF November	Draft Military Doctrine of the RF October 1999	Military Doctrine of the RF April 2000
			• *The RF President is the Supreme C-in-C of the Armed Forces* • *The Ministry of Defence is assigned the development and immediate implementation of military policy* • *The C-in-C Armed Forces exercises direction of the RF Armed Forces (n.b.: Other Troops not mentioned) through the General Staff* • *Coordination of the RF Ministry of Defence with the CIS United Forces Main Command is accomplished through the Council of CIS Ministers of Defence*	• The RF Council of Ministers – RF government is responsible for the state of the RF Armed Forces *and the Other Troops* • The Minister of Defence *directly controls the RF Armed Forces* • The General Staff of the RF Armed Forces has the *operational control of the Armed Forces* • *The Other Troops are directly controlled by the corresponding commanders (chiefs)* • The Security Council RF is responsible for drafting presidential decrees on security issues (n.b.: the SCRF is not listed as a command & control level but as political fundamental)	*security;* provides the equipment of the Armed Forces *and the Other Troops* and directs the preparation of the RF for its defence • The RF Ministry of Defence is in charge *of the organization, development and procurement of the state military organization* • The General Staff is the basic entity for operational command and control of the RF Armed Forces and accomplishes the *strategic planning* for the employment of the Armed Forces *and the Other Troops*	• The RF Government provides the equipment of the Armed Forces and the Other Troops and directs the preparation of the RF for its defence • The RF Ministry of Defence is in charge of the *organization and development of the Other Troops* and procurement • The General Staff is the basic entity for operational command and control of the RF Armed Forces and *coordinates the activities and organizes the joint deployment of the* RF Armed Forces and the Other Troops • *The staffs of the services and the arms accomplish the organization and employment of their forces*

2. Military-strategic principles

Types of conflict (in the order as stated)	1. Armed conflict 2. Local war 3. Regional war 4. *Large-scale* war	1. Global war 2. Regional war 3. Local war 4. Armed conflict	1. Local wars and armed conflicts 2. *Internal* armed conflicts 3. Global war (both conventional and nuclear)	(This paragraph is absent in this military doctrine)	(This paragraph is absent in this military doctrine)	1. *Global* nuclear war 2. *Large-scale* conventional war 3. *Local (civil)* war 4. Armed conflict
Objectives of deploying Armed Forces and the Other Troops	1. *Large-scale (regional)* war 2. Local wars and *international* armed conflicts 3. Internal armed conflicts 4. Peace support and *peace-restoring* operations	1. Conventional global-(regional) war 2. *Nuclear* war 3. Local wars and armed conflicts 4. Internal armed conflicts	• Prevention of war and armed conflicts • Deterrence of potential aggressors	• Prevention of war • Deterrence of potential aggressors • Suppression of aggression • *Defence in all azimuths* • *Non-use of the Armed Forces to accomplish internal political missions*	• Prevention of war • Deterrence of opponents • Suppression of aggression • Defensive strategy	• The prevention of war • Suppression of aggression against the SU or an allied state • Possible allocation of troops for UN peace-support operations • *Defensive strategy*
Ways of employing the Armed Forces and the Other Troops	• Strategic operations, major operations, and combat operations in *large-scale* as well as regional wars • Operations and combat operations in local wars and *international* armed conflicts	• Strategic operations, major operations, and combat operations in a global war and regional wars • Operations and combat operations in local wars and armed conflicts	(This paragraph is absent in this military doctrine)	• Deterrence of potential aggressors • Joint defence or peacekeeping in cooperation with other states in accordance with the UN Charter and other treaties	(This paragraph is absent in this military doctrine)	• The strategic nuclear forces maintain military-strategic parity with US strategic strike forces • The nuclear forces prevent a surprise nuclear attack and guarantee a counterattack

(Table 2.2 continued)

Table 2.2 Continued

Doctrinal themes	Draft Military Doctrine of the USSR, December 1990[b]	Proposed Military Doctrine of the CIS February 1992	Draft Military Doctrine of the RF May 1992	Military Doctrine of the RF November	Draft Military Doctrine of the RF October 1999	Military Doctrine of the RF April 2000
			• *Protection of the rights and interests of Russian citizens and culturally likeminded persons abroad* • *Disaster relief*		• Peace support operations	• *Joint special operations in internal armed conflicts* • *Anti-terror operations* • *Peacekeeping operations*
Missions of the Armed Forces and the Other Troops	• Guaranteeing the inviolability of the borders • Defence of state *sovereignty* • Defence of the territorial integrity	(This paragraph is absent in this military doctrine)	1. Defence of the sovereignty and the territorial integrity of the RF and the CIS 2. *Joint defence based on treaties with other states (alliances)* 3. Maintenance or restoration of international peace in accordance with UN Security Council resolutions 4. *Conflict resolution within the CIS*	1. Defence of the sovereignty and territorial integrity *and other vital interests of the RF* 2. Peace support operations 3. Suppression of internal or border conflicts 4. Disaster relief Tasks are fulfilled by the Armed Forces together with other RF departments, Frontier Troops and Internal Troops	1. Ensuring military security 2. Suppression of aggression towards the RF and its allies 3. Peace support operations 4. Internal armed conflicts 5. Disaster relief	1. Ensuring military security 2. Suppression of aggression towards the RF *and (or) its allies* 3. Internal armed conflicts 4. Peace support and *peace-restoring* operations 5. Disaster relief

Deployment of Armed Forces and the Other Troops abroad	The removal of military bases on the territory of any other state and the deployment of troops explicitly within national boundaries	(This paragraph is absent in this military doctrine.)	• The security interests of the RF and other CIS states may require the deployment of forces outside the RF • Russian forces may be deployed outside its territory in combined or Russian task forces and bases	• RF Armed Forces and Other Troops may be stationed outside its territory as part of combined or Russian task forces and bases	• *Limited contingents of the RF Armed Forces and Other Troops may be deployed in regions of strategic importance,* outside RF territory, as combined or national task forces and bases
3.Military–economic principles (The chapter on 'Military–economic principles' is absent in this military doctrine)			(The chapter on 'Military–economic principles' is absent in this military doctrine)		
Main objective of military–economic ensuring of military security			Timely provide the Armed Forces and the Other Troops of the RF with effective weapons systems to an extent that the vital interests of society and state are ensured	Financial and material guarantees for the state's military organization	To fulfil the demands of the state's military organization with regard to financial and material means
International military cooperation	Contacts in the military field are developed with all interested states by agreements on the prevention of conflict situations	*Russia will cooperate in strengthening (inter)national security and stability with:* 1. CIS 2. *NATO* 3. *OSCE* 4. in other regions than Europe	Cooperation in military security is sought in security structures with: 1. CIS 2. NATO 3. OSCE 4. in other regions than Europe	*To maintain international peace and security the RF cooperates with:* 1. CIS 2. OSCE 3. other states and alliances in	The RF attaches priority importance to the development of military cooperation with member states of the CIS Collective Security Treaty, to establish a unified defence space	The RF attaches priority importance to the development of military cooperation with state parties to the CIS Collective Security Treaty, because of the *necessity to consolidate*

(Table 2.2 continued)

Table 2.2 Continued

Doctrinal themes	*Draft Military Doctrine of the USSR, December 1990*[b]	*Proposed Military Doctrine of the CIS February 1992*	*Draft Military Doctrine of the RF May 1992*	*Military Doctrine of the RF November*	*Draft Military Doctrine of the RF October 1999*	*Military Doctrine of the RF April 2000*
		5. United States 6. other countries by means of the UN	alliances in neighbouring regions 5. on a global scale with all UN member states	neighbouring regions 4. all member states of the UN	ensure collective military security	*the forces towards the creation of a unified defence space and ensure collective military security*
				Military–technical cooperation is aimed at *strengthening RF military–political positions across the world*	Military cooperation is aimed at strengthening of military–political positions of the RF *in various regions of the world*	
Conclusion	The USSR strictly adheres to all international obligations that result from the UN Charter, the Helsinki Final Act, the Stockholm Conference document, the Paris Charter for the new Europe and other agreements and universally recognized norms of international relations	(This paragraph is absent in this military doctrine)	(This paragraph is absent in this military doctrine)	• The RF closely adheres to the norms and principles of international law • The doctrine determines a strictly defensive nature of ensuring the military security of the RF *and its allies*	• The RF guarantees compliance with the norms and principles of international law • The doctrine affirms the strictly defensive direction of its activities for ensuring military security	The RF is dedicated to the deterrence of aggression, the prevention of wars and armed conflicts and fully supports international security and a general peace

Notes

a The citations are mostly not literally derived from the different doctrine documents, but are adapted by the author. Remarkable differences between doctrines are printed in italic. The grouping of related doctrinal aspects as used here is for the purpose of clarity and does not necessarily correspond with the original documents.

b Sources: 'Proyekt dokumenta o voyennoy doktrine', *Voyennaya Mysl'*, spetsial'nyy vypusk, Dec. 1990, pp. 24–8; Klimenko, 'O role i meste voyennoy doktriny v sisteme bezopasnosti Sodruzhestva nezavisimykh gosudarstv'; 'Osnovnyye polozheniya voyennoy doktriny Rossiyskoy Federatsii (izlozheniye)', pp. 3–4; *Sobraniye Aktov Prezidenta i Pravitel'stva RF* (1993), item 4329, p. 4813; 'Dokumenty, Voyennaya doktrina Rossiyskoy Federatsii (proyekt)', *Krasnaya Zvezda*, 9 Oct. 1999, pp. 3–4; 'Voyennaya doktrina Rossiyskoy Federatsii', *Nezavisimoye Voyennoye Obozreniye*, 15, 28 April 2000, pp. 1, 4–5; *Sobraniye Zakonodatel'stva RF* (2000), item 1852, p. 3843.

c The term 'general (all-) national' (*obshchenatsional'nyy*) refers to the entire CIS, see '*Osnovy voyennoy doktriny Rossii (Proyekt)*', p. 11.

d 'Military *danger*' (*opasnost'*) is a state of interstate relations in which the potential possibility of the outbreak of war exists, see '*Osnovy voyennoy doktriny Rossii (Proyekt)*', p. 11.

e 'Military threat' (*ugroza*) is a state of interstate relations in which an immediate danger of the outbreak of war exists, see '*Osnovy voyennoy doktriny Rossii (Proyekt)*', p. 11.

f The term 'other troops, military units and entities' refers to the armed forces of the power ministries, such as the Ministry for Internal Affairs, the Federal Border Guard Service and the Federal Agency for Communications with the presidential apparatus (FAPSI). The term '(RF) Armed Forces' refers to the armed services of the Ministry of Defence.

conventional and nuclear 'no-first-use' declarations, the possible deployment of troops abroad and the strengthening of RF military–political positions throughout the world as an objective for military cooperation. These statements are in contrast to the 'defensive' nature of the doctrine. Although these remarks might be regarded as rhetoric, some CIS neighbours will feel threatened by this assertive attitude. This approach is probably an attempt to regain the status of superpower. Taking into account the RF's economic and military power, this endeavour is not likely to succeed. However, Russia will continue to be an important regional power, especially in the CIS. It is therefore to be expected that these firm views will continue to be expressed in future military doctrines.

Bearing in mind the type of conflicts in the CIS and the RF of the past decade, with regard to *military concepts* a stronger emphasis on preparation for internal and irregular conflicts can be expected in future doctrinal and other security documents. This will most certainly result in the elaboration of new concepts of military action that have been launched in recent years: joint military action by the RF Armed Forces and the Other Troops, as well as training and equipping of the forces for irregular warfare. Likewise it can be expected that the importance of nuclear forces will be further reduced for the benefit of reinforcing conventional forces. As in the last ten years, the future military doctrine of the RF will to a great extent consist of matured standpoints, based upon the perception of (inter) national developments.

Putin's security policy: a comparison of the 2000 issues of the National Security Concept, Military Doctrine and Foreign Policy Concept

According to internationally accepted points of view, national security policy should reflect a coherent and consistent system of political, military, economic and psychological means that a state has at its disposal; an analysis of President Putin's security policy, as it was issued in formal documents in the year 2000; and a discussion of the 2000 edition of the National Security Concept (NSC), the Military Doctrine and the Foreign Policy Concept.[42] Three basic questions will be reviewed: What were the fundamentals of Putin's security policy? Were these viewpoints coherent and consistent? What expectations can be made regarding the advancement of Russia's security policy in the near future?

The NSC was produced by the SCRF and provides an overall view of RF security policy, in which all means available to the state are applied. The Military Doctrine was drafted by the MoD and deals with the military resources of the state. The Foreign Policy Concept was drawn up by the Ministry of Foreign Affairs (MID), and relates to the political and diplomatic means of the RF. Since the NSC is the principle security document, for reasons of unity and clarity the description of the three documents will be offered in the format of the NSC. The structure of the NSC, and thus of the comparison of the 2000 editions of the security documents, is divided into four parts: Russia in the world community,

Russia's national interests, threats to Russia's security and ensuring Russia's security.[43]

Russia in the world community: destabilizing factors

A number of destabilizing factors are consistently mentioned in all documents:

- dominance in the international community of Western states led by the United States;
- unilateral power actions, bypassing the UN Security Council (UNSC), by using concepts such as 'humanitarian intervention' and 'limited sovereignty';
- (international) terrorism;
- organized crime.

The enumeration of destabilizing factors demonstrates an emphasis on *external* aspects. Another striking feature is the prominence of negative references with regard to Western security policy. Over the years, in the three security documents more and more entries have been included relating to this subject. NATO's use of force in the former Yugoslavia (Bosnia and Kosovo), especially, was seen as a clear example of its policy of ignoring Russia, which claimed a decisive role in Europe, as well as of disregarding the UN and the standards of international law. Other concerns were NATO's new Strategic Concept of April 1999 and its enlargement with new member states in the East, adjacent to Russia's borders.

Internal destabilizing factors seem to be of less importance. Terrorism and organized crime are included in all the documents. Two of the three documents mention illegal arms trade and narcotics as well as nationalistic and religious strife as factors. This leads to two conclusions. First, the internal destabilizing factors are not consistent in the security documents. Apparently the security organs had different opinions on the domestic situation. Second, external destabilizing factors outweigh internal ones in RF security policy. The security organs obviously were more focused on international developments.

Russia's national interests

The national interests mentioned in the documents reflect the instruments that the state has at its disposal to achieve the objectives of its grand strategy, i.e. political, military, economic and psychological means. The security documents state that national interests determine Russia's domestic and foreign policies. Additionally, they are meant to ensure the sovereignty of the state. The following points of national interest prevail in the documents:

- primary interests are protection against (international) terrorism, disasters of natural or industrial origin, and the dangers arising from wartime military operations;

- improving economic development and enhancing the standard of living;
- preserving and strengthening of the RF's sovereignty and territorial integrity and strengthening the basis of the constitutional system;
- eliminating the causes and conditions contributing to political and religious extremism and ethno-separatism;
- strengthening Russia's international position as a great power;
- developing mutually advantageous relations, especially with the member states of the CIS;
- cooperation in the military–political area and in the sphere of security through the CIS (Collective Security Treaty), particularly in combating international terrorism and extremism.

The Military Doctrine exclusively deals with the international, military-diplomatic dimensions of national interest. Apparently, the military did not wish to look at, or simply ignored the social-economic aspects of security. This was a short-sighted approach. Russian forces participated in peace-keeping missions in Bosnia (SFOR) and Kosovo (KFOR), in which social-economic aspects were of great importance in reaching a long-lasting settlement of the conflict. Clearly, the Russian military leadership must have been well posted on the concept of 'broad security', which nowadays is an accepted model in international (security) politics. Since the top level of the General Staff was raised in the ideological background of the Cold War, it might very well be possible that hawkish generals stubbornly kept to the outdated and limited views of the military-diplomatic dimension of security. The NSC and Foreign Policy Concept both adhere to the concept of a broad spectrum of security and therefore have corresponding entries on national interests. So in this case the military were out of line.

The national interests as listed are a mixture of entries on *domestic* and *international* matters. Nowadays the perception that security is more than protection with military means against an external aggressor is widely accepted as realistic. 'Chechnya' has made clear to the RF authorities that not only *external* but also *internal* threats exist against national security and that these threats are not confined to the military dimension but also have their roots in political, social and economic dimensions. However, if the RF authorities had taken this interdependence between internal and external national interests seriously, they would have concluded that conflicts of the type of the Chechen war can not be solved by military means. Consequently, in order to ensure a consistent national policy on security not only are military and diplomatic means important, but also social (human rights), economic (development projects, building and maintenance of houses, schools and medical facilities) and political (reform of the bureaucratic apparatus) activities are essential. A stable economic development is a prerequisite for realizing these activities. These basic conditions are, in general terms, reflected in the 2000 editions of the NSC as well as of the Foreign Policy Concept. However, in Russian civic society they had not yet become visible. Probably, this was due to the slow economic development but surely also to the continued presence of a deep-rooted bureaucracy, which led to corruption. Therefore, the implementation of the aforementioned policy intentions in a broad spectrum of security aspects is likely to be a long-term process.

Threats to Russia's security

The RF sees the fulfilment of its political-strategic objectives as well as its internal and external security threatened by a number of factors. In discussing the general roots of threats, the NSC above all points out internal, socio-economic aspects: the poor status of the economy, a failing governmental apparatus, polarization between entities, (organized) crime, corruption and terrorism. These internal aspects are further elaborated in the enumeration of internal threats in the three security documents. Apart from internal threats these documents naturally also recognize external threats. When comparing the three documents the following threats are uppermost:

Internal threats

- extremist national-ethnic and religious separatism and terrorism;
- trans-national organized crime;
- erosion of the territorial integrity of the state by separatist aspirations of a number of constituent entities of the RF, by poor organization of state control, and because of the links between some parts of the executive and the legislature and criminal organizations (corruption).

External threats

- attempts to belittle the role of existing mechanisms for international security of the UN and the OSCE, by economic and power domination of the United States and other Western states;
- attempts to ignore (or infringe on) RF interests and influence in resolving international security problems;
- the strengthening of military–political blocs and alliances, above all the expansion of NATO eastwards;
- NATO's practice of using military force outside the bloc's zone of responsibility without UNSC sanction.

The listed internal and external threats are a logical outcome of the aforementioned destabilizing factors. The entries regarding internal threats are consistently repeated in all three documents. At first sight the provisions on external threats seem to be described much more extensively in the NSC and the Foreign Policy Concept. However, this is a result of the division of the different documents. In the Military Doctrine under the heading 'Destabilizing factors' the remaining internal as well as external threats are mentioned, which are not listed under

77

'Threats'. If this is taken into account then the conclusion can be drawn that the enumerations of threats are, on the whole, similar in all three security documents.

Ensuring Russia's security

In the security part of the documents the various policy dimensions come together. It portrays consecutively the principles of socio-economic and domestic policies (fundamentals and objectives), as well as of foreign and security policies (military security, the use of force and the deployment of forces and troops abroad), for the purpose of achieving the objectives of Russia's grand strategy and of ensuring its national security. As a final point, these parts of the security documents present a hierarchy of the institutions responsible for national security.

Socio-economic and domestic policies

- Decreasing Russia's economic dependency on other states by strengthening state regulation of the economy and by organizing a common economic area in the CIS;
- improving the system of state power of the RF, its federal relations and its local self-government (constituent entities) to reinforce the social and political stability of society;
- guaranteeing strict observance of the law by all citizens, public servants, state institutions, political parties and social and religious organizations to diminish crime, corruption and terrorism;
- adhering to the fundamental principles and rules of international law.

With the exception of the latter entry, the socio-economic and domestic fundamentals are only listed in the NSC. Apart from internal threats and military operations as a result of them, the Military Doctrine does not mingle in domestic affairs, which the MoD apparently considered to be the prime function of other (power) ministries. The Foreign Policy Concept naturally pays a lot of attention to international law, for instance human rights. Considering this as a domestic aspect, one would expect the RF to adhere to these principles and rules in internal affairs as well. However, the consecutive conflicts in Chechnya have demonstrated a different approach, bearing in mind the breaches of the law of armed conflict which have occurred. This leads one to conclude that the RF uses different standards in dealing with external and internal matters.

President Putin regarded the strengthening of central authority as the main solution for the socio-economic problems. In his 'vertical' approach he made an effort to strengthen his grip on developments in these and other fields, by withdrawing power and influence from enterprises (especially of the oligarchs who control vital areas of the economy) and from the constituent entities (governors of the regions) for the benefit of the Kremlin.[44] In this way Putin wanted to increase government revenues (taxes), to finance policy objectives such as the fight against crime and terrorism, as well as to enlarge the influence of the central apparatus on constituent entities, by deploying presidential plenipotentiaries at the regional level. Another objective of the installation of plenipotentiaries was to prevent or neutralize separatist movements. It is doubtful that simply increasing central authority over the regions would result in improvement of the relations between the central and regional powers. Still, reinforcing central authority could also be beneficial for Russia. The RF is a state without a heritage of civic, democratic governance. Yeltsin's period of rule demonstrated that a vast and complicated country such as Russia without steadfast, centralized authority offers certain groups, such as oligarchs and regional governors, the opportunity of abusing power. On the other hand, centralization of power demands guarantees for democratic development, in order to prevent totalitarianism. In this respect it is important to realize that since the introduction of the Constitution of 1993 the powers of the legislature, to properly check the executive (President and government), have been restricted. Theoretically this could lead to unlimited and uncontrolled centralization of powers.

Foreign policy

- Reinforcing vital mechanisms for multilateral management of international processes, above all under jurisdiction of the UNSC;
- partnership with all CIS member states, and development of integration processes within the CIS, as well as implementation of other objectives of Russia's interests regarding the CIS;
- defending and guaranteeing the legal rights and interests of Russian citizens (compatriots) resident abroad or of the Russian-speaking population, in the CIS as well as in the Baltic States.

Reinforcing mechanisms of international security. The RF clearly rejects the leading role in international politics of institutions other than the UNSC. This provision is of course related to the objective of strengthening of Russia's international position. In the UNSC the RF possesses the right of veto and thus is able to block undesirable resolutions. Therefore, the objective of reinforcing Russia's international status can be promoted within the constellation of the UN. However, if NATO were to dominate international politics, the situation would be different. In such an arrangement of the international system, the RF, without right of veto, would be more or less 'dependent' on NATO's policies. This explains the prominence of the UN and the UNSC especially in the relevant entries in the documents.

Advancing regional stability. In the practice of politics, Russia's standpoints on good neighbourhood (partnership) and on regional conflict solution in the CIS get mixed up. On some occasions the RF allegedly has actively encouraged regional conflict, for instance in Abkhazia, followed by an offer of conflict solution, thus making a CIS state, in this case Georgia, dependent on Russia for ensuring its security. Subsequently, this dependency in the field of security was aimed at enhancing RF influence on this state, thus 'ensuring' good neighbourliness.

Protecting Russians abroad. This is a recurring theme of RF foreign policy. In the Foreign Policy Concept this provision is mentioned no less than four times: under the heading 'General principles', under 'Human rights and international relations', and twice under 'Regional priorities', in discussing relations within the CIS and with the Baltic States. The NSC as well as the Foreign Policy Concept, in describing the location of Russians abroad, use the term *za rubezhëm*. This term points at states adjacent to the RF. The expression *za rubezhëm* has an emotional connotation: it refers to something familiar, which binds together.[45] In the consecutive military doctrines a provision on the protection of Russians abroad is also included under the heading 'External threats'. In previous doctrines in describing 'abroad' the same expression was used as in the other two security documents: *za rubezhëm*. However, in the 2000 issue of the Military Doctrine this term has been changed into *inostrannykh*. *Inostrannykh* means out of the country in general, it has a neutral, dispassionate implication. Based on the changed connotation of the term for abroad in the Military Doctrine of 2000 the assumption could be made that the General Staff/MoD became less willing to use force if necessary for the protection of Russian minorities in a foreign country. Considering the term *za rubezhëm*, used in the NSC and in the Foreign Policy Concept, it appears that respectively, the SCRF and, in view of frequent mentions, the MID in particular, attached a higher priority to the position of compatriots abroad than the MoD.

Security policy

With regard to security policy, analysis of the three documents presents three fundamental themes: ensuring military security, methods of using forces and troops and the deployment of forces and troops abroad. These themes generate the following entries, which are only mentioned in the NSC and in the Military Doctrine:

- all forces and facilities available, including nuclear weapons, will be used if necessary to repel armed aggression, if all other means have been exhausted;
- the RF must uphold nuclear deterrence;
- forces and troops are employed in local, regional, international and large-scale conflicts, as well as for peacekeeping operations;
- the interests of Russia's national security may require a Russian military presence in certain strategically vital regions of the world.

Ensuring military security. The NSC and the Military Doctrine permit the use of nuclear weapons to counter aggression. However, the Military Doctrine is more outspoken in this respect: it allows for the use of nuclear arms to repel a conventional attack as well, under certain not specified critical circumstances for national security. Conversely, the Foreign Policy Concept places the emphasis on a desire to lessen the role of military power, mentioning reductions of conventional arms as well as of weapons of mass-destruction, ways to prevent the proliferation of these weapons, and other aspects of arms control, such as confidence and security-building measures. Consequently, in contrast to the other two documents, the Foreign Policy Concept regards nuclear weapons not primarily as a means of deterrence, but as a means of arms control. In this case the MoD, acting in its 'own' field, appears to be the most aggressive institution, with regard to military interests. This attitude is not unexpected, since a decline in the position of the military instrument of national security policy is likely to cause a lessening in the power and influence of the MoD as well. Opposed to the NSC and the Military Doctrine is the point of view of the MID. This difference in approach to security matters could result in an inconsistent foreign policy with regard to stances on international security.

Foreign deployment of forces and troops. The NSC as well as the Military Doctrine consider the deployment of limited contingents of forces and troops abroad justified. It is remarkable in this respect that the NSC specifically mentions naval forces. The doctrine does not bring up naval forces at this spot, although elsewhere it allots a special role to the RF Navy in accomplishing the objectives of the state. Since previous doctrines did not reveal a specific role for naval forces, this provision has to be seen as a new course in security policy. It is likely that the increased contribution of the RF Navy to the implementation of political strategy is related to a purposive campaign of the top level of this service to strengthen its position: in 2000 President Putin endorsed a document on naval policy until 2010, which was further elaborated into a maritime doctrine, published in 2001. In view of the fact that Putin gave his backing to both documents, he apparently was convinced of an essential role for sea power in achieving political-strategic objectives.[46]

Institutions responsible for national security

In the following hierarchy of security organs the first five are listed in at least two of the three security documents. The sixth entry comprises organs which are related to the specific dimensions of the Military Doctrine and the Foreign Policy Concept (*the documents are in parentheses*):

- President (*NSC, Military Doctrine and Foreign Policy Concept*)
  The President is the only authority mentioned in all three security documents. He directs the agencies and forces which ensure RF national security, is Supreme Commander of the RF Armed Forces and as the Head of State represents the RF in international relations;
- Federal Assembly (*NSC, Foreign Policy Concept*)
  The Federal Assembly formulates the legislative basis for national security policy and for foreign policy. However, absent from the Military Doctrine,

this institution is excluded from producing legislative fundamentals of defence policy;

- Government (*NSC, Military Doctrine*)
  The Government coordinates the work of federal executive agencies and executive agencies of RF constituent entities concerning national security, provides the equipment of the Armed Forces and the Other Troops and directs the preparation of the RF for its defence. The government is not listed in the Foreign Policy Concept;

- Security Council (*NSC, Foreign Policy Concept*)
  The SCRF assesses threats to national security, drafts proposals and documents for the President on national security (such as the NSC), coordinates the work of the forces and agencies in ensuring national security and monitors the implementation of policy decisions by federal executive agencies and by authorities in the RF constituent entities;

- Constituent entities (*NSC, Foreign Policy Concept*)
  The constituent entities implement RF legislation and carry out security and international-related decisions of the President, the government, and of the Supreme Commander of the Armed Forces;

- Other institutions (*Military Doctrine, Foreign Policy Concept*)
  In addition to the aforementioned institutions these two security documents include a number of bodies in the hierarchy of security organs, which are only relevant for their specific policy domain:

    - MoD, General Staff, staffs of the services and the arms of the Armed Forces;
    - MID, non-governmental organizations.

In order to establish an efficient government of the state the activities of the executive and the legislature must be well coordinated and congruent to ensure a consistent grand strategy. With regard to the NSC this seems to be the case. On the recommendation of the SCRF the President determines Russia's national security policy, the Federal Assembly takes care of the legal foundation and the government implements this policy. As mentioned before, in this respect it must be remarked that the powers of the legislature to check the executive are rather limited.

In contrast with the NSC the Military Doctrine demonstrates a number of deficiencies in relation to the control of the executive and the legislature over military policy. Parliament and the SCRF are missing in the doctrinal enumeration of security organs. Furthermore, according to the Constitution only the President has the power to sanction the doctrine.[47] Unmistakably, Parliament is set aside. The fact that the SCRF, theoretically the primary security organ, is not formally involved in controlling the military apparatus most likely was deliberate policy by the military to reinforce their own power and influence in this policy dimension. However, Putin's decision to transfer authority over military reforms form the General Staff to the SCRF and to appoint former Secretary SCRF Sergey Ivanov as Minister of Defence were indications that he endeavoured to weaken the power of the military. It was likely that Putin would continue this policy course, which would lead to a formalized contribution of the SCRF in directing military force.

Just like the NSC the Foreign Policy Concept also expresses a consistent control of policy. Apparently except for one point – the government is missing in the list of security organs. This is probably related to the concentration of responsibilities in the area of foreign policy with the President and the Minister of Foreign Affairs. Thus, direct involvement of the government in foreign policy seems to be regarded as superfluous. In addition to this, preparation and implementation of foreign policy is coordinated by the SCRF and corresponding legislation is provided by Parliament.

In conclusion, it is evident that Russia's grand strategy is first of all the prerogative of the President. Without doubt, he is the principal authority with regard to defining and implementing political strategy. His extensive powers in this area are laid down in the corresponding articles of the Constitution.[48] In implementing Russia's political strategy the President is supported by the Federal Assembly, the government and the SCRF.

Conclusions: consistency of RF security policy

The previous paragraph, in analysing the three major security documents, in 2000, provided a portrayal of the framework of the security policy of President Putin. Three security actors, the SCRF, the MoD and the MID, produced these policy documents. A grand strategy can only be efficient and successful if it is based on a coordinated and fine-tuned application of the means which the state has available. Once more, examining the 2000 security documents, I will explain the consistency of Putin's political strategy and a preliminary outlook on the advancement of Russia's security policy. In the concluding chapter the outlook on RF security policy will be further elaborated in view of post-2000 developments in Russia's security and in the international arena.

The three relevant security actors, SCRF, MoD and MID, demonstrate fine-tuned points of view when it comes to external aspects. In other words, these security actors are in accord on their appreciation of external developments and in the responses which RF security policy should present. For example, they all reject Western security policies and refer to the strengthening of recognized security mechanisms (UNSC, OSCE) as the appropriate answer. There are two exceptions to this united approach: the issues of Russians abroad and international security. Whereas the MoD is reluctant to provide military support for the protection of compatriots abroad, the other two actors attach a high priority to this fundamental of security policy. And as to ensuring international security, the MID noticeably has a dissenting view: arms control is more important than nuclear deterrence. These departmental differences could cause strife between these two security actors. However, in spite of these two inconsistent viewpoints, on the whole opinions on the external aspects of security are consistent.

Table 2.3 Comparison of the 2000 editions of NSC, Military Doctrine and Foreign Policy Concept[a]

Themes	National Security Concept January 2000	Military Doctrine April 2000	Foreign Policy Concept June 2000
1. Russia in the world community			
Destabilizing factors for the military–political situation	• *Dominance in the international community of developed Western states led by the United States;* this is especially aimed at applying unilateral solutions, including the use of military force, to key problems in world politics, flouting the fundamental principles of international law • efforts to weaken Russia's position politically, economically, and militarily, as well in other fields • attempts to ignore the interests of Russia in solving major problems in international relations • terrorism poses a threat to world stability	• Extremist nationalist-ethnic, religious, separatist and terrorist movements, organizations and structures • attempts to weaken (ignore) existing mechanisms for ensuring international security, above all the United Nations and OSCE • applying military force *as a means of 'humanitarian intervention'* without UN Security Council sanction, in circumvention of international law • *expansion of the scale of organized crime, terrorism and illegal trade of arms and narcotics*	• *Unilateral actions* can destabilize the international situation, provoke tensions and the arms race, aggravate interstate contradictions, national and religious strife • *the use of force in violation of the UN Charter is unlawful* and poses a threat to the stabilization of the entire system of international relations • attempts to introduce into international parlance such *concepts as 'humanitarian intervention'* and *'limited sovereignty'* in order to justify unilateral power actions *bypassing the UN Security Council are not acceptable*
2. Russia's national interests			
General	Russia's national interests are the sum total of the balanced interests of the individual, society and the state in the economic, domestic, political, social, international and information spheres and in military,	(Not mentioned)	Enhancing the efficiency of political, legal, foreign, economic and other instruments for protecting the state sovereignty of Russia and its national economy in conditions of globalization

Socio-economic	border, ecological and other fields; they are long term in nature, and determine the principal aims of the state and the strategic and current tasks in its domestic and foreign policy • realizing Russia's national interests is possible only on the basis of stable economic development. That is why the national interests of Russia in this field are the crucial ones • the national interests of Russia in the social field lie in guaranteeing the population a high standard of living	(Not mentioned)	• to create favourable external conditions for the steady development of Russia • improving Russia's economy • enhancing the standards of living of the population
Domestic	• upholding the stability of the constitutional system • eliminating the causes and conditions contributing to political and religious extremism, ethno-separatism, and their consequences, i.e. social, inter-ethnic and religious conflicts and terrorism	(Not mentioned)	• to ensure reliable security of the country, to preserve and strengthen its sovereignty and territorial integrity • strengthening the basis of the constitutional system • successfully carrying out democratic reforms • observing individual rights and freedoms
International	• *strengthening Russia's position as a great power* – as one of the centres of influence in a multipolar world • developing mutually advantageous relations, *especially with the member states of the CIS and Russia's traditional partners*	• The RF attaches priority importance to the development of *military cooperation with state parties to the CIS Collective Security Treaty*; because of the necessity to consolidate the forces towards *the creation of a unified defence space* and ensure collective military security	• to achieve firm and prestigious positions in the world community, most fully consistent with *the interests of the RF as a great power, as one of the most influential centres of the modern world*

(Table 2.3 continued)

Table 2.3 Continued

Themes	National Security Concept January 2000	Military Doctrine April 2000	Foreign Policy Concept June 2000
		• the RF executes a *common defence policy with Belarus* in the field of military organization and the development of the Armed Forces of the member states of the Union	• Russia shall seek to achieve a multipolar system of international relations • a *priority* area in Russia's foreign policy is multilateral and bilateral *cooperation with the member states of the CIS* • *relations with European states is Russia's traditional foreign policy priority* • of *key importance are* relations with the *European Union* (EU) • the *intensity of cooperation with NATO will depend on its compliance* with key clauses of the NATO–RF Founding Act of 1997
Military	• defending its independence, its sovereignty and its state and territorial integrity • preventing military aggression against Russia and its allies	(Not mentioned)	• to ensure reliable security of the country • we attach *priority of importance* to joint efforts towards *settling conflicts in CIS* member states and, through the *CIS Collective Security Treaty*, to the development of *cooperation in the military–political area* and in the sphere of security, particularly in combating international terrorism and extremism

Primary interests	Protection against: • terrorism, including international terrorism • disasters of natural or industrial origin and their consequences • the dangers arising from wartime military operations or their consequences	(Not mentioned)	(Not mentioned)
3. Threats to Russia's security			
General causes of internal and external threats	• the state of the national economy • the poor system of organization of state power and civil society • the socio-political polarization in Russian society and the criminalization of social relations • the growth of organized crime • the rising scale of terrorism • the exacerbation of relations between nations and the growing complexity of international relations	(Not mentioned)	(Not mentioned)
Internal threats	• ethno-egoism, ethno-centrism and chauvinism are helping to reinforce nationalism, political and *religious extremism, and ethno-separatism* • *The legal unity of the country is being eroded by separatist aspirations of a number of constituent entities* of the RF, and by poor organization of state control[b]	• the unlawful activities of extremist nationalist-ethnic, religious and separatist and terrorist movements, organizations and structures • attempts to *disrupt the unity and territorial integrity of the state* and to destabilize the internal situation	• the growth of separatism, ethnic-nationalist and religious extremism • the growth of international terrorism, transnational organized crime, as well as *illegal trafficking in drugs and weapons*

(Table 2.3 continued)

Table 2.3 Continued

Themes	National Security Concept January 2000	Military Doctrine April 2000	Foreign Policy Concept June 2000
	linking of some parts of the executive and the legislature to criminal organizations • deep division of society into a few rich and an overwhelming underprivileged majority • the threat to the physical health of the nation as seen in the rise in alcohol consumption and drug use and in the dramatic reduction in the country's birth rate and in average life expectancy *the underfunding of national defence leads to a critically low level of operational and combat training* in the Armed Forces and Other Troops	• attempts to overthrow the constitutional system	
External threats	• attempts by separate states and intergovernmental organizations *to belittle the role of existing mechanisms for the maintenance of international security, primarily the UN and the OSCE* • the danger that the political, economic and military influence of Russia in the world will be reduced • the strengthening of military–political blocs and alliances, above	• interference in RF internal affairs • attempts to ignore (or infringe on) RF interests in resolving international security problems • attempts to oppose the increase of influence of the RF on a global level • the expansion of military blocs and alliances • the introduction of foreign troops (without UN Security Council	• growing trend towards a unipolar structure of the world with the *economic and power domination of the United States* • *stakes are being placed on Western institutions and forums of limited composition, and on weakening the role of the UN Security Council* • *attempts to belittle the role of a sovereign state as the fundamental element of international relations*

all the *expansion of NATO eastwards*
- the possible presence of *foreign military bases and large military contingents in the immediate vicinity of Russian borders*
- the weakening of the processes of integration in the CIS
- the development and escalation of conflicts close to the state border of the Russian Federation and the external borders of the member states of the CIS
- international terrorism has unleashed an open campaign to destabilize the situation in Russia
- *NATO's practice of using military force outside the bloc's zone of responsibility without UN Security Council Sanction, now elevated to the rank of a strategic doctrine, threatens to destabilize the entire global strategic situation*

sanction) to the territory of contiguous states friendly with the RF
- *suppression of the rights of RF citizens abroad (inostrannykh)*

generate a threat of arbitrary interference in internal affairs
- *NATO's present-day political and military guidelines do not coincide with security interests of the RF and occasionally directly contradict them*
- *this primarily concerns the provisions of NATO's new strategic concept, which do not exclude the use of force outside of NATO's Treaty zone without the sanction of the UN Security Council*
- Russia retains its *negative attitude towards the expansion of NATO*
- *the protracted conflict in Afghanistan creates a real threat to the security of the southern CIS borders and directly affects Russian interests*
- Russia, in cooperation with other states concerned, will make consistent efforts to achieve a lasting political settlement of the Afghan problem and interdict the export of terrorism and extremism

4. Ensuring Russia's security

| *Fundamentals and objectives* | • timely prediction, detection and neutralization of external and internal threats | The RF adheres to the fundamental principles and rules of international law | • the *United Nations must remain the main centre for regulating international relations* |

(Table 2.3 continued)

Table 2.3 Continued

Themes	National Security Concept January 2000	Military Doctrine April 2000	Foreign Policy Concept June 2000
	• guaranteeing sovereignty and territorial integrity • *overcoming the Russian Federation's scientific, technical and technological dependence on external sources* • *Improving the system of state power of the RF, its federal relations, its local self-government, tightening up law and order and reinforcing the social and political stability of society* • *Guaranteeing strict observance of the laws by all citizens, public servants, state institutions, political parties and social and religious organizations* • *raising the military potential of the state and maintaining it at a sufficiently high level* • *organizing a common economic area with the member states of the CIS*		• the RF shall resolutely *oppose attempts to belittle the role of the UN and its Security Council in world affairs* • *preservation of the status of the permanent members of the UN Security Council* • *only the UN Security Council has the authority to sanction use of force for the purpose of achieving peace* • other uses of force are unlawful and pose a threat to the stabilization of the entire system of international relations • *to protect the rights and interests of Russian citizens and compatriots abroad (za rubezhëm) on the basis of international law and operative bilateral agreements* • the RF will seek to obtain adequate guarantees for the rights and freedoms of compatriots in states where they permanently reside and to maintain and *develop comprehensive ties with them and their organizations*

Foreign policy objectives	• reinforcing vital machinery for multilateral management of world political and economic processes, above all under jurisdiction of the UN Security Council • *defending the legal rights and interests of Russian citizens resident abroad (za rubezhëm)* • developing relations with the members of the CIS, and *developing integration processes within the CIS in Russia's interests* • adaptation of existing arms control and arms reduction agreements to new conditions in international relations and, if necessary, concluding new agreements, primarily concerning confidence and security building measures	(Not mentioned)	• To promote *elimination* of the existing and prevent the emergence of potential hotbeds of tension and *conflicts in regions adjacent to the RF* • Russia regards as its *most important foreign policy task the combating of international terrorism* • Russia shall collaborate with other states purposefully to combat illegal drug trafficking and the growth of organized crime • *partnership with all CIS member states to take into account in a due manner the interests of the RF, including in terms of guarantees of the rights of Russian compatriots (za rubezhëm)* • *respect by Lithuania, Latvia and Estonia of Russian interests, including in the key question of respect for the rights of the Russian-speaking population (za rubezhëm)*
Ensuring military security	• in the prevention of war and armed conflicts, the RF gives preference to political, diplomatic, economic and other non-military action • *all forces and facilities available, including nuclear weapons, will be used* if necessary to repel armed aggression, if all other means have been exhausted	• ensuring military security • suppression of aggression towards the RF *and (or)* its allies • the RF retains nuclear power status for deterring aggression against the RF *and (or)* its allies • the RF retains the right to use nuclear weapons in response to weapons of mass destruction and	• Russia is prepared to consent to a *further reduction of its nuclear potential* on the basis of bilateral agreements with the United States • Russia will seek preservation and *observance of the 1972 Treaty on the Limitation of Anti-Ballistic Missile Systems (ABM)* – the cornerstone of strategic stability[c]

(Table 2.3 continued)

Table 2.3 Continued

Themes	National Security Concept January 2000	Military Doctrine April 2000	Foreign Policy Concept June 2000
	• Keep up a deterrence capability in the interest of preventing aggression on whatever scale, including when nuclear arms are used against Russia and its allies • *the RF must have nuclear forces for use against any aggressor state or coalition of states* • one of the most important strategic *objectives of military security is the interaction and co-operation with the member states of the CIS*	in response to wide-scale aggression using conventional weapons in situations critical *for the RF*	• The implementation of the *plans of the United States to create a national missile defence system will inevitably compel the RF to adopt adequate measures for maintaining its national security at a proper level* • Russia intends to further promote the strengthening of regional stability by participating in the processes of reducing and limiting *conventional armed forces* • averting the proliferation of nuclear weapons and other weapons of mass destruction
Ways of employing the Armed Forces and Other Troops	• the RF Armed Forces at peacetime strength must be capable of providing reliable *protection for the country from air and space attacks and, together with the Other Troops, of repelling aggression in a local war* (armed conflict) and to fulfil missions in a large-scale war	• Strategic operations, major operations, and combat operations in large-scale as well as regional wars • operations and combat operations in local wars and international armed conflicts • *joint special operations in internal armed conflicts*	(Not mentioned)

	• the RF Armed Forces must carry out peacekeeping duties for the Federation • *the use of military force within the country is permitted in the event of a threat to the life of citizens, to the territorial integrity of the country or in case of a threat to change the constitutional system by force*	• anti-terror operations • peacekeeping operations • disaster relief operations	
Deployment of Armed Forces and Other Troops abroad	*The interests of Russia's national security may require a Russian military presence in certain strategically vital regions of the world; the stationing of limited military contingents (military bases, navy units) in these regions should ensure that Russia is ready to help to establish a stable military-strategic balance of forces in the regions, should give the RF an opportunity to respond to a crisis situation in its initial stage, and should enable the state to meet its foreign policy goals*	Limited contingents of the *RF Armed Forces and the Other Troops may be deployed in regions of strategic importance, outside RF territory,* as combined or national task forces and bases	(Not mentioned)
Command and control institutions of national security policy	• the RF President directs the agencies and forces which ensure RF national security, sanctions action to ensure national security; forms, organs maintaining the national security; delivers directives on national security issues, such as the NSC, and defines trends in foreign policy	• the RF President, Supreme Commander of the RF Armed Forces, directs the organization, preparation and the use of the military organization	• the RF President shall provide guidance of the country's foreign policy and as the Head of State shall represent the RF in international relations

(Table 2.3 continued)

Table 2.3 Continued

Themes	National Security Concept January 2000	Military Doctrine April 2000	Foreign Policy Concept June 2000
	• the RF Federal Assembly formulates the legislative basis for maintaining national security • the RF government coordinates the work of federal executive agencies and executive agencies of RF constituent entities and provides the federal budgeting for programmes of national security • the Security Council (SCRF) assesses threats to national security, operationally prepares related proposals for the President, drafts proposals on ensuring national security, such as NSC provisions, coordinates the work of the forces and agencies that ensure national security and monitors the implementation by federal executive agencies and the authorities in RF constituent entities of related decisions	• the RF government provides the equipment of the Armed Forces and the Other Troops and directs the preparation of the RF for its defence • The RF Ministry of Defence is in charge of the organization and development of the Other Troops and procurement • the General Staff is the basic entity for operational command and control of the RF Armed Forces and coordinates the activities and organizes the joint deployment of the RF Armed Forces and Other Troops • the staffs of the services and the arms accomplish the organization and employment of their forces	• the Federation Council and the State Duma will pursue legislative work to support the foreign policy course of the RF and fulfillment of its international obligations • the RF Security Council shall execute preparation of decisions of the RF President in the area of international security and control over their implementation • The RF Ministry of Foreign Affairs shall provide direct implementation of the foreign policy course approved by the RF President. The Foreign Ministry of Russia shall be in charge of coordination of foreign policy activities pursued by federal bodies of executive power and of control over them • the RF's constituent entities shall promote their international ties in accordance with the Constitution and other legislative acts. The Foreign Ministry of Russia and other federal bodies of executive power shall give aid to the RF subjects in their realization of international cooperation

- federal executive agencies carry out security-related decisions of President and government, and draft enforceable enactments
- executive agencies of RF constituent entities cooperate with federal executive agencies and work jointly with local government agencies in implementing RF legislation and carrying out security-related decisions of President, government and of the Supreme Commander of the Armed Forces

- during the preparation of decisions on the conduct of the state's foreign policy course, the federal bodies of executive power shall cooperate, if necessary, with Russia's non-governmental organizations (NGOs). A broader involvement of NGOs in the sphere of the country's foreign policy activities is consistent with the task of ensuring maximum support by the civic society for the state foreign policy

Notes

a The citations are mostly not literally derived from the different security documents, but adapted by the author. Remarkable differences between the documents or vital entries are in italic. The grouping of related entries as used here is for the purpose of clarity and does not necessarily correspond with the original documents.

b Constituent entities or subjects are administrative authorities within the Russian Federation, below the federal, national level, with specific self-governing legislative, executive and judicial powers.

c The Anti-Ballistic Missile (ABM) Treaty of 1972, agreed between the United States and the USSR, restricted the installation of defence systems against intercontinental ballistic nuclear missiles of both superpowers. See K.A. Nederlof, *Lexicon politiek-militair-strategische termen* (Alphen aan den Rijn (NL)/Brussels: Samson, 1984), pp. 20, 26, 133.

When analysing the standpoints of the security actors concerning internal (domestic) aspects of security, the inconsistencies become more prominent. In this case the actors show disagreement on the nature of internal destabilizing factors. With regard to national interests the positions also tend to differ. For instance, whereas the SCRF and the MID share the nowadays generally recognized idea that the spectrum of security is broader than the military–diplomatic aspect only, the MoD stubbornly sticks to this limited notion.[49] A further point of inconsistency is in threat perception. The NSC perceives the roots of threats to national security in domestic aspects, whereas at the same time all three actors emphasize external instead of internal threats. The often divergent opinions on aspects of internal policy lead to the conclusion that coordination and fine-tuning in this part of security perception is still far from optimal, which could result in an inconsistent domestic security policy.

With regard to the short-term advancement of Putin's security policy, taking into account its consistency, the following can be said. It is expected that, in general, international developments will be answered by a consistent approach, due to the fact that the principal security actors to a large extent agree on these topics. However, Putin has to be aware of the possibility of interdepartmental confrontations between the MoD and the MID. Especially when it comes to decision-making on nuclear arms the danger of differences is vivid. According to the corresponding entries of the security documents, MoD and MID held opposing views on this matter. At the end of 2000 it appeared that Putin had taken the side of the MID – because of the internal threat (Chechnya), priority was shifted from nuclear to conventional military power.[50] In addition to this, shortly afterwards, Marshall Sergeyev, an outspoken proponent of nuclear military power, was replaced as Minister of Defence. This must have decreased this inconsistency in policy perceptions. Even if this was the case, this did not mean that the MoD, which still had a lot of conservative generals, had changed its mind in favour of arms control and consequently of reduction of military power. The matter of the protection of Russian minorities abroad could also become an issue of interdepartmental differences. It is not out of the question that in due course the rights of Russian minorities in one or more of the former Soviet republics will be violated. If so, judging by the adapted provision in the doctrine, one can wonder whether the MoD would be willing to employ military force against the offending state. Since the MID attaches such a high priority to this fundamental, it might urge the MoD to do so. This also might lead to a confrontation between these two actors. Therefore, Putin must be conscious of the differences between the MoD and MID in order to maintain a consistent and cohesive security policy. As mentioned before, the opinions of the security actors differ even more with regard to internal security policy. Putin is faced with the task of establishing consensus among the security actors on the nature of domestic problems and on how to deal with them. After transferring the responsibility for military reforms from the General Staff to the SCRF, it is not unlikely that Putin will bestow on the latter tasks in the area of internal security as well. The SCRF might very well become a binding factor in this field in the form of a 'supreme' security organ that coordinates the activities of the other bodies. Not only by increasing the powers of the SCRF, but also by appointing likeminded functionaries with a security or military background on key positions, Putin endeavours to accomplish his objective of an amplified central control over all policy dimensions. Assuming that this policy will be continued in the coming years, this in turn will strengthen the consistency of Russia's grand strategy.

Notes

1 A.F. Klimenko, 'Osobennosti novoy Voyennoy doktriny', *Voyennaya Mysl'*, 5, (2000), pp. 24–5.
2 V.L. Manilov, *Voyennaya Bezopasnost' Rossii* (Moscow: Probel, 2000), pp. 165, 231–2.
3 V.D. Zabolotin, *Slovar' voyennykh terminov* (Moscow: Kosmo, 2000), p. 161.
4 Manilov, *Voyennaya Bezopasnost' Rossii*, pp. 232–3; pp. 39, 310, 165.
5 'Osnovy voyennoy doktriny Rossii (Proyekt)', *Voyennaya Mysl'*, special issue, 19 May 1992.
6 A.F. Klimenko, 'O role i meste voyennoy doktriny v sisteme bezopasnosti Sodruzhestva nezavisimykh gosudarstv', *Voyennaya Mysl'*, 2, Feb. 1992, p. 16.
7 www.scrf.gov.ru/Documents/2646-1.html
8 S. Rogov, 'Nuzhna li Rossii svoya politika natsional'noy bezopasnosti?', *Nezavisimaya Gazeta*, 45 (6 March 1992), p. 2.
9 N. Malcolm, A. Pravda, *et al.*, *Internal Factors in Russian Foreign Policy* (Oxford: Oxford University Press, 1996), p. 50.
10 C.J. Dick, 'The Military Doctrine of the Russian Federation', *Journal of Slavic Military Studies*, 7, 3, Sept. 1994, p. 504.
11 A. Kassianova, 'Russia: Still Open to the West? Evolution of the State Identity in the Foreign Policy and Security Discourse', *Europe–Asia Studies*, 53, 6 (2001), p. 828.
12 Malcolm, *Internal Factors*, p. 114.
13 J.M. Godzimirski, 'Russian National Security Concepts 1997 and 2000: A Comparative Analysis', *European Security*, 9, 4 (2000), p. 76.
14 G. Miranovich, 'Geopolitika i bezopasnost' Rossii', *Krasnaya Zvezda*, 30 July 1999, p. 2, and 31 July 1999, p. 2.
15 The Russian security elite was especially disturbed about the responsibility that NATO grants itself in its Strategic Concept for the maintenance of security and stability within the Euro-Atlantic area. In this way NATO permits itself the use of military force, without the consent of the Security Council of the United Nations, in a region of which the boundaries are not mentioned. See *The Alliance's Strategic Concept* (Brussels: NATO Office of Information and Press, 1999), p. 14. In Russian eyes, and with the experience of 'Kosovo', 'Chechnya' could very well be the next conflict for NATO to intervene in. Therefore Russia considered this Concept to be a threat for its national interests.
16 Manilov, *Voyennaya Bezopasnost' Rossii*, p. 231.
17 Malcolm, *Internal Factors*, p. 107.
18 Godzimirski, 'Russian National Security Concepts', pp. 75–6.
19 V. Chernov, 'Natsional'nyye interesy Rossii i ugrozy dlya ego bezopasnosti, Boris Yel'tsin utverdil kontseptsiyu vneshney politiki RF', *Nezavisimaya Gazeta*, 29 April 1993, pp. 1, 3.
20 A.C. Lynch, 'The Realism of Russia's Foreign Policy', *Europe–Asia Studies*, 53, 1 (2001), p. 24.
21 M.A. Smith, *Russia and the Far Abroad 2000*, F72 (Camberley: Conflict Studies Research Centre, 2000), p. 27.

22 *Strategic Survey 2000–2001*, (Oxford: Oxford University Press International Institute for Strategic Studies, 2000), p. 122.
23 A.L. Adamishin, 'Naskol'ko bezopasna nyneshnaya Yevropa?', *Nezavisimaya Gazeta*, 2 Nov. 2000, p. 3.
24 Draft RF Military Doctrine 1992, see 'Osnovy voyennoy doktriny Rossii (Proyekt)'. As to Manilov's statement, see 'Novaya Voyennaya doktrina Rossii – adekvatnyy otvet na vyzov vremeni', *Krasnaya Zvezda*, 8 Oct. 1999, p. 1. Presidential decree regarding the 2000 doctrine: 'Ukaz Prezidenta Rossiyskoy Federatsii ob utverzdenii Voyennoy doktriny Rossiyskoy Federatsii', *Krasnaya Zvezda*, 25 April 2000, p. 1. Colonel-General Valery Manilov was First Deputy Chief of the RF General Staff and acting chairman of the working group for the draft Military Doctrine of 1999.
25 For definitions of the doctrine see 'Osnovy voyennoy doktriny Rossii (Proyekt)', p. 3; and Zabolotin, *Slovar' voyennykh terminov*, p. 53.
26 M.E. Glantz, 'The Origins and Development of Soviet and Russian Military Doctrine', *Journal of Slavic Military Studies*, 7, 3 (1994), p. 461.
27 Ibid., p. 473.
28 A. Pel'ts, 'Nuzhna novaya voyennaya doktrina', *Krasnaya Zvezda*, 6 Nov. 1996, p. 1.
29 A. Korbut, 'Rossiya utochnyayet Voyennuyu doktrinu', *Nezavisimoye Voyennoye Obozreniye*, 40 (163), 15 Oct. 1999, p. 1.
30 'Osnovy voyennoy doktriny Rossii (Proyekt)', p. 2.
31 'Osnovnyye polozheniya voyennoy doktriny Rossiyskoy Federatsii (izlozheniye)', *Krasnaya Zvezda*, 19 Nov. 1993, p. 4.
32 Regarding the openness of doctrinal debate, see Glantz, 'The Origins and Development of Soviet and Russian Military Doctrine', pp. 459–60. Concerning views of officers who felt excluded from the doctrinal debate, see Klimenko, 'O role i meste voyennoy doktriny v sisteme bezopasnosti Sodruzhestva nezavisimykh gosudarstv', p. 12.
33 On the restricted publication of the 1993 doctrine, see C.J. Dick, *The Military Doctrine of the Russian Federation*, Occasional Brief 25 (Camberley: Conflict Studies Research Centre, 1993), pp. 1–2. On the doctrinal workgroup and Manilov's support for publication in full, see 'Novaya Voyennaya doktrina Rossii – adekvatnyy otvet na vyzov vremeni'.
34 Klimenko, 'O role i meste voyennoy doktriny v sisteme bezopasnosti Sodruzhestva nezavisimykh gosudarstv', p. 14.
35 Malcolm, *Internal Factors*, pp. 312–19.
36 'Osnovy voyennoy doktriny Rossii (Proyekt)', p. 7.
37 Klimenko, 'O role i meste voyennoy doktriny v sisteme bezopasnosti Sodruzhestva nezavisimykh gosudarstv', p. 15.
38 Malcolm, *Internal Factors*, p. 112.
39 *Military Balance 2000–2001*, p. 109.
40 Malcolm, *Internal Factors*, pp. 312–19.
41 'Doktrina budet utochnyat'sya', *Nezavisimoye Voyennoye Obozreniye*, 13, 13 April 2001, p. 1.
42 See the following sources for the contents of the 2000 editions of the three principle security documents:
   National Security Concept (January 2000):
   Russian: 'Kontseptsiya natsional'noy bezopasnosti', *Nezavisimoye Voyennoye Obozreniye*, 1 (14 January 2000), p. 1.
   www.scrf.gov.ru/Documents/Decree/2000/24-1.html
   English: www.fas.org/nuke/guide/russia/doctrine/gazeta012400.htm
   Military Doctrine (April 2000):
   Russian: 'Voyennaya doktrina Rossiyskoy Federatsii', *Nezavisimoye Voyennoye Obozreniye*, 15 (28 April 2000).
   www.scrf.gov.ru/Documents/Decree/2000/706-1.html

English: www.freerepublic.com/forum/a394aa0466bfe.htm
Foreign Policy Concept (June 2000):
Russian: 'Kontseptsiya vneshney politiki Rossiyskoy Federatsii', *Nezavisimoye Voyennoye Obozreniye*, 25 (14 July 2000), p. 4.
www.scrf.gov.ru/Documents/Decree/2000/07-10.html
English: www.fas.org/nuke/guide/russia/doctrine/econcept.htm
43 See Table 2.3, Comparison of the 2000 editions of NSC, Military Doctrine and Foreign Policy Concept.
44 M.A. Smith, *Putin's Regime: Administered Democracy*, E108 (Camberley: Conflict Studies Research Centre, 2000).
45 As explained to the author by Irina Kirilova, lecturer in Russian studies, University of Cambridge, at a Wilton Park conference, March 2001.
46 'Principles of RF Naval Policy, as Confirmed by presidential Decree, 4 March 2000', *Nezavisimoye Voyennoye Obozreniye*, 11 (184), 31 March 2000, pp. 1, 4; 'Morskaya doktrina Rossiyskoy Federatsii na period do 2020 goda', *Nezavisimoye Voyennoye Obozreniye*, 28 (250), 3 Aug. 2001, p. 4; S.J. Main, *Russia's Military Doctrine*, Occasional Brief 77 (Camberley: Conflict Studies Research Centre, 2000), p 7.
47 'Konstitutsiya Rossiyskoy Federatsii', *Rossiyskaya Gazeta*, 25 Dec.1993; www.gov.ru:8104/main/konst/konst0.html, art.83, para. H.
48 'Konstitutsiya Rossiyskoy Federatsii', arts 80, 84 and 85.
49 For the broad concept of security, see *NATO Handbook* (Brussels: NATO Office of Information and Press, 1995), pp. 39–40. 'Broad security' explains that in addition to the traditional dimension of security, of the military–diplomatic field, other dimensions of security also have to be taken into account. The concept of broad security recognizes four security dimensions: military–diplomatic (national interests, territorial integrity and sovereignty), social (human rights, democracy and freedom), economic (prosperity, welfare and development) and ecological (health, liveableness).
50 *Military Balance 2000–2001*, pp. 109–10.

3

STRUCTURE OF AIR POWER
Development, organization and status of air forces

Introduction

The portrayal of the structure of air power leads us to the level of military strategy. This chapter forms the bridge between the national security policy, drafted by the Kremlin and the General Staff in Moscow and situated at the level of grand strategy, and the practice of security policy, for instance in Chechnya, at the operational and lower levels, which will be described in Chapter 4. According to the theory of levels of strategy, military doctrine, which was depicted in Chapter 2, is also located at this level of strategy. However, the predominantly political-strategic nature of Russian military doctrine causes this policy document to be more closely related to grand strategy than to military strategy.

This chapter elaborates on the consequences of the Kremlin's national security policy for the organization, combat readiness and reforms of air power. In addition to this, the thought processes on the use of air power, derived from domestic and foreign experiences, will be explained, as well as the tasks of air power which were the result. However, before expanding on these themes, the expression 'Russian air power', being the central focus of this chapter, has to be explained. 'Air power' can be described as the ability to project military force in the third dimension, air and space, in order to realize political and military objectives. In the Russian setting the matériel constituent of air power, military aviation, is divided among a number of departments.[1] With regard to the MoD, not only the Air Forces VVS (*Voyenno-Vozdushnyye Sily*) had fixed aircraft at their disposal; the Air Defence Forces VPVO (*Voyska Protivovozdushnoy Oborony*) were also an independent service of the RF Armed Forces. Furthermore, the Ground Forces had an army aviation branch, ASV (*Aviatsiya Sukhoputnykh Voysk* or *Armeyskaya Aviatsiya*), while Navy and Strategic Missile Forces also possessed flying elements. Rotary wing (helicopters) was not subordinated to the VVS, but to the ASV. Some of the power ministries also had military aviation units at their disposal. For instance, MVD (Internal Troops) and Border Guard Service (Border Troops) made a contribution, although rather limited, to the air component. Since VVS and ASV possessed the lion's share of military aviation the emphasis in this chapter will be on those two elements of Russian military aviation.

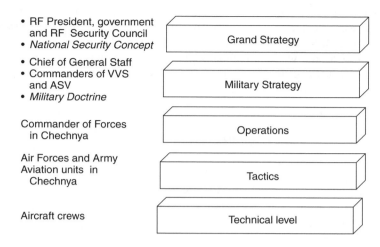

- RF President, government and RF Security Council
- *National Security Concept*

Grand Strategy

- Chief of General Staff
- Commanders of VVS and ASV
- *Military Doctrine*

Military Strategy

Commander of Forces in Chechnya

Operations

Air Forces and Army Aviation units in Chechnya

Tactics

Aircraft crews

Technical level

Figure 3.1 Command and control at the military-strategic level.

Genesis and development of Soviet–Russian air power

On 12 August 1912 at the instigation of the Duma a military aviation branch was founded by creating a corresponding main directorate at the General Staff. Thus air power was started in Russia. Nearly 80 years later, at the time of the collapse of the Soviet Union, at the end of 1991, developments initially went in a direction that gave the impression that the CIS would take over the Soviet integrated military structure, including united air forces. Soon afterwards, when a number of CIS member states strove for independence in the military field as well by creating national armed forces, the idea of united CIS armed forces turned out to be an illusion.

In 1991 the Soviet VVS had more than 11,000 aircraft at its disposal. According to the first RF VVS commander-in-chief, Colonel-General Pëtr Deynekin, Russia's part of this Soviet heritage amounted to 5,000 aircraft and 14,000 pilots. In total the RF received about 60 per cent of the former Soviet VVS assets and half of its airbases.[2] In addition to the larger part of the former Soviet air units, Russia also obtained the bulk of maintenance facilities, aircraft factories and design bureaus. In the USSR, the Belarusian and Ukrainian Military Districts (MDs) formed the frontline towards the west, which was the strategic reason for deploying the most modern aircraft types as well as a large part of the strategic bomber force in these districts. The geographic disposition of the RF, in the heart-land of the former USSR, meant that in 1992 Russia inherited only a limited number of these sophisticated weapon systems, since most of them were obtained by the former frontline districts Belarus and Ukraine, as well as by Kazakhstan. For instance, to Russia's displeasure, Ukraine and Kazakhstan received more than half of the strategic bombers. Russia was especially annoyed that the RF, as legal successor to the USSR, considered itself entitled to claim the strategic bomber force because of its status of nuclear power. For many years to come Russia and Ukraine would continue their dispute over the possession of these aircraft. Only in 1999, did Ukraine transfer 11 bombers to Russia, to pay for gas supplies.[3]

Organization of the VVS

Components of the VVS

The various components of the VVS will now be described, according to the build-up of the VVS in the year 2000. At that time, the VVS, true to Soviet tradition, consisted of three main elements. First, the tactical air force FA (*Frontavaya Aviatsiya*), air force units which were operationally under the command of the MDs, but administratively subordinated to the VVS staff. Next, the strategic bomber or long-distance force DA (*Dalnyaya Aviatsiya*) and finally VVS's transport force VTA (*Voyenno-Transportnaya Aviatsiya*), which were both under direct command of the VVS. The Air Defence Forces, VPVO, amalgamated with the VVS in 1998, under the name of VVS. Subsequently, the PVO air units were incorporated into the FA in the MDs. The last component, army aviation ASV, was an arm of the Ground Forces until it was resubordinated to VVS in 2003.[4]

Number of aircraft and personnel

At the end of the 1990s, the VVS had more than 2,100 operational aircraft at is disposal, 1,600 of which were fighter-bombers and interceptors (FA and PVO), some 225 strategic bombers (DA) and almost 300 transport aircraft (VTA). The personnel strength amounted to 185,000 servicemen. Over 1,000 training aircraft as well as aircraft in storage were left out of the account. The distribution of aircraft over the various elements of VVS was as follows: 27 per cent FA, 38 per cent PVO, 15 per cent DA and 20 per cent VTA. Around the year 2000 the ASV comprised 1,500–2,000 helicopters.[5]

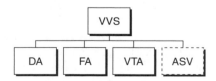

Figure 3.2 VVS components.

102

Main types of fixed and rotary-wing aircraft

Judging by the use of air power in the Chechen conflict, the most important aircraft of military aviation, making up its combat force, were:[6]

FA   Su-24M *Fencer-D* fighter-bomber (*bombardirovshchik*) and Su-25 *Frogfoot* ground attack aircraft (*shturmovik*)

PVO   Su-27/30 *Flanker* air defence interceptor (*istrebitel*)

DA   Tu-22M3 *Backfire* strategic bomber (*dalniy bombardirovshchik*)

ASV   Mi-24 *Hind* combat helicopter (*boyevoy vertolët*)

Organizational structure of air force formations

The build-up of air units, of VVS as well as of other services with aviation components, was usually as follows. The elementary air unit was the air regiment (*aviapolk*), consisting of three squadrons (*eskadrilya*), a personnel strength of 1,500–1,700 servicemen and generally stationed at one airbase. Three air regiments formed an air division (*aviadiviziya*). Out of 2–3 air divisions an air army (*vozdushnaya armiya*) was shaped. On 11 December 1997 the structure of a combined air army of VVS and PVO, which was to be the standard composition of the VVS units within a MD, was laid down by first deputy Chief of the General Staff, Colonel-General Valery Manilov.[7]

FA – tactical air force

The FA consisted of three components: fighters, bombers and reconnaissance (recce) aircraft. The main tasks of the FA covered conducting air attacks in operational depth, providing air support to ground operations and securing friendly troops and objects against air attacks.

In 1994 within the VVS staff an FA Command was formed, which was in charge of FA air armies in the MDs. In 1997 this command had already closed down. Subsequently, the VVS staff itself, in its capacity of administrative control over FA units, generated directives, instructions and regulations for these units. So, as of that time, functional control over FA units was exercised by VVS staff in Moscow, while operational command was lodged in the MDs. The operational command over FA units, exercised by the MDs, was evidence of the fact that since the beginning of Soviet–Russian military aviation the main task of the air forces had consisted in providing air support for ground operations.

Each MD had its 'own' air force at its disposal. In general this was made up of an air army, usually composed of a fighter division, a bomber division and a division or command of PVO, supplemented with recce, ground attack, electronic warfare (EW) and transport units.[8]

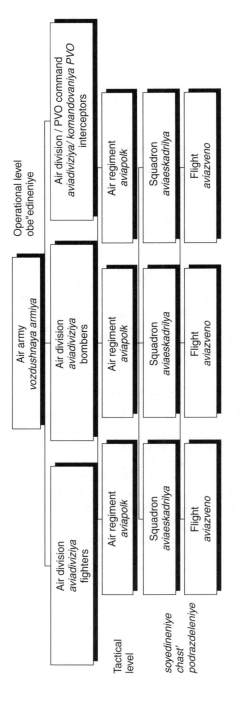

Figure 3.3 Structure of a VVS and PVO air army of a Military District.

DA – strategic bomber force

The DA, also referred to as *strategicheskaya aviatsiya*, included two parts: a bomber component and a recce component. The DA was assigned to destroy military objects in deep enemy hinterland, as well as to conduct operational and strategic recce. For conducting its missions the DA had conventional as well as nuclear weapons available. At the collapse of the USSR Russia had obtained 42 per cent of the nuclear bombers. In 1998 the VVS changed the designation of the DA into the 37 (Strategic) Air Army.[9]

As of 1998 the pattern of exercises showed that Russia's military and political leadership, for the first time since the disintegration of the Soviet Union, were taking an interest in the strategic, intercontinental employment of this bomber force. DA bombers conducted missions up to North America and Japan to test the readiness of Western air defence systems. In June 1999, in the massive exercise *Zapad-99*, the DA again demonstrated its capacity to use strategic bombers for intercontinental missions. The VVS Commander-in-Chief, Colonel-General Anatoly Kornukov, stated that this exercise was meant to show the power of the RF Armed Forces in general and the combat readiness of air power especially, in reaction to NATO's air attacks on Kosovo.[10] This unique position, which was bestowed upon the DA, had a positive result on its readiness status: in 2000 80 per cent of the bombers were ready to conduct operational missions. Unmistakeably, the DA formed a vital element in the efforts of RF security policy to strengthen Russia's position in the international arena and regain the status of superpower.[11]

VTA – transport force

The transport fleet of the VTA was tasked to drop airborne troops, to relocate forces, to supply arms, fuel, food and other logistic resources, as well as to evacuate wounded and ill servicemen (medevac). In the 1990s the contribution of the VTA to VVS missions had grown, due to the Russian involvement in operations in the CIS and as a result of the domestic Chechen conflict.

In 1955 the VTA attained independent status within the VVS. In 1998 the VTA was renamed into 61 Air Army. Consecutive reorganizations have diminished the size of the transport fleet by one-third, when older aircraft types were thrown out. Because of the intensive use of VTA assets in internal and regional conflicts, but also for commercial flights, that generated foreign currencies, the average number of annual flying hours for VTA pilots amounted to 50, which was much higher than that of pilots of other components of the VVS.[12]

VPVO – air defence forces

The assets of the VPVO were assigned to neutralize the enemy in the air, as well as to secure administrative, economic and industrial centres, units of other services and vital military and civil objects against air attacks. In 1954, as a consequence of the threat of the US strategic bomber force, the VPVO became an independent service of the RF Armed Forces. In 1998 this status was lost again, when the VPVO and VVS were combined.[13]

ASV – rotary wing force

The main tasks of the ASV consisted of providing air support and tactical air recce at the instruction of ground force commanders; transport, dropping and fire support of tactical airborne units; conducting EW missions; and dropping of mines. In the 1990s because of its involvement in internal (Chechnya, Dagestan) and regional (CIS) conflicts the emphasis in ASV missions shifted from support to combat tasks. The weight of rotary wing in air power increased accordingly, because of the increasing demands for mobile and rapid deployment of ground and airborne troops. The ASV made helicopters available to each MD. At army level, army aviation ASV in general contributed with two air regiments, comprising a mixture of combat and transport helicopters, *Hinds* and *Hips* respectively.[14]

The intensive use of rotary-wing aircraft in the aforementioned conflicts had consequences for its utilization. Already in 1993 in the Russian defence paper *Krasnaya Zvezda* a complaint was published by a prominent colonel-pilot. He criticized the deplorable state of the helicopter fleet, which was outdated and obsolete. Furthermore, this pilot stated his unease about the fact that rotary-wing aircraft lacked instruments for operating under conditions of bad weather and limited visibility. He also revealed that more than half of the helicopter accidents were the result of construction errors, and that obsolescence and wastage, as well as the absence of replacements, would cause a reduction of the helicopter fleet by one third in the year 2000. The pilot blamed the VVS for the lack of new helicopters, because the VVS, instead of the Ground Forces to which ASV belonged, controlled the procurement budget.[15] These statements were made by one colonel-pilot. However, his opinions, due to his experience and prominent position in the ASV, could not be easily disregarded by the military authorities. Furthermore, the fact that the official defence newspaper listed this critical portrayal of the state of affairs of the ASV was an indication of its authenticity. Possibly the ASV command supported the publication of these complaints in order to convince the military–political leadership to allocate more finance to improve conditions.

At the end of the 1990s, as a consequence of deficient maintenance and insufficient spare parts, only some 400 of a total of 1,500 helicopters were ready for operational use; 80 per cent of helicopter losses were caused by crews having insufficient flying skills, technical failures and human error during the flight. In 1999 the ASV commander, Colonel-General Vitaly Pavlov, stated that modernization of the helicopter fleet had to be based on existing air frames, i.e. *Hind* and *Hip*, which were 15–20 years old. He preferred this approach to introducing new helicopter types, because for the price of one state-of-the-art helicopter five existing air frames could be modernized.[16]

From its foundation at the end of the 1950s until 1977 ASV had been a part of the Ground Forces. From 1977 to 1990 ASV was administratively subordinated to VVS, although the helicopter units remained under operational command of the MDs. On 30 July 1990 the ASV was granted the status of an independent arm of the Ground Forces.

On 19 August 2002 an Mi-26 *Halo* heavy transport helicopter was shot down by Chechen fighters while approaching the airbase of Khankala, near Groznyy. In this incident, which the Russian press, because of its size, titled 'The second *Kursk*' 118 people lost their lives. This occurrence would have far-reaching consequences for the command and control of air power. The following day Colonel-General Pavlov was relieved of his command over ASV. A week later sources within the MoD revealed that ASV was to be transferred from Ground Forces to VVS during the current year. The reason for this decision was the alleged misuse of helicopters by commanders of ground troops, for instance by overloading them, as had been the case with this *Halo*.[17] Pilots of helicopter regiments confirmed this tendency of overloading helicopters. Loading conditions were violated because of a shortage of available helicopters.

The withdrawal of the helicopter fleet from the Ground Forces did not receive general agreement. Obviously its former commander was an outspoken opponent of this decision. Pavlov considered this transfer of command as a serious misstep, that would damage the RF Armed Forces as a whole. In his opinion, the use of rotary wing in warfare, such as in the war in Afghanistan, had proved that by its nature ASV belonged to the Ground Forces. According to Pavlov the negative consequences of this resubordination would be a reduction in flying hours, deterioration of coordination between air power and commanders of ground troops and a lowered effectiveness of air support for ground operations. Besides objections from the top of ASV, officers in the helicopter units also protested against the transfer to the VVS. Their opposition had to do with the expected long process of adapting to new demands, instructions and habits, which in VVS were different from the common procedures in ASV although officers at this level also recognized the advantage of the resubordination; flight security requirements in VVS were much higher than in their present position as an arm of the Ground Forces.

Support for the objections against resubordination came also from an unexpected direction, from the esteemed Russian air power expert, retired VVS Major-General Valentin Rog. He agreed that ASV, because of its tasks, should be considered an inalienable element of the Ground Forces, just like the infantry and artillery. According to Rog, the importance of ASV, as a component of the Ground Forces, was found in joint action with artillery and missile troops, which formed the coordinated firepower in support of combat operations. For planning and establishing tactical cooperation the status of ASV as an arm of the Ground Forces was indispensable. Rog recognized the following problems for the use of

ASV after its transfer to the VVS. In the situation where the ASV was an arm of the Ground Forces a commander of ground troops could give orders directly to a helicopter unit, which meant a minimal loss of time. When ASV was a component of VVS, time would be spent in drafting procedures to allocate staff, crews and helicopters from VVS to an army commander of the Ground Forces. Another point raised by him was that VVS had its own technical service, armaments service and training institutes at its disposal. ASV did not have such services and institutions and would be an outsider within the organizational structure of VVS. Finally, Rog stated that the logical continuation of this principle of centralized command and control of air power would demand the transfer of the other elements of military aviation, for instance those of the Navy and of the MVD as well to VVS. Apparently his comment was noticed at the MoD. In January 2003 it became known that the MoD was drafting a study on the idea of transferring additional components of military aviation from other services and troops to VVS.[18]

Consequently, the decision to resubordinate the ASV from Ground Forces to VVS was met by fierce opposition, naturally from inside ASV but also from outsiders such as Valentin Rog. Apart from emotional arguments the objections were in particular with regard to the belief that disconnecting ASV from the Ground Forces would complicate tactical-operational cooperation with units of the latter. This line of reasoning seemed justified. On the other hand, the point was made by the VVS that centralized command and control of air power as a whole, of fixed as well as rotary wing, would optimize its effectiveness. Both opinions were legitimate. The decision was a military–political choice between one of the two options. In January 2003 VVS commander Colonel-General Vladimir Mikhaylov reported to the Minister of Defence that the transfer of ASV to VVS had been completed. Thus VVS capacities were reinforced with more than 80 helicopter units, of which 20 air regiments, 2,000 helicopters and 20,000 servicemen.[19]

Combat readiness

Reductions in military expenditures over several years resulted in a falling level of combat readiness as a consequence of the deteriorating status of personnel and material of the RF Armed Forces as a whole. Regarding air power, while foreign air forces usually received 30 per cent of the defence budget, the VVS share of this budget dropped from 20 per cent in 1992, to 15–17 per cent in 1996 and to around 10 per cent in the year 2000 (related to this was the fact that prior to their amalgamation, the separate budgets of VVS and VPVO amounted to 22–23 per cent of the defence budget). According to the independent military–political weekly, *Nezavisimoye Voyennoye Obozreniye*, this budget level was only 40–50 per cent of the minimal sum necessary for maintaining VVS.[20] The heavy reduction of the VVS budget resulted in the following consequences for personnel and material.[21]

Personnel

Decreasing flight readiness of aircraft damaged the flying capabilities of air crews, especially with regard to pilot training and maintenance of flying skills. material shortcomings caused reductions in routine flights and large-scale exercises. Annual flying hours are considered to be an important indicator for assessing the combat readiness of an air force. The average number of flying hours per VVS pilot (*godovoy nalët lëtchika*) fell from 73 hours in 1993, to 60 hours in 1995 and to 29 in the year 2000. In 1996 the VVS commander, Deynekin, provided another indication of the problems in flying proficiency. According to him, in that year the annual flying hours of FA, DA and VTA pilots were respectively 28, 43 and 63 per cent below standard. His successor, Anatoly Kornukov, mentioned a further reduction of flying hours, from 55 per cent flying hours below standard in 1998 to 65 per cent below standard in 1999. In addition to the low average of annual flying hours, another indicator of low combat readiness of VVS was that some air regiments allegedly did not carry out any flights whatsoever in a period of two years. Furthermore, in the year 2000, 400 pilots out of the total number of 1,500 who left flying schools since 1995 had not made a single flight since their graduation. Allegedly only 30–40 per cent of all pilots were capable of conducting combat missions. The limited possibilities of maintaining flying skills also affected the morale of pilots.[22]

Besides deteriorating working circumstances, VVS personnel and their families increasingly had to face a decline in social-economic conditions. Problems in housing for military families became structural. In 1992, 22,000 VVS families lacked accommodation, of which 3,500 were pilots. Around the year 2000 this number had increased to 23,000, which was 35 per cent of all VVS families. In addition to this, 45,000 air force families were forced to live in deficient housing. The bad working and living conditions gave rise to a flood of resignations among VVS officers. Based upon these deplorable conditions for themselves and their families 32,000 officers resigned between 1998 and 2000, 4,500 of whom were junior officers who had joined the forces from 1995 to 1999. The harsh circumstances also brought about problems of discipline, corruption and other forms of criminality.[23] The consequences of deplorable social-economic conditions were visible not only in VVS but in the RF Armed Forces as a whole as well as in the Other Troops of the power ministries. The deteriorating circumstances were not

Table 3.1 Development of annual flying hours per pilot

Year	Amount of flying hours	FA	DA	VTA
1993	73	40	80	100
1995	60	40	80	—
2000	29	18	20	50

new but dated from the end of the Soviet era. It was evident that since that time military and political authorities apparently had priorities other than solving the misery of servicemen.

Material

Shortcomings in maintenance and lack of fuel as well as spare parts for aircraft strongly affected the combat readiness of air force units. From 1996 to 1999 VVS received only 30–40 per cent of the necessary fuel, which in 1996 limited the number of flying hours actually carried out to 45 per cent. Some of the problems in maintenance of aircraft were related to the large diversity of air frames, some 35 different types. At the end of the 1990s, of the 2,000 operational aircraft of the FA, DA and VTA allegedly only 50–60 per cent were combat ready. Kornukov claimed that of the 36–54 aircrafts per air regiment only 6–10 were fully combat ready.[24]

Another negative development on the utilization and combat readiness of military aviation was the ageing of air frames. The supplies of new aircraft continued to drop. At the end of the 1990s, of the total aircraft park, 48 per cent of air frames were more than 15 years in use, 23 per cent 10–15 years, some 28 per cent 5–10 years and 1 per cent less than 5 years. Taking into account these numbers, not surprisingly the VVS commander Kornukov considered only 5 per cent of the aircraft as 'state-of-the-art'. VVS staff expected that the state of the air frames would enter a critical phase in 2005, in which year a large part of the aircraft park would be out of date for operational use.[25]

Viewpoint of VVS commanders

Initially the leadership of the VVS did not want to face the seriousness of the problems in which military aviation found itself. In this respect, in 1993 the VVS commander-in-chief, Colonel-General Pëtr Deynekin, claimed that reports on cutbacks in the number of flights and an increase in accidents were incorrect. He stated that these accidents were exclusively a consequence of violations of flight

Table 3.2 Aircraft deliveries to the VVS

Year	Number of aircraft received
1992	77
1993	66
1994	29
1995	31
1996	19
1997	6
1998	none

Table 3.3 VVS commanders

Name	Period in function
Deynekin, Pëtr	September 1992 – January 1998
Kornukov, Anatoly	January 1998 – January 2002
Michaylov, Vladimir	As of January 2002

security regulations and therefore were not caused by shortcomings in maintenance and flying proficiency. Apparently these critical news items were unwelcome to this VVS commander, since he could be held responsible for these failures. However, Deynekin did acknowledge shortcomings in spare parts, fuel, oil and lubricants. Furthermore, as one would expect, he proved to be a proponent of improved living conditions for VVS personnel, for instance by increasing salaries and providing more and better housing. In spite of the promises the short-comings which were recognized in 1993 would increase in the following years. Anatoly Kornukov, who succeeded Pëtr Deynekin in 1998, was rather explicit in his remarks on the current state of affairs and the future of VVS. In 1999 he stated that further reductions in personnel and material of VVS were unacceptable, that this would damage combat readiness and would obstruct the tasks laid upon VVS. The next year Kornukov testified that continuation of the current deficient VVS budget would mean the end of the VVS within a period of six or seven years. In the same year, the Collegium of the MoD, its highest consultative body including the commanders of all services, came to the conclusion that VVS could no longer accomplish all its assignments.[26]

In spite of these alarming reports the deplorable circumstances in which VVS found itself did not change. The reason for this had to do with the fact that the pri-orities of the military–political leadership were power and influence, embodied in preparation for massive large-scale and nuclear warfare. Modern perceptions of warfare, including a dominant position for air power in conflict resolution and corresponding state-of-the-art equipment, had to yield to these conservative lines of thought.

Reforms and reorganizations

During the Cold War the Soviet Union directed its military efforts towards the West. The ending of strained relations between East and West forced Russia's VVS to adapt former Soviet strategic concepts, which would entail huge conse-quences for Russia's order of battle. The USSR having lost the air defence belt when the Warsaw Pact collapsed, as well as the cover of the forward airbases of the former front MDs of Belarus and Ukraine, left this in heritance to the RF. This demanded a radical revision of the defence structure of Russian airspace. Another consequence of the end of the Cold War was the withdrawal of Russian forces from Eastern Europe. From 1990–93 the USSR and its successor state the RF withdrew 300 air force units, 700 aircraft, 100 helicopter and 30,000 servicemen from Czechoslovakia, Hungary, Poland, Germany and the Baltic States. More than half of the units and 500 aircraft were redeployed in the Moscow Military District (MOMD). A further outcome of the end of the Cold War was the implementation of the Treaty on Conventional Forces in Europe (CFE). According to this arms control treaty the USSR and subsequently the RF were obliged to reduce arms, which were tied to specified limits. In the treaty this was referred to as treaty limited equipment (TLE). As a result of this, aircraft too had to be demolished. Taking into account Yeltsin's initial pro-Western course in politics, it was unlikely that Russia would endanger (economic) cooperation with the West by not complying with the CFE Treaty.

In 1993 VVS commander Deynekin stated that the main objective of the reform plan of the VVS until 2000 was creating, based upon existing air units, a mobile service of the RF Armed Forces, with a balanced structure and modern aircraft. In this way VVS would be able to carry out the tasks set by the political and military leadership, in accordance with the increased importance of air power in ensuring the stability of the state.[27] In his description of the terms of reference of the VVS Deneykin expressed a correct understanding of the position and capabilities of VVS, as an element of military strategy in support of national security policy. However, developments in the following years would prove that the dualistic nature of RF security policy would thwart the envisaged direction of the VVS towards becoming a mobile, modern equipped air force.

Reform phases

Reforms of Russian air power were implemented in three phases. In the first phase, 1991–92, due to the loss of the integrated military structure with the other former Soviet republics, VVS was forced to form its own headquarters and to review its order of battle as well as the organizational structure of units and airbases. Because of the collapse of the USSR the position of the Military Districts of Moscow, St. Petersburg (LEMD) and North-Caucasus (NCMD) had changed from rearward to border (or front) MDs. The air component of these rear MDs consisted mainly of flying schools and training regiments. The status of front MDs required transition from training to operational units. In the second phase of reforms this intended reorganization would be completed. The conversion of these units together with the withdrawal of air force units from Eastern Europe would become the most acute problem for, the VVS. This was caused by a shortage of sufficiently equipped airbases, aircraft shelters, private housing and staff buildings. This resulted in overpopulated airbases, which lacked space for the construction of additional facilities as well as a sufficient quantity of public utilities (heating, water and electricity). In turn, this brought about the aforementioned appalling social-economic conditions for servicemen and their families.

In the second phase, 1993–95, the VVS further implemented the earlier initiatives, for instance by completing the withdrawal of air force units from former

Warsaw Pact states and former Soviet republics. In addition to this the VVS created new units, realized reductions in personnel strength and revised its training system. As early as 1992 Colonel-General Deynekin announced the intention of bringing all VVS units under the four commands of FA, DA, VTA and Reserve & Training.

In the third phase, as of 1995, the VVS reviewed its network of airbases. Owing to the heritage of the Soviet focus on the Western strategic direction, the majority of approximately 100 Russian airbases were deployed within a zone of 300 km of its western border. Thus, there was no proportional distribution of airfields over the country. Half the airbases were in urgent need of repairs and renovation. In addition to these changes the VVS in this phase of reforms implemented new systems of logistics and training.[28]

Amalgamation of VPVO and VVS

The decision to unite the VPVO and VVS was not taken hurriedly. This process was started on 4 November 1994, when the then Secretary of the Security Council (SCRF), Oleg Lobov, called a meeting on this subject. Present at this meeting were two general officers, who later on would play a dominant role in RF security policy: Lieutenant-Generals Anatoly Kvashnin and Valery Manilov. In January 1995, as a follow-up to this meeting, VVS commander Deynekin published a document on the status and future of VVS, in which the merger of the VPVO and VVS was recommended. Following this, moves towards a decision on unification for these two services developed swiftly. In October 1996 the proposal for amalgamation was on the desks of the Chief of the General Staff (CGS) and of the Minister of Defence. Furthermore, in December 1996 the institute ISKRAN of the Russian Academy of Sciences (RAS) organized a conference on military reforms, at which Makhmut Gareyev, President of the Academy of Military Sciences, spoke out in favour of an armed forces structure of three services: ground, air and naval forces. On 4 July 1997, at a meeting of the Federation Council, Russia's Upper House, Minister of Defence Igor Sergeyev officially announced the decision to fusing VPVO and VVS, which was to be realized in 1998.

Remarkable in the process of decision-making regarding the merger was the involvement of a fair number of prominent security actors. In addition to the aforementioned General Kvashnin (General Staff) and General Manilov (SCRF) and the self-evident contribution of VVS staff members, CGS and Minister of Defence, scientific institutions such as RAS and the Academy of Military Sciences were also engaged in the debate. This case of decision-making underlines the fact that RF security policy was determined by a small circle of prominent security actors, representing military, political and scientific institutions. The legislature was excluded from this decision-making process.

The main reasons for deciding to combine the VPVO and VVS were to be found in an analysis of the structure of foreign armed forces, in which air defence generally was carried out by the air force. Next, there was a budgetary need to proceed to reduce equipment and personnel, to dispose of duplications in organization and assignment of duties, and to aim at an increase in centralized command and control of air power and a subsequent rise in the efficient use of resources. With the discontinuance of the VPVO as an independent service of the RF Armed Forces, PVO units, just like FA units, were placed under operational command of the MDs. The merger of PVO units into VVS was accompanied by radical reductions in these two former independent services. From 1998 to 1999 reductions cut the formal total personnel strength from 318,000 to 185,000 servicemen, i.e. more than 40 per cent. Furthermore, 580 units and 20 airbases were disbanded.[29]

The amalgamation of the VPVO and VVS was not an unqualified success. At the end of 1998 a retired VVS colonel raised a number of disadvantages of the union. First, the fact that PVO units kept their stations, which, because of the distance between them and their counterparts in the VVS, made cooperation in unified VVS/PVO air armies complicated. Second, he found that PVO units were assigned missions, such as escorting VVS units, which were alien to their primary task of air defence. Finally, the colonel pointed at shortcomings in computerized command and control, since the systems of the PVO and VVS were not tuned in to one other. One-and-a-half years later the Chief of the VVS Staff gave his opinion on the merger.[30] As positive aspects of this synergy he mentioned the realization of a joined policy of procurement, improvement in the training of officers and the achievement of a coupled command and control system, which the colonel in 1998 still considered to be deficient. However, the Chief of the VVS Staff also observed negative consequences of unification. For instance, the capacity for the air defence of vital military, economic and administrative objects was diminished, just as the level of combat readiness. The time needed for full deployment of PVO formations had increased. To counter these negative effects and problems in other areas, this military authority announced the following measures, which were to be realized within the next 10–15 years: modernization of the computerized command and control system, procurement of state-of-the-art avionics (instruments for operating under limited flying conditions), EW and intelligence systems, precision-guided munitions (PGMs, *vysokotochnyye oruziya*), including cruise missiles, and modern aircraft for the FA (interceptors, fighter-bombers and ground attack aircraft) and VTA. However, the fact that the priorities in the defence budget were of a different order would cause problems for the realization of this 'shopping list'.

VVS structure as of 1998

In March 1998 Colonel-General Kornukov, who had recently succeeded Deynekin as commander-in-chief of VVS, presented a new organizational structure for the air forces, after the merger of the VPVO and VVS.[31] The four VVS commands, which were founded during the second phase of reforms, were to be closed down. The VVS headquarters, which since 1997 carried out administrative command over FA (operational command by the MDs), received in 1998 direct control over DA and VTA, which were reorganized into 37 and 61 Air Army respectively. Besides these

Table 3.4 Review of air force reforms 1991–99

Year	Event
1991–95	• Headquarters RF VVS formed
	• Transformation of training units into combat units
	• Withdrawal of air force units from Eastern Europe and the former USSR
1993–95	• Formation of DA, VTA, FA and Reserve & Training commands
1997–98	• Discontinuance of DA, VTA, FA and Reserve & Training commands
	• Name alteration of DA into 37 (Strategic) Air army
	• Name alteration of van VTA in 61 Air army
1998–99	• Amalgamation of VPVO and VVS

two air armies this new structure of the VVS comprised a VVS/PVO District Moscow. The VVS units of the MDs were organized into mixed VVS/PVO air armies or air corps. In addition to a new organizational structure, in his reform plan Kornukov also mentioned new terms of reference. The revision of tasks presented by Kornukov corresponded to a great extent with the recommendations which his predecessor Deynekin had made after the first Chechen conflict, focusing on the effective use of air power in local conflicts. With regard to this topic, Kornukov and Deynekin emphasized centralized command and control of air power. Another opinion was that initially the use of air power should be directed at achieving air superiority. Furthermore, the traditional single task of air power of providing air support for ground operations was broadened with an assignment of duties which was more in line with modern Western views on air power. Thus tasks such as air attacks, air fights, special combat missions including tactical dropping of airborne troops, air transport of equipment and personnel, air recce, EW, and demonstrations of force, were added to the traditional tasks of Soviet/Russian air power. What is more, tasks had to be carried out on the basis of joint efforts, i.e. integrated and coordinated actions of the RF Armed Forces and Other Troops of the power ministries. Not surprisingly, the operations of VVS in the second Chechen conflict corresponded with the revised tasks as presented by Kornukov.

Results and perspective

In the 1990s, just as the other services of the armed forces, the VPVO and VVS were forced to cut their strength in arms and personnel. Because of the amalgamation of the VPVO and VVS the total personnel strength of these two services dropped from 400,000 in 1993 to less than 185,000 servicemen in the year 2000.[32] However, the radical reorganizations in military aviation did not produce additional financial resources for a rise of combat readiness. The VVS remained deprived of financial means to overcome shortcomings in the areas of personnel (training and living conditions) and material (maintenance and replacements). Russia's security establishment retained its focus on nuclear power status and large-scale warfare, at the expense of the VVS and other conventional forces.

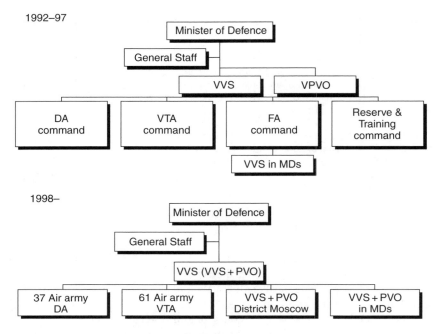

Figure 3.4 Development of the organizational structure of air forces.

Thoughts on the use of air power

Russia was and is a continental power. This fact had consequences for the build-up of the RF Armed Forces. Until well after the Second World War the assignment of duties as well as the thought processes regarding Soviet air power would be concentrated on air support for ground forces, instead of specific kinds of air warfare, such as air campaigns, air superiority and strategic bombardments. I will now examine the views of the VVS leadership on the use of Soviet and Russian air power in Afghanistan in the 1980s, in Chechnya in the 1990s, as well as Western experiences in using air power in the Gulf and in the Balkans. In conclusion, the policy of VVS in applying these lessons learned in tasks and procurement, as well as the position of military aviation as a part of security policy, will be examined.

Command and control, air-to-ground operations and air superiority

The history of Soviet and Russian military aviation shows a recurring fight for control over the use of air power between the VVS and Ground Forces. As early as the First World War two contrasting principles of command and control of air power in providing air support for ground operations became clear. One was *centralized* control (*printsip tsentralizovannogo upravleniya aviatsionnymi obyedineniyami*), in which air force units were under operational command of the MDs but under direct functional command of the commander-in-chief of VVS. The other principle was *decentralized* control (*printsip detsentralizovannogo upravleniya aviatsionnymi obyedineniyami*), in which these units, especially those of the FA, were subordinated to the (Ground Forces) commanders of the MDs. This dispute over the control of air power was to become a constant theme in the debates on command and control over the armed forces. In the First World War air force command won the day; command and control over air power came in the hands of the air force commander. However, in the years preceding the Second World War and during the first year of USSR involvement, until May 1942, control over air power belonged to the Ground Forces. This brought about a strongly decentralized organization of command and control, in which commanders of MDs, army corps and other formations of Ground Forces were in charge of air force units. This decentralized control over air power proved to undermine its effectiveness. As a result of this in spring 1942 the military leadership re-established command and control by the VVS. Subsequently, the VVS formed air armies. In the 1980s and 1990s the traditional debate on control over air power revived. In 1980, the decision to subordinate the FA and ASV to the MDs (a process of decentralization), in fact meant a return to the situation on the eve of the Second World War. This decision entailed the end of independent air armies; VVS units were now part of the structure of an MD. A further splitting into smaller units took place by disconnecting FA and ASV in the MDs. These changes in the command and control structure had a number of negative consequences. Not only control over the use of air power, but also the management of air force units in the MDs became more complicated. Command levels run from the MDs to Ground Forces Staff and from Ground Forces Staff to VVS Staff. Such an organizational structure hampered a clear, consequent and fast command and control over air power. Furthermore, this decentralized structure also created problems in carrying out maintenance of airbases and equipment, because the distribution of tasks between Ground Forces and VVS was not always obvious. Additionally, the split command over air force units complicated the introduction of avionics, PGMs and the training of personnel. In 1988 the Defence Council of the USSR put an end to the decentralized structure of command and control, by reinstating the old (centralized) structure of pre-1980 and by resubordinating FA units to the air armies of the MDs. Another development in the competition for control over air power occurred in 1990, when the ASV, which had been an element of VVS since 1977, was transferred to the Ground Forces, to be installed as an independent arm of this service. In 1997 another change in control over air power took place. After the discontinuance of the FA Command, FA units were brought under operational command of the MDs, but this time preserving the air army structure, and VVS maintaining administrative control over these units. As mentioned earlier, the most recent developments in this field were the amalgamation of VPVO and VVS in 1998 and the transfer of ASV from Ground Forces to VVS in 2002.[33] The leadership of VVS has never made a secret of its view that for optimizing effective management of air power centralized control by VVS was a prerequisite. The VVS considered the ideal organizational structure to be one in which the VVS commander-in-chief would have centralized functional command over the air units and FA units would be under operational command of the MDs. The VVS commanders, Deynekin and Kornukov, as well as air power expert Rog believed that this concept was the best way of controlling air armies, of concentrating air power means in all necessary directions and in as limited a time as possible, for introducing computerized command and control and logistical systems, for optimizing training, as well as for cooperation with other services of the RF Armed Forces, aviation industries and research institutes.

Another point of view of Deynekin and Kornukov was that VVS has always regarded Anti-Surface Force Air Operations (*aviatsionnaya podderzhka voysk*, APV) as its primary task. For instance, in the Second World War 43 per cent of the sorties (*samolëto-vylet*) of FA and DA were assigned to APV missions. Irregular conflicts, such as the Soviet intervention in Afghanistan (1979–89) and the Chechen conflict, confirmed the significance of APV. Of vital importance for carrying out this task was achieving and preserving air superiority (*zavoyevaniye i uderzhaniye gospodstva v vozdukhe*), also referred to as Counter-Air Operations. In carrying out these essential tasks the VVS leadership regarded the merger of VPVO and VVS as a positive step towards further centralization of air power. In this unified structure of air forces air operations would no longer be classified by the type of units (PVO or VVS) and aircraft, but by the type of action: offensive operations (*vozdushnyye nastupatelnyye operatsii*) or defensive operations (*vozdushnyye oboronitelnyye operatsii*). Ways for further centralization of command and control of air power were constant factors in the thinking of the VVS. Needless to say, the transfer of ASV to VVS and an MoD study on the possibility of further reassignment of elements of military aviation to VVS, were welcomed by the VVS leadership as fulfilment of their views on modern use of air power.[34]

Soviet, Russian and Western experiences in using air power

Afghanistan

The management of the Soviet VVS can best be described by a fixation on logged procedures. This applied especially to the organization and working of operational flying missions. Scrupulous implementation of the instructions set by VVS Staff in Moscow seemed to have a higher priority than achieving an optimal standard of readiness of aircrews and aircraft. The combat experience of VVS units in Afghanistan would change this attitude. Combat conditions in this country did not allow for rigorous following of procedures. Unit commanders did not bother about paperwork, neglected superfluous (security) procedures and concentrated on combat readiness and optimal use of air power. Pilots as well as unit commanders regarded avoiding red tape as liberation. Even more, they were convinced that after returning from their tour of duty their aim should be to transform VVS completely, based on their experiences in Afghanistan. Having experienced freedom of action there, on their return to the USSR these officers would no longer accept the bureaucratic, rigid, centralized working methods. However, the VVS leadership considered this attitude of commanders and pilots as a threat to their own position. Consequently, VVS Staff decided to prevent this rebellion against the ruling class, by disbanding air units after their return from Afghanistan and redeploying their officers all over the country.[35] So, fearful of having their authority undermined, the VVS leadership purposely silenced vital operational lessons learned from officers serving in Afghanistan. Thus, valuable experience concerning the use of air power in irregular warfare was lost. The Chechen conflicts of the 1990s would demonstrate that disregarding the very useful lessons learned was a serious shortcoming in VVS leadership at that time.

Western experiences

In the Gulf War of 1991 the Coalition Forces carried out shattering air attacks. In correspondence with this concept a strong air group was formed, consisting of fighters, fighter-bombers, combat helicopters, strategic bombers, EW and recce aircraft, tankers and flying command posts (AWACS). Control of the use of air power was centralized at one authority. The attack of the multinational force started with achieving air superiority in the theatre of war, and was followed by an air campaign (*vozdushnaya kampaniya*). One of the first lessons of this conflict was that ground forces could only be deployed successfully after air power had cleared the way through an air offensive. The leadership of the Russian air force took these conclusions into account. According to the VVS commander, Deynekin, in the first Chechen conflict (1994–96), by introducing dedicated air groups (*aviatsionnaya gruppirovka*), centralized control of air power by the various commands of VVS had proved to be the most effective model of air warfare. In both Chechen conflicts the VVS formed a dedicated air group. However, in the first Chechen conflict, because of the rushed start of the military operation and the consequent unclear lines of command, the control of air power was not centralized. In the second Chechen conflict this was the case: operational control over the joint air component of VVS, ASV and military aviation of the troops of the power ministries was concentrated under one general of the Joint Military Staff. After the mishaps in the first Chechen conflict, the lesson learned, that ground troops should enter the battlefield only after preparatory air operations, was activated at the start of the second conflict in 1999.

The Western use of air power was further developed during the conflicts in former Yugoslavia. In August/September 1995, in Bosnia, NATO's operation *Deliberate Force* demonstrated another method of using modern air power. Using PGMs, the air component shelled vital targets in the rear of the (Bosnian–Serbian) opponent.

This tactic of air warfare would also be followed by the VVS. In autumn 1999, during the conflict in Dagestan, the VVS also attacked vital targets in Chechnya. According to VVS commander, Kornukov, NATO's air campaign in Kosovo in spring 1999, *Allied Force*, gave once more evidence to the fact that air power had accomplished a decisive position in solving current conflicts. His predecessor, Pëtr Deynekin, in 1996 had pointed out the vital contribution of air power in the Gulf War of 1991, when after 37 days of using air power, the ground forces needed only 100 hours to force the Iraqis to sign a truce.[36] Kornukov's statement, attaching a decisive role to air power in conflict resolution, was remarkable. Until then VVS commanders as well as air power experts had designated air support for ground operations as the primary task of air power, which signified that the use of air power was subjected to land warfare. Now, seemingly 'infected' by current air power thinking in the West, the leadership of VVS recognized the broader use of air power and a role for air power independent of ground operations.

Air power in local conflicts

Based upon the aforementioned Soviet, Russian and Western air power experiences, general Deynekin came up with a number of recommendations on the effective use of air power in local conflicts:[37]

- centralized control of air power in principle; assignment of duties by the joint commander to the VVS commander, who in turn assigns tasks through the air component commander and the chiefs of the Commands of FA, DA and VTA;
- in the initial phase of a conflict air power is directed exclusively at achieving and preserving air superiority;
- air power can be used in the form of air attacks (*aviatsionnyye udary*), air fights (*vozdushnyy boy*), special combat missions (*spetsialnyye boyevyye polëty*), for instance tactical airborne landings (*desantirovaniye takticheskikh vozdushnykh desantov*), air transport of personnel and equipment (*perevozka voysk i boyevoy tekhniki po vozdukhu*), air recce (*vozdushnaya razvedka*), EW (*sozdaniye radiopomekh*), medevac (*evakuatsiya ranenykh i bolnykh*), as well as demonstration of force (*demonstrativnyye deystviya*);
- exclusion of sole use of air power; applying air power on the basis of joint actions, coordinated and operating together with other services of the armed forces and troops of the power ministries. Joint action is specifically important with regard to cooperation of intelligence gathering organs of air and ground forces and intelligence services, concerning transparency in targeting and in relation to joint operations of ASV and VVS;
- all-weather and limited visibility capabilities for material (avionics) as well as personnel (training);
- application of PGMs; in doing so, VVS would be able to strike targets more effectively, with fewer pilots, less equipment and a decrease in losses of servicemen as well as of civilians.

Deynekin's recommendations were not in vain. The use of air power in the second Chechen conflict showed the application of most of his points. This was especially the case with his arguments on centralized command and control of air power, the various methods of air warfare, as well as unified and coordinated action of military aviation together with other defence forces and the Other Troops of the power ministries. However, in the case of proposals which demanded additional financial resources, such as measures to improve combat readiness of material and personnel and the procurement of PGMs, they would not be applied in the second Chechen conflict, because of continuous budgetary problems and other priorities.

Implementation of lessons learned

The successful and dominant contribution of air power in the Gulf War of 1991 and in NATO's air attacks in Bosnia in 1995 and Kosovo in 1999 changed the viewpoint of the VVS leadership with regard to the set of tasks and the position of air power. Air power now had larger significance than simply providing air support for ground operations in a large-scale conflict situation. The aforementioned lessons learned, emphasizing the increased importance of local conflicts and the simultaneous decreased role of large-scale conflicts, were implemented in awarding a higher priority to flying skills. As a result of this line of thought, FA pilots would receive more flying hours, at the expense of the flying hours of PVO and DA pilots. Furthermore, the VVS intended to change the emphasis of DA assignments from strategic, large-scale operations to local conflicts. However, the military–political leadership had a different opinion. In their view, the DA was intended primarily as a means of displaying (nuclear) power.[38]

Furthermore, the VVS leadership was of the opinion that the 'Chechen factor' should also be reflected in the modernization plans of the aircraft park. The prominence of local conflicts was the reason for VVS to give priority to modernizing the FA and ASV. Next the VTA and finally DA would be in line for replacements. This policy was rational and realistic and was a sign of decision-making in correspondence with the current spectrum of threats for the RF. Not large-scale warfare, with a possible role for nuclear arms and subsequently of DA, but irregular, local warfare, such as in Dagestan and Chechnya, with the FA and ASV as vital elements of air power, was the most likely conflict situation Russia had to cope with.[39]

With regard to the position of the VVS, its leadership now stated that the recognized increased importance of air power should be reflected in the concepts of warfare, by declaring the role of VVS as spearhead. This point of view was also brought forward from an unexpected direction. Already in 1994 strategy expert army general Makhmut Gareyev assured that in modern warfare air power was to receive a vital role. In his opinion at the start of a conflict massive air strikes (*massirovannye aviatsionnye udary*) would play a decisive role, because without them successful action of ground troops would be impossible. For such a method of warfare coordination and tuning among the defence forces was necessary. Furthermore, he stated that under these circumstances air power means would have to be directly subordinated to the overall commander.[40] With this view Gareyev proved to be far-sighted. Precisely the aspects of initial use of air power, cooperation among MoD forces and power ministries troops and the positioning of an air component under central command and control, would turn out to be important causes for failed military action in the first Chechen conflict, but also for more successful warfare in the second conflict.

Air power had reached the status of a key factor in solving local armed conflicts and ensuring national security in general. Valentin Rog noticed that the strengthened role of air power was confirmed in the editions of 2000 of NSC and Military Doctrine, in which the latter for the first time mentioned specific types of air warfare, such as air campaigns and operations.[41] The VVS leadership perceived that the enlarged importance of air power should be rendered into a raise of financial means. The level should be comparable to that of Western air forces, which was 25–30 per cent of the defence budget, instead of the 10 per cent of the RF defence budget in 2000.[42] This ambition was laudable but not realistic, since the military–political leadership attached greater value to other assets, especially those which had to do with demonstrating Russia's nuclear potential.

Notes

1 For air power definitions, see G. Teitler, J.M.J. Bosch, W. Klinkert *et al.*, *Militaire strategie* (Amsterdam: Mets & Schilt, 2002), pp. 141–3. In describing the air forces, one of the services of the RF Armed Forces, I will do so by its Russian abbreviation VVS. The other components of military aviation of the Armed Forces and of the Other Troops will also be referred to by their specific names, for instance, army aviation ASV.

2 Ye. Agapova, 'Rossiya bez kryl'ev – ne Rossiya', *Krasnaya Zvezda*, 15 Aug. 1992, p. 1; V.G. Rog, 'Put' Rossiyskoy voyennoy aviatsii', *Nezavisimoye Voyennoye Obozreniye*, 26 (296), 2 Aug. 2002, p. 1; P.S. Deynekin, 'Vremya reshitel'nykh deystviy', *Aviatsiya i Kosmonavtika*, Jan. 1993, p. 2, and 'Problemnyye voprosy stroitel'stva i primeneniya voyenno-vozdushnykh sil Rossii', *Aviatsiya i Kosmonavtika*, May 1996, p. 3; V.G. Rog and A. Drobyshevskiy, 'Improvizatsiy ne bylo', *Nezavisimoye Voyennoye Obozreniye*, 47 (220), 15 Dec. 2000, p. 4.

3 P.S. Deynekin, 'U rossiyskikh VVS budut tol'ko noveyshiye samolëty', *Izvestiya*, 24 March 1993, p. 6; M.M. Oparin, 'Dal'nyaya aviatsiya i bezopasnost' Rossii', *Armeyskiy Sbornik*, 10 (1999), p. 30; A. Chernorechenskiy and S. Sokut, 'Vykhod iz shtopora otkladyvayetsya', *Nezavisimoye Voyennoye Obozreniye*, 2 (175), 21 Jan. 2000, p. 3; and S. Sokut, 'Kurs na lokal'nyye konflikty', *Nezavisimoye Voyennoye Obozreniye*, 4 (226), 2 Feb. 2001, p. 3.

4 M. Khodarenok, 'Zatyanuvsheesya pike', *Nezavisimoye Voyennoye Obozreniye*, 8 (278), 15 March 2002, p. 4. For an explanation of the resubordination of ASV from Ground Forces to VVS, see pp. 106–8, 'ASV – rotary wing force'.

5 *Military Balance 2000–2001*, pp. 124–5; P. Butowski 'Air Force Must Look Up as Training Hits a Low', *Jane's Defence Weekly*, 2 Aug. 2000, p. 22; A.M. Kornukov, 'Zavoyevat', uderzhat', podderzhat'', *Armeyskiy Sbornik*, 12 (1998), p. 32; 'Aviatsiya poiznosilas'', *Nezavisimoye Voyennoye Obozreniye*, 38 (308), 25 Oct. 2002, p. 3; and 'Doklad o perekhode', *Nezavisimoye Voyennoye Obozreniye*, 1 (316), 17 Jan. 2003, p. 3.

6 Kornukov, 'Zavoyevat', uderzhat', podderzhat'', p. 33. See also Appendix II: Main Russian aircraft types used in the Chechen conflicts.

7 Sokut, 'Kurs na lokal'nyye konflikty'; and Rog, 'Improvizatsiy ne bylo'. See Figure 3.3: Structure of a VVS and PVO air army of a Military District. This is generalized structure and therefore not a standard organization for each Military District. Sources used for this figure are *Military Balance 2000–2001*, pp. 124–5; CFE; J. Lake, 'Order of battle: Russia's Air Forces today', *Combat Aircraft*, Oct.–Nov. 1998, pp. 702–12; V.G. Rog, 'Vozdushniye operatsii uprazdnit' nel'zya', *Nezavisimoye Voyennoye Obozreniye*, 38 (211), 13 Oct. 2000, p. 1, and 'Improvizatsiy ne bylo'; H. Nikunen, *The Current State of the Russian Air Force*, 28 Nov. 2001, www.sci.fi/~fta/ruaf.htm. See also 'Note on Strength of Russian Military Formations', p. xvi.

8 S.F. Akhromeyev, *Voyennyy Entsiklopedicheskiy Slovar'* (Moscow: Voyenizdat, 1986), p. 787; B. Lambeth, *Russia's Air Power in Crisis* (Washington, DC: Smithsonian Institution Press, 1999), p. 43; and Lake, 'Order of battle: Russia's Air Forces today', p. 707.

9 Akhromeyev, *Voyennyy Entsiklopedicheskiy Slovar*, p. 221; Deynekin, 'U rossiyskikh VVS budut tol'ko noveyshiye samolëty'; and M.M. Oparin, 'Ot "Ilyi Muromtsa" do Tu-160', *Nezavisimoye Voyennoye Obozreniye*, 50 (173), 24 Dec. 1999, p. 1.

10 Butowski, 'Air Force Must Look Up as Training Hits a Low'; V. Aleksin and O. Finayev, 'V nebe nad Kavkazom', *Nezavisimoye Voyennoye Obozreniye*, 36 (159), 17 Sept. 1999, p. 2; Oparin, 'Dal'nyaya aviatsiya i bezopasnost' Rossii' and 'Ot "Ilyi Muromtsa" do Tu-160'; Chernorechenskiy, 'Vykhod iz shtopora otkladyvayetsya'; A.M. Kornukov, 'Voyenno-Vozdushnyye Sily – eto i shchit, i mech', *Vestnik Vozdushnogo Flota*, 7–8 (1999), p. 9.

Five Military Districts contributed to the exercise *Zapad-99*: LEMD, MOMD, NCMD, the MDs Volga and Ural, as well as three fleets of the RF Navy, adding up to 7,000 servicemen in total. Belarusian military units also participated in the exercise. The air forces contributed with air assets of VVS and PVO. The air assets were combined into an *ad hoc* air army. The central focus of the scenario of this command-post exercise was a large-scale conflict. See S. Babichev, 'I prikrytiye, i karayushchiy mech', *Krasnaya Zvezda*, 25 June 1999, p. 1; Kornukov, 'Voyenno-Vozdushnyye Sily – eto i shchit, i mech'. The emphasis on large-scale warfare revealed that at that moment at least a part of the military leadership still regarded this type of conflict more important than irregular, internal conflict, such as in Chechnya.

11 S. Lefebvre, *The Reform of the Russian Air Force* (Camberley: Conflict Studies Research Centre, 2002), p. 8; and V.G. Rog, 'Oriyentir – neyadernoye sderzhivaniye', *Nezavisimoye Voyennoye Obozreniye*, 38 (260), 12 Oct. 2001, p. 4.

12 Akhromeyev, *Voyennyy Entsiklopedicheskiy Slovar*, p. 144; Lefebvre, *The Reform of the Russian Air Force*, pp. 9–10.

13 Akhromeyev, *Voyennyy Entsiklopedicheskiy Slovar*, pp. 153–4. In paragraph 3.4 'Reforms and reorganizations' I will explain the amalgamation of VPVO and VVS.

14 Akhromeyev, *Voyennyy Entsiklopedicheskiy Slovar*, p. 43; Lake, 'Order of Battle: Russia's Air Forces Today', p. 710.

15 A. Novikov, 'The Russian Helicopter Fleet – What Will It Be?', *Krasnaya Zvezda*, 3 Feb. 1993, p. 2; S. Sokut, 'Osmysleniye Chechenskogo opyta', *Nezavisimoye Voyennoye Obozreniye*, 29 (251), 10 Aug. 2001, p. 3.

16 'Aviatsiya poiznosilas''; I. Kedrov, 'Staryye vertolety resayut novyye zadachi', *Nezavisimoye Voyennoye Obozreniye*, 40 (163), 15 Oct. 1999, pp. 1, 3; and V. Yuzbasyev, 'A Show of Punishment Instead of a True Investigation of the Mi-26 Crash', *Moskovskiye Novosti*, 10 Sept. 2002, p. 3.

17 Kornukov, 'Zavoyevat', uderzhat', podderzhat'', pp. 30–1; V.G. Rog, 'Zlovrednaya kon'yunkturshchina', *Nezavisimoye Voyennoye Obozreniye*, 43 (313), 6 Dec. 2002,

p. 4; S. Suleymanov, 'V poiskakh vinovnykh', *Nezavisimoye Voyennoye Obozreniye*, 31 (301), 6 Sept. 2002, p. 3; L. Slonov, 'War in Chechnya continues', *Former Soviet Union Fifteen Nations: Policy and Security*, 8 (2002), pp. 4–5; 'Peremeny v aviatsii', *Nezavisimoye Voyennoye Obozreniye*, 30 (300), 30 Aug. 2002, p. 3; Ye. Matveyev, 'Tridtsat' pyatyy: v srednem federal'nyye voyska terjayut v Chechne po vertoljotu v mesyats', *Nezavisimoye Voyennoye Obozreniye*, 30 (300), 30 Aug. 2002, p. 1; V. Mukhin, 'Sergei Ivanov Quoted the President as Saying that the Mi-26 Catastrophe Was Another *Kursk*', *Nezavisimaya Gazeta*, 9 Sept. 2002, p. 1; 'Lichnyy kontrol' nachal'nika GSh', *Nezavisimoye Voyennoye Obozreniye*, 32 (302), 13 Sept. 2002, p. 1; and A. Khrolenko, 'Bez platy za strakh', *Nezavisimoye Voyennoye Obozreniye*, 1 (316), 17 Jan. 2003, p. 6.

On 12 Aug. 2000 in the Barents Sea the nuclear submarine *Kursk* sank, as a result of an accident with a torpedo. In this disaster the same number of servicemen were killed as in the shooting down of the *Halo*. See W. Parkhomenko, 'The Russian military in the wake of the Kursk tragedy', *Journal of Slavic Military Studies*, 14, 4 (2001), p. 35.

18 Slonov, 'War in Chechnya continuous'; Khrolenko, 'Bez platy za strakh'; Rog, 'Zlovrednaya kon"yunkturshchina'; 'Doklad o perekhode'.

19 'Lichnyy kontrol'nachal'nika GSh'; 'Doklad o perekhode'. Taking into account the fact that the (official) statements on this subject varied, my estimate of the number of helicopters of the ASV in the 1990s is between 1,500 and 2,000. Sources: see 'Aviatsiya poiznosilas'' and 'Doklad o perekhode'.

20 S. Sokut, 'Perspektivy razvitiya boyevoy aviatsii', *Nezavisimoye Voyennoye Obozreniye*, 29 (251), 10 Aug. 2001, p. 1; and Khodarenok, 'Zatyanuvsheesya pike'.

21 Lefebvre, *The Reform of the Russian Air Force*, p. 10; Deynekin, 'Problemnyye voprosy stroitel'stva i primeneniya voyenno-vozdushnykh sil Rossii', p. 4; Chernorechenskiy, 'Vykhod iz shtopora otkladyvayetsya'; A. Drobyshevshkiy and S. Babichev, 'Boyegotovnost' trebuyet raskhodov', *Krasnaya Zvezda*, 17 July 1999, p. 1.

22 According to NATO air force standards, 180 flying hours are required for a skilled fighter pilot. *Military Balance 1995–1996*, p. 115; Chernorechenskiy, 'Vykhod iz shtopora otkladyvayetsya'; P.S. Deynekin, 'Basic Directions of Air Force Organizational Developments and Training under Present Conditions', *Voyennaya Mysl'*, 7 (1993), p. 4, and 'Problemnyye voprosy stroitel'stva i primeneniya voyenno-vozdushnykh sil Rossii', p. 4; S. Sokut, 'Dal'she sokrashchat' VVS nel'zya', *Nezavisimoye Voyennoye Obozreniye*, 31 (154), 13 Aug. 1999, p. 1; C. Covault, 'Russian Air Force Faces Deepening Crisis', *Aviation Week & Space Technology*, 5 March 2001, p. 63; 'V VVS nekomu letat'?', *Nezavisimoye Voyennoye Obozreniye*, 38 (211), 13 Oct. 2000, p. 1; Sokut, 'Kurs na lokal'nyye konflikty'; Khodarenok, 'Zatyanuvsheesya pike'; and Lefebvre, *The Reform of the Russian Air Force*, p. 16.

23 Agapova, 'Rossiya bez kryl'ev – ne Rossiya', p. 2; Khodarenok, 'Zatyanuvsheesya pike'; 'V VVS ne khvatayet ofitserov', *Nezavisimoye Voyennoye Obozreniye*, 37 (210), 6 Oct. 2000, p. 1; and Lefebvre, *The Reform of the Russian Air Force*, p. 10.

24 V. Matyash, 'S trevogoy i nadezhdoy', *Krasnaya Zvezda*, 3 Dec. 1996, pp. 1–2; Drobyshevshkiy, 'Boyegotovnost' trebuyet raskhodov', pp. 1–2; Covault, 'Russian Air Force Faces Deepening Crisis', p. 60; Khodarenok, 'Zatyanuvsheesya pike'; 'Park VVS stareyet', *Nezavisimoye Voyennoye Obozreniye*, 26 (199), 21 July 2000, p. 1; Sokut, 'Perspektivy razvitiya boyevoy aviatsii'.

25 Drobyshevshkiy, 'Boyegotovnost' trebuyet raskhodov', p. 2; A. Dobrovol'skiy, 'VVS budut spasat' svoyu tekhniku', *Nezavisimoye Voyennoye Obozreniye*, 18 (141), 14 May 1999, p. 6; V. Aleksin, 'Aviatsiya v "shtopore"', *Nezavisimoye Voyennoye Obozreniye*, 4 (164), 22 Oct. 1999, p. 6; Chernorechenskiy, 'Vykhod iz shtopora otkladyvayetsya'; 'Park VVS stareyet'.

With respect to the obsolete state of aircraft one has to consider that the service life of Russian aircraft is shorter than that of Western military aircraft. This shorter service life dates back to the Cold War when the Soviet Union aimed at massive use of aircraft and realized that many would be destroyed. Therefore, a long service life for aircraft was not necessary. See C.J. Dick, 'Military Reform and the Russian Air Force 1999', *Journal of Slavic Military Studies*, 13, 1 (2000), p. 8.

26 Agapova, 'Rossiya bez kryl'ev – ne Rossiya', p. 2; Deynekin, 'Vremya reshitel'nykh deystviy'; Sokut, 'Dal'she sokrashchat' VVS nel'zya', p. 3 and 'Kurs na lokal'nyye konflikty'; Chernorechenskiy, 'Vykhod iz shtopora otkladyvayetsya'; 'VVS ne boyegotovy?', *Nezavisimoye Voyennoye Obozreniye*, 49 (222), 29 Dec. 2000, p. 1; and Khodarenok, 'Zatyanuvsheesya pike'.

27 Deynekin, 'Vremya reshitel'nykh deystviy'; N.T. Antoshkin, 'Speech at the RNLAF Base Leeuwarden on 20.4.93', in R.W. Dellow, *Organization and Equipment: Priorities for the Russian Air Force*, B52 (Camberley: Conflict Studies Research Centre, 1993); Deynekin, 'Basic directions of air force organizational developments and training under present conditions'.

28 Antoshkin, 'Speech at the RNLAF base Leeuwarden on 20.4.93'; Deynekin, 'Basic directions of air force organizational developments and training under present conditions' and 'Reform of the air force is a must', *Military News Bulletin*, 8 (1996), pp. 7–8; Agapova, 'Rossiya bez kryl'ev – ne Rossiya', p. 1; Yu. Gavrilov and S. Babichev 'Ne teryat' temp, zavershit' nachatoye', *Krasnaya Zvezda*, 12 Aug. 1998, pp. 1–2.

29 *Military Balance 2000–2001*, pp. 124–5; CFE; 'Improvizatsiy ne bylo'; A.M. Kornukov, 'To Preserve and Build Up Combat Capabilities', *Military News Bulletin*, 3 (1998), pp. 8–9; Gavrilov 'Ne teryat' temp, zavershit' nachatoye'; 'Pri ob"yedinenii VVS i PVO budet sokrashcheno 40% boyevogo sostava', *Interfaks*, 29, 11 Feb. 1998, p. 3.

30 A. Krasnov, 'Nash argument protiv MAU', *Vestnik Vozdushnogo Flota*, Nov.–Dec. 1998, p. 18; B. Chel'tsov, 'VVS ishchut svoyë mesto v trëkhvidovoy strukture vooruzhënnykh sil', *Nezavisimoye Voyennoye Obozreniye*, 29 (202), 11 Aug. 2000, p. 1.

31 A.M. Kornukov, 'Teoriya stroitel'stva novykh VVS', *Nezavisimoye Voyennoye Obozreniye*, 10 (84), 13 March 1998, p. 1 and 'Aviatsionnaya podderzhka voysk: gospodstvo v nebe – uspekh na zemle', *Krasnaya Zvezda*, 11 Nov. 1998, p. 2; Gavrilov 'Ne teryat' temp, zavershit' nachatoye'. See Figure 3.4: Development of the organizational structure of air forces.

32 *Military Balance 1990–2001*; CFE.

33 Rog, 'Put' Rossiyskoy voyennoy aviatsii'; Deynekin, 'Problemnyye voprosy stroitel'stva i primeneniya voyenno-vozdushnykh sil Rossii', *Aviatsiya i Kosmonavtika*, May 1996, p. 5; Deynekin, 'Reform of the air force is a must', p. 7; Kornoekov, 'Aviatsionnaya podderzhka voysk: gospodstvo v nebe – uspekh na zemle', p. 2, and 'Zavoyevat', uderzhat', podderzhat'' pp. 30–1.

34 Deynekin, 'Problemnyye voprosy stroitel'stva i primeneniya voyenno-vozdushnykh sil Rossii', pp. 3, 7; V.G. Rog, 'Vozdushnoye nastupleniye i vozdushnaya oborona', *Armeyskiy Sbornik*, 11 (1997), p. 4; Kornukov, 'Teoriya stroitel'stva novykh VVS', pp. 1, 3, and 'Aviatsionnaya podderzhka voysk: gospodstvo v nebe – uspekh na zemle'; Rog, 'Put' Rossiyskoy voyennoy aviatsii'.

35 Lambeth, *Russia's Air Power in Crisis*, pp. 96–7.

36 Rog, 'Vozdushnoye nastupleniye i vozdushnaya oborona'; Deynekin, 'Problemnyye voprosy stroitel'stva i primeneniya voyenno-vozdushnykh sil Rossii', pp. 7–8; and Sokut, 'Dal'she sokrashchat' VVS nel'zya'.

37 Deynekin, 'Problemnyye voprosy stroitel'stva i primeneniya voyenno-vozdushnykh sil Rossii', pp. 10–11.

38 Sokut, 'Kurs na lokal'nyye konflikty'.

39 Sokut, 'Osmysleniye Chechenskogo opyta'.

40 M.A. Gareyev, 'Yadernym oruzhiyem problem ne reshit'', *Krasnaya Zvezda*, 5 Aug. 1994, p. 2.
41 Rog, V.G. 'Bor'ba za gospodstvo v vozdukhe', *Nezavisimoye Voyennoye Obozreniye*, 3 (225), 26 Jan. 2001, p. 4; 'Voyennaya doktrina Rossiyskoy Federatsii', *Nezavisimoye Voyennoye Obozreniye*, 15, 28 April 2000, pp. 1, 4–5; *Sobraniye Zakonodatel'stva RF* (2000) item 1852, p. 3843.
42 Deynekin, 'Problemnyye voprosy stroitel'stva i primeneniya voyenno-vozdushnykh sil Rossii', pp. 4, 7–10; Kornukov, 'Teoriya stroitel'stva novykh VVS', p. 3, and 'VVS kak faktor natsional'noy bezopasnosti', *Krasnaya Zvezda*, 12 Nov. 1999, pp. 1–2.

4

IMPLEMENTATION OF AIR POWER – WAR AROUND CHECHNYA

The conflicts in Chechnya (1994–96), Dagestan (Autumn 1999), Chechnya (1999–) and an assessment of the use of air power

Introduction

In this chapter the central theme is the implementation of air power and the actual use of the air forces. In the previous chapters the higher (military–political) levels of strategy were described. In this part the remaining levels, operations, tactics and technical level, will be presented. The themes of earlier chapters return here in analysing subjects such as the application of the various levels of strategy in the Chechen conflicts, the performance of security actors, the use of air forces in an irregular conflict and the relationship between military doctrine and the practice of warfare. Since the latter is one of the basic questions of this book, the account of this section will be included in the next chapter on conclusions.

The purpose here is not to provide a comprehensive study of these conflicts but to focus, in particular, on the use of Russian air power and the Chechen response to the use of military force.

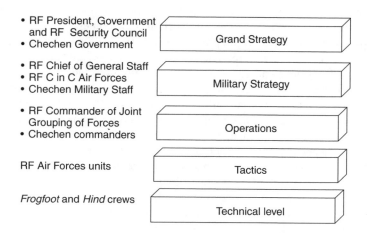

- RF President, Government and RF Security Council
- Chechen Government

Grand Strategy

- RF Chief of General Staff
- RF C in C Air Forces
- Chechen Military Staff

Military Strategy

- RF Commander of Joint Grouping of Forces
- Chechen commanders

Operations

RF Air Forces units

Tactics

Frogfoot and *Hind* crews

Technical level

Figure 4.1 Levels of strategy in the conflicts in Chechnya and Dagestan.

Chechnya: background

Chechnya is a small Russian republic. To really understand the Chechen conflict two points are important. First, the Chechens have a history of showing fierce resistance against Russian occupation, which goes back to the expansion of the Russian tsarist empire in the nineteenth century. Second, to the Chechens clan adherence is more important than a one nation state.

Geography

Chechnya forms a part of the North Caucasus, which in the south borders on the Trans-Caucasian republics of Georgia, Armenia and Azerbaijan, in the west on the Sea of Azov and in the east on the Caspian Sea. The population of the North Caucasus consists of approximately 16 million people, divided over more than 100 nationalities. Russians, who form the largest entity, live mostly in the northern part. The North Caucasian republics of the Russian Federation, such as Chechnya and Dagestan, are dominated by non-Russian nationalities. The area of Chechnya is about half the size of The Netherlands. Chechnya is adjacent to Georgia, the RF republics of Dagestan and Ingushetia, as well as to Russia proper. In 1989 Chechnya had over 1 million inhabitants, 90 per cent of whom were ethnic Chechens.

Economic and social development

Chechnya and its surroundings, such as Azerbaijan, are rich in oil. In 1893 the oil industry was set up on a large scale, by constructing pipelines to the Caspian and to the Black Sea. Oil production brought petrochemical and chemical industries to Chechnya. Other industrial branches that developed included those dealing with building material, forestry and the construction of machinery.

In spite of the industrialization process the majority of the Chechen population remained active in agriculture. The dominant social organization is the clan. Chechens belong to some 135–50 clans.[1] Immigration and the forced collectivization of the agricultural sector caused the Chechens to retire within themselves in resistance to Russian and communist rule. The consequences of this were a rise in religious (Muslim) brotherhoods and nostalgia for the traditional village and clan structures, manners and traditions.[2] Here both prominent characteristics of Chechens come together: an aversion to Russian reign but also a preference for the clan over loyalty to a one nation state. Recent history makes it clear that as a result of a lack of 'national feeling' and in the absence of the 'foreign invader', Chechens will fight against each other. For instance, President Dudayev as well as his successor Maskhadov have experienced a number of assassination attempts. Under Maskhadov, in particular, central power was weak and warlords ruled over large parts of Chechnya.

128

History

In 1853, after many years of heavy fighting, Chechnya was conquered by tsarist Russia. However, this did not mean that Chechen resistance against Russian occupation ended. During the Russian Revolution of 1917 the Chechens fought against tsarist troops as well as against the Red Army. In the 1930s, because of the enforced agricultural collectivization, Chechen opposition was once again strong. In 1944, when Stalin suspected the Chechens of collaborating with the Nazis, half a million Chechens and Ingushetians were deported to Central Asia. In 1953, after Stalin's death, a slow process of rehabilitation started for the Chechens, in which Chechens and Ingushetians gradually returned to their home ground. In the 1970s and 1980s the combination of religious, anti-communist and anti-Russian sentiments, as well as of ethnic pride and a sense of historical injustice, gave rise to increasing demands for autonomy and ultimately full independence from the USSR. On 27 October 1991, the Chechens, taking advantage of the disarray after the attempted *coup d'état* in Moscow in August, chose their leader Dzhokhar Dudayev as the first Chechen President.[3] By doing so, although not officially, Chechnya declared itself *de facto* independent from the USSR. Due to the disorder after the break-up of the USSR, it was not until 1994 that RF President Yeltsin deemed it necessary to respond to this secession. By supporting the opposition against Dudayev's regime the Kremlin thought that internal struggle among the Chechens would bring a more pragmatic leader in power, one who would be willing to negotiate with Russia. Apart from deliberations with the opposition, the RF had installed an economic blockade around Chechnya and had strengthened its deployment of forces in this region. In the meantime, the growing instability caused many Russians to leave Chechnya.[4] As of summer 1994, the growing opposition against Dudayev escalated into the break-out of civil war in Chechnya. This time Russia intervened; the Russian government supplied the opposition forces with tanks and military personnel to operate them. On 26 November 1994, after the failed invasion of anti-Dudayev troops into Groznyy, Russian involvement was proved by television pictures, in which captured Russian soldiers were shown.[5] On 29 November, by issuing an ultimatum to Dudayev, Yeltsin made the first move towards using Russian armed forces. On 9 December, Yeltsin instructed his government to use all means available in order to disarm the Chechen fighters.[6] This was the start of the first Russian–Chechen war.

The first Chechen conflict (1994–96)

Course of the conflict

On 11 December 1994 three columns of Russian forces marched into Chechnya. Two invaded from North Ossetia – a western attack axis from Vladikavkaz and a northern one from Mozdok. The third, eastern attack axis was started from Kizlyar in Dagestan.[7] The advance into Chechnya did not go as smoothly as expected. Immediately after leaving the assembly areas the Russian forces met with severe resistance. At the end of December, after an exhausting march, the RF assault force arrived on the outskirts of Groznyy. The invasion of the Chechen capital, on New Year's Eve, turned out to be a catastrophe. The RF troops, which were not trained for urban, or for irregular warfare, suffered heavy casualties. This urban warfare excluded the use of substantial mechanized formations in which the Russian officers were trained. In this type of warfare initiative was expected from lower tactical commanders, who were unable to fall back on orders from higher levels. The outcome was that the statement of the Minister of Defence and airborne Army-General Pavel Grachev, claiming that Groznyy would be conquered by one airborne regiment within 24 hours, proved to be false.[8] Only by uninterruptedly conducting bombardments was access gained to Groznyy. No earlier than January 1995 when additional training for urban warfare was set up and the use of units of dedicated special forces were introduced into the battle, could control be taken over Groznyy.

Because of the fact that only a few citizens had left the city prior to the Russian attack, the bombardments of Groznyy resulted in many civilian casualties. Already in March 1995, 40,000 civilians had been killed and 250,000 had fled. Increasingly the Russian forces were criticized for their lack of success and for creating many innocent victims. Although the Russians managed to occupy the cities, the countryside remained in the hands of the Chechen resistance. However, as a result of heavy casualties, and several hostage situations as well as the recapture by the Chechens of cities, such as Groznyy in August 1996, the Russians were forced to sign a truce. Defeated, the last Russian forces left Chechnya in December 1996. Estimates of the number of casualties in the first Chechen war differ according to the (official, independent or non-Russian) sources used. Bearing this in mind, the numbers are approximately as follows: 4,000–6,000 RF soldiers were killed and 20,000–30,000 wounded. Of the Chechen fighters, 2,000–3,000 allegedly died, as well as some 50,000 civilians. Finally, over 400,000 Chechens fled the theatre of war.[9]

Russian grand strategy: actors and objectives

Retaining Chechnya within the constellation of the Russian Federation was important for *economic*, *domestic*, as well as *geostrategic* reasons. The economic element of course had to do with obtaining oil. Russia expected a further growth in the oil production in the region around the Caspian Sea. Therefore, control over the oil fields in Chechnya and the pipeline network, which runs through Chechnya, was essential for the Russian economy and thus for RF authorities. Domestic grounds were related to the Chechen separatist tendencies. A successful secession of Chechnya from the RF might become an example to other RF republics wanting to gain sovereignty. In the end this might undermine the existence of the RF itself. Another internal aspect was that Yeltsin had to cope with increasing criticism of his leadership. A short armed conflict against Chechnya, resulting in a decisive victory, would strengthen Yeltsin's power and enlarge his chances for a second term in (presidential) office. A third reason was in the field of geostrategy. Russia endeavoured to maintain its influence over the CIS states on its southern border, i.e. the Trans-Caucasian republics of Georgia, Armenia and Azerbaijan, as a potential 'buffer zone' for threats from the south. Iran and Turkey also showed interest in this region. Instability and separatism in the RF republics would damage the maintainence and strengthening of Russian influence in the Trans-Caucasian region.

Russia's Security Council (SCRF) had actually taken the decision to invade Chechnya. In particular, the representatives of the MoD and of the power ministries in this body were responsible for this decision. As a rule the collegium of the MoD, its highest institute of deliberation, to which all commanders-in-chief of the services belonged, would have been informed of this decision by MoD Minister Grachev. However, in this case, probably in order to avoid disputes, this procedure was not followed.[10] A number of high-ranking officers, among them the first deputy chief of the Ground Forces, Colonel-General Eduard Vorobyev, the commander of the 14th Army in Moldova, Lieutenant-General Aleksandr Lebed, as well as the deputy Ministers of Defence, Boris Gromov, Georgy Kondratyev and Valery Mironov, turned against the use of military force in Chechnya, mainly because the combat readiness of the forces was allegedly insufficient. When Vorobyev was ordered by Grachev to take over the command of the invasion force this general refused. Subsequently he was fired.[11] Hence the military leadership was not in agreement concerning the decision to invade Chechnya. A likely assumption is that Grachev, because of the very limited preparation time before the assault was due, purposely refrained from updating the MoD collegium in order to avoid any possible opposition against the decision, and to put forward further resolutions regarding the attack on Chechnya. The argument of the opponents regarding the lack of combat readiness seemed legitimate. Combat readiness was severely damaged as a result of the break-up of Soviet military power and the subsequent annual reductions of the RF defence budget since 1992. Undoubtedly these generals also must have raised objections to the use of MoD forces in an internal conflict, which was by tradition a task for the Internal Troops and other military formations of the power ministries, whereas the RF Armed Forces were traditionally tasked for warfare against foreign opponents.

The use of force against Chechnya allegedly was not planned to be long lasting or intensive warfare, but instead to take the form of a quick and vigorous demonstration of force to depose Dudayev and to replace him by a Russian-inclined regime.[12] That way Russian authority over Chechnya would be restored.

Russian military strategy: command and control structure

The overall command of the operation was not in the hands of the military, but, probably to justify it as a case within the boundaries of the Geneva conventions, 'ending unrest within the territory of the state', was led by the Minister of

Nationalities.[13] Apart from the RF Armed Forces of the MoD, troops of the Ministry of Internal Affairs MVD (*Ministerstvo Vnutrennykh Del*) and of the Federal Service for Counter-Intelligence FSK (*Federal'naya Sluzhba Kontrrazvedki*) took part in the operation.[14] The Russian invasion contingent, of some 40,000 military in total, consisted of MoD forces (Ground Forces, Airborne Troops and Naval-Infantry Troops), Internal Troops (*Vnutrennyye Voyska*) of the MVD, Border Troops and units of the FSK.

MoD Minister Grachev was responsible for the actual deployment of forces and troops. A working group under the command of Lieutenant-General Anatoly Kvashnin of the General Staff was charged with planning and conducting the operation. The commander of the Military District North Caucasus (NCMD) held the actual command and control of the military contingent. However, at the end of December 1994, probably due to lack of success so far, Grachev personally took over direct command of the military operation in Chechnya. He appointed Lieutenant-General Kvashnin as his deputy.[15]

Nonetheless, the chain of command was unclear. Although the SCRF did intervene in the implementation of the operation, no explicit command and control structure had been defined in advance. On 25 January 1995, at a meeting of the SCRF, Grachev stated that the military part of the operation had been concluded. Subsequently, he transferred authority over the operation from the MoD to the MVD.[16] However, MoD, MVD and other security organs did not act alongside but separate from each other, in Moscow as well as in the theatre of war. The area of operations missed a supreme level of command, a so-called Joint Staff of MoD forces and Other Troops of the power ministries. The commanders of the various components of the military contingent (Ground and Air Forces, Other Troops)

Table 4.1 Force comparisons at the start of the first Chechen conflict

Belligerent	Personnel strength land forces	Material air forces
Russian Federation	40,000 regular forces and troops: mechanized divisions; airborne and naval-infantry units; Internal Troops; Border Troops; units of the FSK and special forces	140 combat aircraft; 55 transport and combat helicopters: 25 *Hinds*, 28 *Hips* and 2 *Halos*; 30 transport aircraft
Chechnya	12,000–13,000 guerrilla fighters	Over 260 aircraft, 100 of which were ready to fly: mainly trainers; a couple of combat aircraft, helicopters and transport aircraft

Sources: A. Geibel, 'Caucasus Nightmare', *Armor,* March–April 1995, p. 11; G. Isenkov, 'VVS zadachu vypolnili', *Armeyskiy Sbornik*, No. 3 March 1995, p. 42; A. Yavorskiy, 'Lëtchikam ne dali razvernut'sya', *Nezavisimoye Voyennoye Obozreniye*, No. 48 (171), 10 December 1999, p. 5; and A. Korbut, 'Ucheba v boyu', *Nezavisimoye Voyennoye Obozreniye*, No. 50 (173), 24 December 1999, p. 2.

took decisions individually, without consulting the others. They responded directly to the Minister of Defence or to the leadership of their own department. At a later stage, forces of the different services of the RF Armed Forces were united under a single command, but the troops of the power ministries maintained their separate command structures.[17] The reason for the lack of cooperation amongst the services of the Armed Forces and between them and the Other Troops, which became explicit in the unclear structure of command and control of the Chechen operation, is to be found in rivalry. The commanders of the various forces and troops contended with each other in order to improve their status. The shortcomings in the field of coordination and fine-tuning of decisions would become the prime cause of the Russian defeat in the first Chechen conflict.

Russian operational level: organization of air power

Command and control structure

For the use of air power in Chechnya an air component was available, which primarily consisted of two elements: fixed-wing aircraft of the Air Forces VVS (*Voyenno-Vozdushnyye Sily*) and rotary wing (helicopters) of army aviation ASV (*Aviatsiya Sukhoputnykh Voysk*, or *Armeyskaya Aviatsiya*). As mentioned above, helicopters were not subordinated to the VVS, but to the ASV. Apart from these principle elements, military aviation units of MVD and Border Troops also made a, although rather limited, contribution to the air component.[18]

For the efficient conducting of air operations by the VVS, the tactical air force FA (*Frontavaya Aviatsiya*) formed an *ad hoc* air group (*aviatsionnaya gruppirovka*), consisting of units of the 4th Air Army of the NCMD, complete with reconnaissance (recce), ground attack, transport and strategic bomber units from other military districts.[19] Helicopters of three different air regiments of the NCMD were unified in an impromptu air group, corresponding to the arrangement of the VVS aircraft. *Hind* combat and *Hip* transport helicopters were divided into two squadrons of each type; the *Halo* heavy transport and *Hip* command and control helicopters were grouped as independent flights. The command and control *Hips* came from the Military District Volga, and the *Halos* also belonged to units outside the NCMD. According to the commander of the ASV, Colonel-General Vitaly Pavlov, 60 per cent of the helicopter pilots were veterans of the war in Afghanistan.[20] As mentioned above, not only the MoD but also the MVD contributed to the air component, with 12 *Hips* and an unknown number of *Halos*. No data were released on the size and structure of the air element of the Border Troops.[21] In December 1994 the larger part of the air component was deployed at the airbase of Mozdok. After the occupation of Chechen territory part of the rotary and fixed-wing aircraft was redeployed to bases in Chechnya, such as Groznyy-North. Transport aircraft flew missions from Mozdok and Vladikavkaz, rotary-wing elements were stationed at Mozdok and Kizlyar.[22]

For the purpose of coordination between air and land forces, 40 forward air-controllers (FACs) were available.[23] The FACs sent their data to the airbase Khankala, where these were brought together, processed and analysed. Subsequently, Khankala transmitted the assessments to the airbase of Mozdok, on the basis of which the allocation of VVS (FA) and ASV elements for air operations was decided.

Force build-up

In December 1994 the starting position of the RF air component was comparable to that of the land component – a distinct superiority of weaponry and manpower over the Chechens. The air component comprised, among other elements, 140 combat aircraft and 55 helicopters. The already strong air component was strengthened even further – in March 1995 the number of helicopters was increased to 105, 55 of which were *Hind* combat helicopters.[24] Judging from the enormous superiority in fighting power, resulting from the disproportion between Chechen and Russian force strengths, successful use of air power was to be expected.

VVS had the following fixed-wing aircraft at its disposal for air-to-ground support: the Su-25 *Frogfoot* ground-attack aircraft, the Su-17/22M *Fitter* and the Su-24M *Fencer-D* fighter-bombers. *Fencers* and *Frogfoots* formed the backbone of combat power in the air. For air recce tasks the Su-24MR *Fencer-E* and the MiG-25RBK *Foxbat-D* were available. Su-27 *Flanker* and MiG-31 *Foxhound* interceptors, aircraft which did not belong to the VVS but to the Air Defence Forces VPVO (*Voyska Protivovozdushnoy Oborony*), conducted counter-air missions.[25] Strategic bombers of the type Tu-22Ms *Backfire*, subordinated to the strategic bomber force of the VVS, DA (*Dalnyaya Aviatsiya*), were also used in this conflict. Finally, the VVS transport force VTA (*Voyenno-Transportnaya Aviatsiya*) took care of transport of equipment and personnel by using the An-12 *Cub*, An-22 *Cock*, An-26 *Curl*, An-124 *Condor* and the Il-76 *Candid*. Early warning against air threat as well as air command and control was carried out by the A-50 *Mainstay*.[26] The rotary-wing component of ASV consisted of the Mi-24 *Hind* combat helicopter, the Mi-8 *Hip* transport and Mi-9 *Hip* command and control helicopter, as well as the Mi-26 *Halo* heavy transport helicopter.

Russian tactical level – application of air power

The use of air power in the first Chechen conflict was carried out in three phases. The first phase consisted of preparations for the invasion, in the form of recce and transport missions (Supporting Air Operations). The second phase was aimed at achieving air superiority (Counter-Air Operations). The third and final phase encompassed support for advancing land forces (Anti-Surface Force Air Operations and Strategic Air Operations). After the summer of 1995, when the principal cities Groznyy, Gudermes and Argun had fallen into the hands of the Russian forces, the number of combat missions was reduced drastically.[27]

Counter-Air Operations

Before air support for ground operations could be started air power was first aimed at achieving and preserving air superiority. Air superiority was essential to counter the potential threat of Chechen air attacks against Russian nuclear and conventional power stations, industries, administrative centres, storage depots of nuclear weapons, air bases and other military objects (Defensive Counter-Air, DCA). On 1 December 1994, *Frogfoots* carried out attacks on three Chechen airbases, in which the complete Chechen air force was neutralized. Chechen resistance against these attacks proved to be minimal.[28]

After this, the Chechen air threat against advancing Russian ground troops had to be dealt with (Offensive Counter-Air, OCA). Air support to the Chechens, possibly from surrounding countries, had to be prevented by non-stop missions of two to six *Flankers* and *Foxhounds*, conducting combat air patrols (CAPs), in which *Mainstays* secured air traffic over Chechnya. On the ground, radar units of the VPVO completed the threat spectrum of VVS, by providing data on the lower part of the air space.

Anti-Surface Force Air Operations

Another primary task of air power was to provide air support for ground troops – offensive air support (OAS). By conducting OAS missions, buildings, command posts, armoured vehicles, bridges, roads, depots (training) camps and industrial complexes were destroyed. Not earlier than June 1995, when the fighting had moved to less densely populated areas, OAS missions were conducted prior to the advancement of ground troops. The reason for this reluctance to carry out air attacks in urban areas was because of public opinion, which received mostly uncensored media reports on the fighting and for whom civilian casualties were unacceptable. Although the VVS commander-in-chief Colonel-General Pëtr Deynekin categorically denied the frequent accusations of VVS attacks on non-military targets, media reports gave evidence to the fact that air attacks caused many victims among the population.[29]

Strategic Air Operations

The images of civilian casualties made a deep impression on Russian and inter-national public opinion, proving the cruelty which accompanied Russia's invasion of Chechnya. The possibility that Russian public opinion would change course and reject the use of force, which would subsequently affect support for the President, more than once caused Yeltsin to stop the air bombardments. This ban on bombing, for instance, was issued from 24 December 1994 until 3 January 1995.[30] At a later stage, domestic as well as foreign criticism of the operations in Chechnya was silent, which opened the way for strategic bombardments. Gradually, due to the lack of success of the RF troops, the morale of the Chechen population and the Chechen fighters became targets – punishment bombardments were conducted on urban areas. According to the RF authorities *Backfires* were used exclusively for target illumination with flares and for dropping propaganda leaflets on Groznyy, as part of psychological warfare. However, independent sources stated that the DA also conducted bombardments on Chechen troop concentrations. Other strategic targets for the VVS were power stations, Dudayev's presidential palace, in which his military staff was situated, the television tower and the media centre of Groznyy.[31]

Supporting Air Operations

The VVS transport component, VTA, made a vital contribution to the build-up of the Russian invasion in Chechnya. Around 1 December 1994, 38 *Cub* transport aircraft flew equipment and troops to Mozdok and Vladikavkaz. After the take-over of Groznyy, the VTA also flew transport missions to the airfield of Groznyy-North.

In addition to combat missions, helicopters of the ASV were used for the transport of airborne and general infantry units, for recce, escort, provisioning, communications, medical evacuation (medevac), as well as for (combat) search-and-rescue (CSAR) missions. Besides transport missions the VVS conducted supporting air operations in the form of recce, battle damage assessment and target illumination.[32]

Tactics

For fear of anti-aircraft artillery, helicopters usually were excluded from urban areas. Their tasks were mainly limited to transport and provisioning missions. In using helicopters for combat missions the element of surprise was the most important tactic for outwitting to counter anti-aircraft defence: by approaching targets from different sides and at low altitude, by manoeuvring randomly before an attack and by changing course rapidly after making an assault. In doing so, helicopters were backed especially by mutual fire support and by means of diverting anti-aircraft artillery, such as electronic warfare and flares.[33]

Failures, problems and losses of air power

The outcome of the use of air power in the first Chechen war varied but on the whole had to be characterized as a failure. Air supremacy did not guarantee a victory on the ground; air power did not have a decisive impact on Chechen resistance. Because of shortcomings in training and equipment, as well as lack of experience operating in urban surroundings, the effectiveness of the OAS was highly unsuccessful. Another sign of failure was that there were frequent attacks on own troops. The reasons for these blue-on-blue attacks or fratricide were: insufficient flying training, shortcomings in cooperation among forces and troops, a lack of precision-guided munitions (PGMs), which accounted for only 2.3 per cent of the total amount of ammunition used by VVS and ASV, malfunction of obsolete weaponry, as well as lack of modern avionics for operating in darkness and under bad weather conditions. Another reason for fratricide was that the pilots were unaware of where the front line of the own troops was. Commanders of ground troops were reluctant to informing the air force of their positions, realizing that the Chechens intercepted Russian communications. Interception of RF military reports also damaged the command and control of air operations. For fear of interception, messages were frequently transmitted incompletely, which resulted regularly in the inappropriate use of military means.[34] Another reason for the lack of success of OAS missions was political limitations. As mentioned earlier, the air barrages on Groznyy, which caused many innocent victims, were criticized by Russian public opinion as well as by the international community. The negative domestic responses to this type of war came from generals, the Union of Soldiers' Mothers, parliamentarians and the mass media, which refused to accept false information on these events from RF authorities. Criticism from outside came from international organizations, such as the EU, NATO and the OSCE, as well as the Council of Europe.[35] As mentioned earlier, initially Yeltsin was influenced by this criticism and temporarily stopped the bombardments. However, the objective of limiting further civilian casualties was largely dashed by operating with obsolete and insufficiently maintained *matériel* and by the low level of training of air crews, who caused a lot of collateral damage. The strategic bombardments did not have much effect on the morale of the Chechen fighters, or that of the Chechen population.[36]

In carrying out the air campaign of the invasion of Chechnya, the following problems arose. At the military-strategic level, the intensive use of air power in Chechnya meant that means (material, fuel, maintenance and ammunition) had to be withdrawn from other units of military aviation, thus diminishing the (combat) readiness of the remainder of the VVS and ASV. Bad weather conditions hampered the use of air power, especially of *Frogfoots*. *Fencers* possessed better target acquisition instruments for operating under these conditions.[37] Procurement of additional navigation and target acquisition equipment, which could lift these limitations, was not possible for lack of financial resources. The budgetary limitations brought about additional consequences, which limited the effectiveness of air power. There was, for instance, a shortage of ammunition, fuel and spare parts, which caused reduced readiness as well as unnecessary losses of aircraft. The average annual flying hours of combat pilots of the VVS, 30 hours, was below internationally recognized standards of combat readiness. For ASV pilots the number of flying hours was 40–50, whereas the ASV commander Pavlov stated that 100–150 hours was required.[38] Hence aircrews were inadequately trained for operational deployment. The low level of combat readiness among pilots was one reason for the number of innocent victims: in fear of Chechen anti-aircraft defence RF pilots more than once released their bomb load before reaching the target. Another problem was target acquisition, which was hindered in urban areas, in which the exact location of the enemy was often unclear, thus increasing the chances for blue-on-blue attacks. Due to the lack of modern detection equipment light-armed guerrillas proved to be difficult targets. The VVS commander, Deynekin, as well as ASV commander, Pavlov, frequently made public statements regarding their concern over the low level of combat readiness, caused by constant cuts in the defence budget.[39]

In spite of the aforementioned shortcomings and problems, losses of aircraft were limited. In December 1995, one year after the start of the invasion of Chechnya, the losses of VVS fixed wing numbered one *Fencer*, two *Frogfoots*, as well as 24 aircraft damaged. The losses of the rotary wing of the ASV were more extensive. Until July 1995, five *Hips* and seven *Hinds* were lost and 30 helicopters were damaged. In August 1996, at the end of the first Chechen conflict, the AVS losses had increased to at least 14 helicopters lost, seven *Hips* and seven *Hinds*. At this stage the losses of fixed wing remained equal, although at least 26 VVS aircraft had been damaged.[40]

Successes of air power

In the first seven months of the conflict military aviation carried out 9,000 sorties, consisting of 5,000 air attacks and over 600 recce missions. At the closing stages of the war, in August 1996, the number of sorties of the VVS allegedly was 17,000 : 14,000 by the FA, over 170 by the DA and more than 3,000 by the VTA. A positive outcome of this huge number of sorties was the rise in combat experience of RF pilots.[41]

The successes of air power were predominantly in the field of Counter-Air Operations and Supporting Air Operations. By destroying 166 aircraft and damaging over 100, within 24 hours, the Chechen air force was neutralized. This removed the air threat for the VVS as well as for the ground troops. The intensive use of CAPs during the entire period of the conflict made any possible air support for the Chechens from abroad impossible. The VTA's input of air transport was impressive. The VTA allegedly transported 20,000 troops to the area of operations, which was half of the total RF military contingent. In addition to this, the VTA also transported more than 1,000 pieces of equipment.[42]

One tactical success of air power, which had strategic implications, must be mentioned. On 22 April 1996, Chechen President Dudayev was killed by the VVS. Dudayev, allegedly because of using his satellite phone, was detected by a *Mainstay*. Subsequently, a *Frogfoot* was directed to the target, and, by launching a missile ended the life of the Chechen President. Accordingly, the VVS conducted a successful tactical mission encompassing strategic consequences – a serious blow was dealt temporarily to the Chechen military–political leadership.[43]

Chechen strategy and operations

At the political-strategic level President Dudayev's policy was aimed at preserving the *de facto* independent position of Chechnya. Because of the overwhelming

Russian superiority in arms and troops, at the operational and tactical levels this objective was transformed into guerrilla warfare.

Land warfare

In the war on the ground after the loss of Groznyy, in January 1995, the Chechen fighters withdrew to the mountains in the south. From here they operated by using guerrilla tactics, such as hit-and-run raids, ambushes, the use of snipers and bomb attacks. Taking account of Russian superiority, in general direct fighting contact with hostile troops was avoided. In doing so, the Chechens skilfully took advantage of the Russian weak spots, for instance by attacking in bad weather conditions and in darkness, which limited the use of air power. Another tactic was the use of hostage-taking, especially the hostage-taking, operations in Budënnovsk of June 1995 and Pervomayskoye in January 1996, in which the Russian troops failed and were humiliated. These were substantial Chechen successes, due to the negative consequences they entailed on the morale of the troops and on public support for the war. Apart from more or less 'primitive' guerrilla tactics the Chechens also applied modern (electronic) warfare, in the form of the aforementioned interception and diversion of Russian communications. Many Chechen fighters were well informed on Russian tactics and procedures, because they were trained at Russian military institutions or had undergone conscription into the Soviet/Russian armed forces. Obviously guerrillas were also capable of waging modern warfare. It is doubtful whether the Russian military leadership had considered this in planning the invasion of Chechnya.[44]

Air warfare

For air power Dudayev had at his disposal over 260 airplanes, mainly trainers (149 L-29 *Delfin* and 111 L-39 *Albatros* aircraft), a couple of combat aircraft (two MiG-15 *Fagot* and and three MiG-17 *Fresco* aircraft), six An-2 *Colt* transport airplanes and two Mi-8 *Hips* which were abandoned in 1992 by the VVS at the former Soviet flying school of Armavir and at a former flying training centre of the paramilitary organization DOSAAF. The combat aircraft were stationed at the airbases of Khankala and Kalinovskaya. The remaining aircraft as well as three unidentified helicopters were located at the airfield of Groznyy-North. One hundred of the total number of aircraft were ready for combat operations, of which at least one squadron consisted of *Albatros* trainers, i.e. 12 aircraft. However, to fly these, only 40 trained pilots were available.

The Chechen anti-aircraft defence system was unorganized and lacked radar equipment. The anti-aircraft artillery comprised eight to ten pieces of ZSU-23/4 mechanized systems, six pieces of ZSU-23/2 static guns, machineguns displayed on trucks and man portable missiles. It was not unusual for Chechen fighters to deploy their anti-aircraft artillery in urban areas, amongst the population.[45] This made Russian pilots reluctant to attack and, if they did, and it resulted in civilian casualties and collateral damage, the Chechens publicly rebuked the Russians for violating the laws of armed conflict. Another effective Chechen tactic against Russian air power was the killing of FACs. The Chechens traced FACs systematically and used snipers to take their lives. By using this tactic the effective use of air power in support of Russian ground operations was severely hindered.[46]

Summary

Russian strategy and warfare

At the political-strategic level (grand strategy) level especially, President Yeltsin and MoD Minister Grachev had been in favour of solving the 'Chechen problem' by military means. The absence of broader decision-making and consensus in the military–political discourse, as well as a lack of preparation time before force was used brought about a high number of casualties among the Russian troops in the initial phase of the conflict. On paper the starting position seemed favourable for the Russians. The RF military contingent numbered three times the size of the Chechen contingent. Furthermore, whereas the Chechens were armed mainly with small arms and a limited number of mechanized *matériel*, the Russians had a large number of heavy armour and air power at their disposal. However, the numerical and *matériel* weaknesses of Dudayev's troops were compensated for by high morale and strong defences. Although, as a result of their superiority in arms and troops, the Russians managed to occupy the larger part of Chechnya, they were not capable of providing an effective response to guerrilla warfare. Russian forces and troops were still focused on the large-scale warfare of the Cold War.

Another shortcoming at this level of strategy was in the field of psychological warfare. The Russian military–political leadership had overlooked the proper preparation for war of its troops as well as of its population.[47] The Chechens did not refrain from using this factor to their advantage. The morale of the Russian troops quite soon dropped when confrontation with the hostile local population made it clear to the soldiers that they were not operating as a peacekeeping contingent for restoring law and order, as they had been told. Witnessing heavy air bombardments on Groznyy took away the last bit of hope in the peacekeeping nature of the operation, thus further damaging the morale of the Russian troops.

Another aspect of failure at this level was the lack of political objectives for the situation in Chechnya after the fighting was brought to a close. In the end military occupation became untenable, from a military stand point, as well as from the point of view of public support. Yeltsin was forced to accept Russia's military defeat as well as a return to the *de facto* independent status of Chechnya.

At the military-strategic level the lack of a unified command and control system caused grave problems. There was no formal command and control connection between the SCRF in Moscow and the forces in the field. The unity of command which normally would be in the hands of the General Staff was broken because, in an *ad hoc* way, responsibility was transferred to the MoD and the power ministries. At the level of the theatre of war, command and control was also unclear, which affected the cooperation between forces and troops. Although initially the operation was led by the commander of the NCMD, at his headquarters in Mozdok this general was monitored by Minister of Defence Grachev and representatives of the General Staff, as well as by members of the SCRF, among them the other 'commanders' of the invading troops, and of the power ministries MVD and FSK. In total some 100 generals from Moscow mingled in Mozdok with operational affairs.[48]

This defective command and control was also displayed in the application of air power. Often cooperation between the staffs of the VVS and ASV, for the purpose of joint use of fixed and rotary wing, failed. Thus the aforementioned problems in coordination and fine tuning between forces and troops of the land forces also emerged in the air component. Not just simply because they were unwilling but also to counter the constant reductions in their budgets, MoD forces and troops of the power ministries were engaged in competition, in order to gain a favourable position with the military–political leadership. Clearly, joint operational action was not self-evident for Russia's forces and troops.[49]

A further shortcoming at this strategic level was the starting date of the operation. This date concurred with the rotation point of conscription classes, which meant that the most experienced servicemen could not be employed, because their two years of service had just come to an end. The majority of conscripts, who had to take part in the action, had one year of military experience, which affected the combat readiness of the military contingent in a negative sense. Due to this rotation point of conscript classes, but also to the fact that combat readiness was low as a result of the cuts in defence spending, units were formed often only just before operational employment, which meant that team-building and training standards at unit level were completely absent. In addition to these reasons, the starting date of the invasion was also a bad choice because of the deteriorating weather conditions at this time of year.

Another shortcoming was in the field of intelligence. Insufficient intelligence gathering, underestimating Chechen resistance and overestimating Russian military capabilities were the grounds for a rather wide off the mark assessment of the course of battle by the RF military leadership. As mentioned earlier, the Russian military did not anticipate that the Chechens would make use of modern methods of warfare, using their experience as former Soviet/RF conscripts.

The low level of combat readiness of *matériel* and personnel set off by structural cuts in the budgets of the MoD and power ministries was one more shortcoming at this strategic level. Communications equipment, for instance, caused a lot of problems. This equipment was obsolete, of insufficient quality and was not secured against hostile interception. The low level of combat readiness also had consequences for command and control. As mentioned, because of shortages of *matériel* and servicemen, most units were not standard but organized *ad hoc*, out of different units. Considering the short timeframe between decision-making and the actual invasion there was no time available to improve the combat readiness and cooperation among units. This affected the efficiency of command and control.

A final shortcoming was in the planning of the operation, which was far from complete. According to the plans, MoD forces would encircle Groznyy, disarm Dudayev's troops and subsequently transfer command to the Internal Troops, who would enforce law and order until negotiations led to a new pro-Moscow regime in Chechnya. This scheme did not include any contingency plans for unexpected developments, such as setbacks and fierce resistance.[50]

At the *operational and tactical levels* it became obvious that the effectiveness for operations in urban areas of fixed-wing aircraft, and in particular the *Frogfoot* which was specialized in close-air-support (CAS) missions, was much higher than that of rotary wing, i.e. combat helicopters. For instance, in comparison with the *Hind* the *Frogfoot* offered more protection for the aircrew, had a superior reach and speed, as well as better manoeuvrability. Although it should be stated that combat helicopters did operate satisfactorily outside of urban areas. Even so, a rather large number of combat helicopters was shot down. Their low velocity made them easy targets for the primitive but quite effective mobile anti-aircraft weapons of the Chechens. Therefore, it seemed that in the spectrum of air power the eminent position of the combat helicopter in irregular warfare (e.g. the *Hind* in the war in Afghanistan) was to be replaced by fixed-wing aircraft dedicated for CAS missions, for example the *Frogfoot*.[51]

Keeping the Afghan war in mind, this conflict once again gave evidence of the fact that thorough analysis of guerrilla tactics and comprehensive intelligence gathering, for instance on anti-aircraft positions, were indispensable for an effective use of air power in irregular warfare. The reason that the RF VVS in particular was not capable of applying the lessons learned from Afghanistan was that the command of the Soviet VVS considered the 'liberal' attitude of veteran pilots as a threat to its existence and consequently had refrained from incorporating their experiences into tactical directives for air warfare. A further aspect at this strategic level was the use of FACs to ensure good air–ground cooperation. The FAC system was not as effective as it was supposed to be. One explanation for this shortcoming was the lack of knowledge and subsequent lack of awareness among tactical commanders of the land component regarding the possibilities and limitations of the use of air power. Other reasons for the inadequacy of the FAC system were the restricted number of FACs deployed in the area of operations (because of which not all battalions had an FAC at their disposal as planned), insufficient training, and equipping FACs with out-dated communications instruments, which did not always work in the mountainous area of Chechnya and which could easily be intercepted by the opponent.[52]

The hopelessness of the conflict lowered the morale of the Russian troops. This also entailed violations of the law of armed conflict by Russian servicemen, such as looting and rape. It also gave rise to corruption – Russian soldiers sold weaponry to Chechen fighters. To a large extent the media were able to carry out unrestricted coverage of these breaches of humanitarian law and of the humiliating and failing performance of the Russian military. This resulted in a loss of support among the Russian public for continuing the war.[53]

Chechen strategy and warfare

At the political-strategic level the Chechens made good and scrupulous use of the fact that the media were free to report on the cruelty of the fighting and the many civilian victims it caused. The Chechens used this media coverage as an instrument of psychological warfare, as propaganda to gain support of the international community against the Russian invasion, as well as to influence Russian public opinion to reject further killing of Chechens but of Russian soldiers also.

At the operational and tactical levels the overwhelming Russian superiority in arms and troops forced the Chechens to resort to irregular, guerrilla warfare. The Russian forces and troops were trained for conventional, large-scale warfare, and hence had not anticipated this type of conflict. In conducting hit-and-run attacks, in hostage-taking and conducting electronic warfare against the Russian air-to-ground cooperation, the Chechens demonstrated that they possessed effective tactics against a numerically superior enemy, especially as this type of warfare severely damaged the morale of the Russian troops.

The conflict in Dagestan (August–September 1999)

Background and course of the conflict

Dagestan is a republic within the Russian Federation, three times the size of Chechnya, with a population of just over 2 million and 30 different, primarily Muslim, ethnic groups. In August and September 1999 Russian forces conducted three operations in Dagestan. The RF forces had to counter two assaults from Chechen Islamic insurgents in two districts of Dagestan and to put an end to Islamic rule, which had been set up in a different area of Dagestan the previous year.[54]

Tensions had risen in the border region between Chechnya and Dagestan early in August 1999. The first operation of the Russian forces was in response to an invasion by groups of armed Islamic fighters, possibly around 1,500 men, led by the Chechen field commanders Basayev and Hattab, who from 2 August had infiltrated from Chechnya into the Botlikh and Tsumadin districts of western Dagestan, occupied some villages and declared the area to be under Islamic law. The second operation of the Russian forces, commencing on 29 August 1999, was in an area consisting of the villages of Chabanmakhi and Karamakhi in the central Dagestani district of Buynaksk, to bring an end to Islamic control, which had been installed there a year before. On 5 September RF forces were employed for the third time, on this occasion to counter a second incursion by a force of the order of 2,000 Chechen Islamic fighters in the Novolaksk district, north of the earlier invaded districts. After two incursions and a number of (sniper) attacks on Russian troops on the border between Dagestan and Chechnya, the conflict escalated to Chechnya. On 7 September Colonel-General Valery Manilov, first deputy Chief of the Russian General Staff, officially announced the first air attack on Chechnya.[55] After some 45 days of fighting the insurgents were driven back to Chechen territory. According to the Russian authorities, 1,500 rebels were killed during the operations. The joint RF forces lost approximately 300 men, and close to 1,000 were wounded.

Russian grand strategy: actors and objectives

At the political-strategic level of the RF, two actors were deeply involved in the operations in Dagestan. Vladimir Putin, recently appointed Prime Minister, regularly expressed his views in the media on the official policy towards the conflict and visited the area together with the Chief of the General Staff (CGS), Army-General Anatoly Kvashnin, on 27 August.[56] CGS General Anatoly Kvashnin kept a close watch on the execution of the military operations and accompanied Putin and the Minister for Internal Affairs, MVD, Vladimir Rushaylo, on visits to the conflict area. As early as 17 August, Kvashnin announced that, if necessary, enemy bases inside Chechnya would be targeted.[57]

From the start of the counter-insurgency operations media coverage was restricted. According to official sources the reason for media limitations was to prevent the enemy from acquiring intelligence on the course of action. Another reason must have been to give the Russian population the impression of a smooth operation and to keep up the morale of the forces. A third reason was to prevent the rebels from spreading propaganda.[58]

The objectives that the military–political leadership set out for the RF armed forces were to cut off the rebels' fuel and financial base in Chechnya (illegal gasoline trading), to destroy their main arsenals and training centres in Chechnya and to prevent further incursions.[59] Another objective was to put an end to the already existing independent Islamic rule in a central district of Dagestan. In sum, RF law and order was to be restored over all of Dagestan.

Russian military strategy: command and control structure

The Russian forces involved in the operations in Dagestan initially consisted of Ground and Air Forces of the RF MoD and Internal Troops of the MVD. The ground component, with an original strength of 4,000, increased to 10,000 men at the end of the operations, was to begin with made up of two brigades, 136 Brigade (MoD) and 102 Brigade (MVD). During the conflict reinforcements were sent comprising airborne and naval infantry units from distant locations such as the Siberian Military District and the Northern Fleet.[60]

At first, operational command of the RF forces, i.e. MoD and MVD forces, was given to the MVD. However the commander in chief of the Internal Troops,

144

Colonel-General Vyacheslav Ovchinnikov, who himself led the operation, had no experience in commanding troops of different RF departments (MVD and MoD).[61] Already during the conflict the inadequacies of the MVD troops and their failure to properly coordinate became public when an army commander of the Ground Forces uttered this complaint in the media. This meant that MVD troops had to cope with fierce resistance, as they were not used to the procedures of calling in the necessary artillery fire support or close air support. Therefore the situation demanded a change of command. On 17 August command was transferred from the MVD to MoD in order to improve the conduct of the operation repelling the incursion. CGS General Anatoly Kvashnin put Colonel-General Viktor Kazantsev, commander of the North Caucasus Military District (NCMD), in command of the Joint Grouping of Forces in Dagestan. On 27 August, after finishing the first operation in the Botlikh and Tsumadin districts, operational command was returned to the MVD to start the second operation in the Buynaksk district of central Dagestan. On 4 September, following a meeting attended by MVD Minister Rushaylo, CGS Kvashnin and Commander NCMD Kazantsev, command of the Joint Grouping of Forces was once more transferred from the MVD back to MoD. Lieutenant-General Gennady Troshev, Deputy Commander NCMD, would now lead the second operation of the Russian forces, in the Buynaksk district.[62]

Russian operational level: organization of air power

Command and control structure

The Russian air component in the Dagestan operation consisted of two parts. The Russian Air Forces VVS formed the larger part of the air component of the RF troops. The other part was made up of army aviation ASV. The VVS component of the RF forces operating in Dagestan was commanded by the 4th Air Army, headquartered at Rostov-na-Donu. Later a forward HQ for the VVS component was placed in the Dagestani capital Makhachkala. Coordination was established with MVD forces to make preparations for cooperation between ASV, VVS and air assets of the MVD. Mozdok, close to the western border of Chechnya and earmarked as the main operational base, was linked to mobile command and coordination posts in the front line of the ground troops.

Force build-up

The assets that the ASV deployed in the Dagestan operation were especially the Mi-24 *Hind* combat helicopter and the Mi-8 *Hip* transport helicopter. The ASV also employed the Mi-26 *Halo* heavy lift helicopter. VVS input consisted of the Su-25 *Frogfoot* fighter-bomber, Su-27 *Flanker* fighters, Su-24M/MR *Fencer D/E* fighter-bomber/reconnaissance aircraft, An-30 *Clank* photo-recce aircraft and

A-50 *Mainstay* early warning aircraft. The backbone of the air component in Dagestan consisted of *Hip* and *Hind* helicopters (ASV) and Su-25 *Frogfoot* fighter-bomber aircraft (VVS). VVS quickly sent reinforcements to the conflict area. Between 12 and 15 August, 16 aircraft were flown over to the airfield at Makhachkala.[63] In the end the number of *Hinds* had risen to more than 120 helicopters. The total number of air assets used in the Dagestan operation, i.e. helicopters and aircraft, amounted up to 300 by mid-September.[64]

Russian tactical level: application of air power

Counter-Air Operations

Flankers fulfilled CAP missions, to prevent reinforcements reaching the rebels by air. The Chechen rebels did not have an organized air-defence system with radar and missiles. Their air-defence armament essentially consisted of some man-portable SAMs (surface-to-air missiles), heavy machine-guns and ZSU-23/2 twin-barrel anti-aircraft guns on trucks. The Chechens did not possess an air component, so the Russian air forces had air supremacy in this operation. Therefore counter-air operations could be limited to CAPs, as mentioned above, and occasionally suppression of enemy air defences (SEAD), during OAS missions and supporting air operations.

Anti-Surface Force Air Operations

Fencer-D and *Frogfoot* aircraft and *Hind* helicopters conducted OAS and air interdiction (AI) missions. *Frogfoots* attacked targets such as bunkers and mortar positions. Apart from attacks against strongholds, *Frogfoots* were also used to mine mountain roads. Another task was to cut off the supply routes of the rebels between Dagestan and Chechnya. To achieve this objective *Frogfoots* carried out missions on rebel camps and supply bases in the border area. By performing tactical air reconnaissance (TAR) missions, and thus supplying targeting, terrain and other intelligence, *Fencer-E* aircraft supported OAS and AI of fighters and combat helicopters.

Supporting Air Operations

ASV's *Hip* helicopters were used to deliver special (*Spetsnaz*) and conventional airborne units behind enemy lines, to transport airborne command and control posts, for medevac, CSAR and, lastly, recce purposes. In these missions *Frogfoots* provided cover for the *Hips* by means of SEAD and CAS. *Halos* took care of supply and transport tasks. The *Clanks* conducted photo-recce missions. And finally *Mainstays* provided airborne early warnings over Dagestan and Chechnya.

Tactics

Hinds operated in combat groups of two or four, attacking from a height of 3,500 to 4,000 m, with steep diving descents down to tens of metres, followed by surprise pop-ups from different directions, with one pair covering the other two after attack. Thus suppressive attacks on rebel positions were conducted. Two to four *Fencer-Ds* or two to four *Frogfoots* generally carried out tasks such as 'search-and-destroy' or 'bomb-storming' missions. The former, flying at high altitudes (at least 3,500 m), and therefore protected against portable air defence systems, often bombarded with high-precision weapons. The *Frogfoots* attacked from lower altitudes (1,000–3,000 m) and with their high-manoeuvrability, normally used conventional arms in the bombardments.[65]

Failures of air power

On 12 August, due to a lack of awareness, one MVD *Hip* came under fire, and among others three MVD generals were wounded.[66] Two other helicopters were destroyed approaching the Botlikh landing strip. A second mistake was the accidental bombing of a village in Georgia, by a VVS *Frogfoot*. A third error was in the field of friendly fire (blue-on-blue attacks). An MVD detachment was attacked by the VVS.[67] To a large extent these failures in using air power were the result of shortcomings in cooperation between the VVS, ASV and MVD. In reviewing the operations in Dagestan, the Russian military leadership concluded that in future operations these shortcomings could be avoided by creating a single system of aviation control in joint operations. Another measure to improve coordination in the use of air power was to install FACs in ground component units.[68] During the operations in Dagestan four to six helicopters and one to three fixed-wing aircraft were lost.

Successes of air power

The ASV and VVS had flown more than 1,000 combat sorties in which four to six helicopters and one to three fixed-wing aircraft were lost.[69] By demolishing fortifications, bridges, supply and ammunition stores, destroying or mining all major routes between Dagestan and Chechnya, the air component had played its part in achieving the expressed military–political objectives.

Chechen insurgents: strategy and operations

With regard to the political-strategic level it must be stated that both commanders of the Chechen insurgents, Basayev and Khattab, seemed to operate independently of the Chechen government of President Maskhadov. The Chechen fighters invaded Dagestan with the objective of changing it into an Islamic state, seceded from Russia. Following this, their next objective would be unification with Chechnya in order to form an Islamic republic. The Chechen intruders misjudged their potential support in Dagestan for establishing an Islamic state in that republic. The ethnic diversity in Dagestan and historic confrontations between Chechens and Dagestani worked against local support. In some villages the Chechen fighters had to face resistance from local inhabitants even before Federal forces arrived. Since Basayev and Khattab apparently operated independently, the military-strategic level was absent. Both commanders were active only on the lower levels of strategy.

Concerning the operational and tactical level it was rather remarkable that the Chechen insurgents in Dagestan changed their methods of warfare a number of times. First they invaded in the form of an irregular raid, not as conventional armed forces. This was of course due also to their mostly light armament. Because of the lack of local support, after occupying some areas of Dagestan they resorted to building fortified strongholds to defend themselves against Federal troops. This can be considered as a form of regular warfare. Being outnumbered and badly equipped, the insurgents were not capable of launching counter-offensives against the Russian forces. However, being aware of the limitations of the Russian forces under bad weather and night conditions, they took advantage of this by operating especially under these circumstances. After they had been forced to leave the occupied villages and return to Chechnya, the insurgents again changed over to partisan warfare;[70] for instance, by using snipers, mining roads and laying ambushes. With regard to air defence it was mainly luck rather than well-prepared defence, which enabled them to shoot down some helicopters and aircraft.

Conclusions

Russian strategy and warfare

On the grand strategy level it was remarkable that it was not RF President Yeltsin but Prime Minister Putin who took the lead in the operations in Dagestan. Two reasons can be advanced for the fact that Putin became deeply involved in the Dagestan conflict. First of all, it indicated his interest in security affairs, being a former intelligence officer. Second he was climbing the ladder of the political hierarchy. Victory in Dagestan would promote his career. Another point of interest at the political-strategic level was how the media were dealt with. The RF authorities restricted media coverage on the operations in Dagestan. In the first Chechen conflict, unrestrained reporting by the press, especially of civilian casualties, had a negative impact on public opinion and on the morale of the soldiers. Due to political demands it also limited military operations, especially with regard to targeting. By controlling the media the Russian authorities were successful in information warfare.

Regarding the military-strategic level, it turned out that the command and control structure of the joint Federal Forces failed on various occasions. Since the

MVD forces were not capable of handling the situation, operational command was moved a number of times between the MVD and MoD. Undoubtedly this must have had a negative influence on the outcome of the operations. Bearing in mind similar experiences during the first Chechen conflict, the failures in coordination during the operations in Dagestan proved that cooperation between MVD and MoD troops was still insufficient. Just as in 1994–96, MoD and MVD units learned to cooperate with each other only when in battle.

At the operational level one must conclude that the original ground component of the Federal forces, consisting of two brigades, was not capable of defeating the insurgents. Reinforcements had to come from distant peacetime locations and from elite forces such as airborne and naval infantry troops. This was an indication of the low level of combat readiness of a large part of the Russian armed forces.

Another observation at this level is that the air component made a number of mistakes, mostly due to shortcomings in coordination between the VVS, ASV and MVD. With regard to the use of air power, coordinated mission planning between VVS, ASV, Ground Forces and MVD troops should already, prior to the Dagestani operations, have been considered imperative for achieving joint military objectives and avoiding blue-on-blue attacks.

Overall, in spite of a number of shortcomings, the operations in Dagestan were successful. This was especially due to a change of conduct at the tactical level, compared to the 1994–96 conflict. The Dagestani operations showed that the Federal forces had altered their tactics. Only after heavy artillery and air bombardments did ground forces start their assault to destroy the rebels.[71] Modern, high-tech precision arms, part of the RF defence capability, were used, especially in the initial bombardments. In the first Chechen conflict modern weapons were used less and ground forces were often in direct contact with the enemy from the very beginning. This approach had resulted in a high casualty rate and had affected morale. The new approach of employing ground troops only after initial artillery and air bombardments seemed to be more successful.

Strategy and warfare of the Chechen insurgents

At the political-strategic level the Chechen insurgents incorrectly assessed popular support for Islamic rule in Dagestan. In addition to lack of public support, in some cases Dagestanis actively resisted them. The lack of Dagestani support was probably due to the ethnic diversity of the population, who were not united in favour of secession from Russia. Nor did the majority of the Dagestani people feel drawn towards radical Islamic ideas that were propagated by the Chechen intruders.

With regard to the operational-tactical level, after losing the battles in three successive operations, the intruders were driven back to Chechen territory. It can be concluded that apart from defending fortified strongholds, which was an example of regular warfare, the Chechens operated mainly as insurgents, using tactics of irregular warfare.

The second Chechen conflict (October 1999–)

Setting between the first and second conflict

From 1996 until 1999, Chechnya regained its independent status. However, the situation in Chechnya during this interbellum turned out to be one of vulnerability, poverty, danger, violence, internal division, chaos and anarchy. Chechnya's *de facto* sovereignty was not recognized by the international community, therefore it found itself isolated. Chechnya had become a failed state. The common features of a self-ruling entity, i.e. certain basic institutions and facilities, were missing. It lacked a central governmental apparatus and corresponding institutions, such as a national government supported by the majority of the population, police, armed forces and national electricity and telephone networks. Another aspect of Chechnya as a failed state was the fact that national borders had lost their significance, because gradually only boundaries between clans and warlords were decisive.

Chechnya's population was divided over the institutional establishment and the future of this entity. In fact, it was ruled by a criminal anarchy of clans and of warlords, commanders of armed elements, who used violence to enlarge their political-economic status. Chiefs of clans and warlords determined matters in their region, notwithstanding the formal government in Groznyy. Chechnya became a centre of anarchy, in which abductions, especially of foreigners, turned out to be the major source of income for local warlords. From 1996 to 1999 some 700 people were abducted, many of whom were found dead. Furthermore, organized crime prospered, particularly the trade in arms and narcotics. As mentioned earlier, President Maskhadov, just as his predecessor Dudayev, experienced a number of assassination attempts. A successful attempt might have created another civil war, as was the case before the Russians carried out their first invasion in 1994. In spite of the internal differences, most of the Chechens agreed that a return to external, Russian rule should be avoided.[72] After the first conflict Groznyy was left in ruins. Roads were hardly practicable, schools and medical facilities scarcely existed, and some 400,000 Chechens were unemployed but armed. Increasingly radical Muslim organizations, with roots in the Arab world, were able to expand their influence on the Chechen population, because of their approach of the problem of poverty. Subsequently, mosques were built and children received an Islamic education. At the forefront of this Islamization of Chechen society was an extreme Islamic movement, called *Wahhabism*. Their objective was to turn Chechnya into an Islamic state.

Russia refrained from involving itself in Chechen affairs and let things drift. In spite of its statements on establishing a social-economic support programme for the Chechen population, which might have countered the dangerous extreme Islamic tendencies, the RF failed to provide financial resources. Providing only minimal financial support for the rebuilding of Chechnya and diverting oil pipeline routes round Chechnya made of Chechnya's deplorable economic circumstances even worse and further inspired Chechen feelings of aversion towards

Russia. The anarchistic, violent nature of the Chechen failed state more and more became a threat to the rest of the (North) Caucasus and to other states around the Black and the Caspian Seas. In October 1999 Russian forces for the second time would invade Chechnya.[73]

The two problems I described in the introduction to this chapter, which complicate the solving of the Chechen struggle, i.e. clan adherence over nationalistic loyalty and fierce Chechen resistance against Russian occupation, have so far hampered any attempt to establish solid governance over Chechnya, either by the Russians or by the Chechens themselves.

The course of the second Chechen conflict

I will divide the course of the conflict into five phases. The air campaign in September 1999 was followed by the installation of a security cordon in northern Chechnya (October–November 1999), after which a larger part of Chechnya was occupied, including Groznyy (November 1999–February 2000). Then came the fourth phase, which was conquering the mountainous part, south of Groznyy (March 2000–January 2001), and finally the fifth phase, which was restoring Russian Federal law and order, under command of the internal security service, FSB (*Federal'naya Sluzhba Bezopasnosti*) (January 2001–present).

Phase one: the air campaign (September 1999). For weeks Russia mounted an air campaign against Chechnya in which not only the insurgents, withdrawing from Dagestan, were targeted, but also strategic objectives such as telephone and electricity infrastructures, water reservoirs and the airport of the capitol, Groznyy. Tactical targets destroyed were military bases, bridges, roads and vehicles. Although denied by the VVS commander-in-chief, Colonel-General Anatoly Kornukov, many civilians were killed as a result of the air strikes.[74]

Phase two: the installation of a security cordon in northern Chechnya (October–November 1999). Putin's statement, that the authority of Chechen President Maskhadov and of his government was illigimate, on 1 October, was the signal to start the ground campaign. The objective was to capture territory to establish a security zone as far as the river Terek, north of Groznyy, officially to prevent any further incursions into RF territory. The Russian forces used 'go-slow' tactics, sending in infantry only after heavy artillery and air barrages, to avoid the heavy casualties of the first Chechen conflict. On 15 October, the commander of the Joint Grouping of Forces, General Kazantsev, announced that the security zone, comprising one-third of Chechnya, was complete. After this, and although officially denied, Russian troops made efforts to encircle Groznyy in preparation for an invasion of the Chechen capital. On 12 November, Gudermes, Chechnya's second largest city, was taken. At the end of that month Russian forces largely surrounded Groznyy and held more than 50 per cent of Chechnya.

Phase three. This was the occupation of the larger part of Chechnya, including Groznyy (November 1999–February 2000). On 4 December, Groznyy was fully blockaded by Russian troops. By 13 December, the Russians had regained control of Groznyy's airport. As of the next day, Russian forces met fierce resistance in advancing into the outskirts of Groznyy. On 3 February 2000, the Federal forces held half of Groznyy. During the following days 2,000 Chechen fighters pulled out of their capital into the southern mountains. The Russians had recaptured Groznyy.

Phase four: the battle for the southern mountains (March 2000–January 2001). From mid-February 2000, the VVS bombed Chechen positions in the southern mountains, where around 8,000 fighters were believed to be in hiding. The Chechen benefited from the mountainous terrain in their hit-and-run attacks on the Russian troops. Still lacking a sufficient counter-insurgency doctrine, the Russian forces were unable to deal with the Chechen guerrilla tactics and to complete the operation.

Phase five: the swift transition from a military operation to an FSB-led anti-terrorist operation (January 2001–present). In January 2001, President Putin announced that the military campaign in Chechnya had been successfully completed and that this allowed the turning over of command of the 'anti-terrorist operation' from the military to the FSB.[75] The FSB would further restore RF law and order in Chechnya by employing special units (*spetsnaz*) to conduct extensive search-and-destroy operations against rebel groups and their commanders. Although Russian officials claimed that the military conflict had ended, the Chechens continue their guerrilla warfare not only in the southern mountains, but also throughout Chechnya and even by bomb attacks and incursions into Dagestan and Ingushetia. In September 2002, three years after the second Chechen conflict had begun, the official total number (MoD forces and troops of the power ministries) of Russian soldiers killed was 4,500, which was comparable with the loss of 4,000–6,000 servicemen in the first Chechen conflict. Also, according to Russian officials, at that moment 12,500 Russians were wounded and nearly 14,000 Chechen fighters had been killed.[76]

Russian grand strategy: actors and objectives

Economic, *internal* and *external politics*, as well as *military* and *ideological* grounds gave rise to the second Russian invasion of autumn 1999. The motives for this invasion can be divided into structural and opportunistic ones. Structural motives are present in the fields of the economy, geostrategy and internal politics. The *economic* drive was due to the presence of oil in the area of the Caspian Sea, in the vicinity of Chechnya. Oil was and is an important source of income for Russia. Therefore, Russia had an economic interest in safeguarding its oil pipelines in the vicinity of Chechnya and the petrochemical industries on Chechen territory. Furthermore, Russia considers the Caucasus to be of vital *strategic* importance, as it leads to Turkey and the Middle East. In order to maintain its influence in that area, a stable southern border, on which Chechnya is situated, was an essential prerequisite. Concerning *internal* politics, Russia considered the secession of Chechnya as a threat to its integrity. This could create a domino effect of separatism; other entities within the RF might follow this example, which eventually could lead to the break-up of the RF.

Second, opportunistic motives can be found in the fields of internal, military and ideological politics. Regarding *internal* politics, as I described in my conclusions on the Dagestani conflict, in autumn 1999 Putin was on his way to becoming the leader of the country. In August, in a television speech, Yeltsin had announced Putin as his successor for the presidency. Although at that time no official statements were made on Putin as a candidate for the presidential elections, which were to take place in 2000, a successful campaign in Chechnya would strengthen his position for obtaining this office. The *military* motives were twofold. First, the Russian generals were vindicated in having their revenge for the humiliating defeat they suffered in the first Chechen conflict in 1996. Second, the top brass wished to increase the defence budget with the intention of modernizing and strengthening the armed forces. A victory in Chechnya would increase their influence in the Kremlin in order to achieve this target. Finally, the *ideological* argument was the threat of Islamic fundamentalism, which has been a constant theme in Russian foreign as well as domestic policy. Internationally, Russia pointed at the Islamic terror attacks in Central Asia, developments in Afghanistan, and domestically, at the incursions by Islamic extremists in Dagestan and the installation of Islamic rule in Chechnya. Often these developments have been portrayed as connected, and especially to Osama bin Laden's terror network.

The most likely direct motives giving rise to the decision to use military force against Chechnya, were the aforementioned incursions of Chechen insurgents into Dagestan and a number of bomb attacks in Russia. One explosion occurred in Dagestan, three in Moscow, and one in Volgodonsk, all between 31 August and 16 September 1999.[77] Russian authorities justified the invasion using the Chechen incursions and the bomb blasts as reasons. However, to this very day no

Table 4.2 Force comparisons at the start of the second Chechen conflict

Belligerent	Personnel strength land forces	Material air forces
Russian Federation	100,000 regular forces and troops	Combat aircraft (number unknown); 68 transport and combat helicopters (among them 32 Mi-24 *Hinds*); transport and recce/intelligence aircraft
Chechnya	20,000 guerrilla fighters	Two Mi-8 *Hips* and one An-2 *Colt* transport aircraft

Sources: Yu. Golotyuk, 'Groznyy bombili', *Izvestiya*, 24 September 1999, p. 1; A. Korbut, 'Ucheba v boyu', *Nezavisimoye Voyennoye Obozreniye*, 50 (173), 24 December 1999, p. 2; Ye. Matveyev, 'Tridtsat' pyatyy: v srednem federal'nyye voyska terjayut v Chechne po vertoljotu v mesyats', *Nezavisimoye Voyennoye Obozreniye*, 30 (300), 30 August 2002, p. 1; M.J. Orr, 'Russia's Chechen war reaches crisis point', *Jane's Intelligence Review*, October 2000, p. 17; Ye. Smyshlayev, 'Vertolety nad Chechney', *Nezavisimoye Voyennoye Obozreniye*, 38 (211), 13 October 2000, p. 6.

proof has been given that Chechens were behind the bomb attacks. On the contrary, quite often the FSB is accused of these terror attacks. Another point of interest is that the invasion of Chechnya was well organized, which makes it unlikely that it was a sudden decision to use military force. Probably a reason was found for conducting an already planned military campaign.

Russian military strategy: command and control structure

At the outset of the second invasion into Chechnya, in October 1999, the estimated number of the forces, the majority being MoD troops, was 100,000. In August 2000 the Joint Grouping of Forces consisted of 80,000 men, of whom 50,000 were MoD troops.[78] In January 2001 it was announced that the total personnel strength of the forces in Chechnya, MoD and MVD troops and *militsia* (military organized police), was to be reduced to 50,000–60,000 men. However, in November 2002 the number of servicemen was still 80,000.[79]

Initially the Joint Grouping of Forces, under the command of Colonel-General Kazantsev, Commander NCMD, conducted the operations in Chechnya. The Joint Grouping of Forces was divided into five parts: the western, northern, eastern, southern and Groznyy (later Argun) groups. Each group consisted of MoD troops (Ground and Air Forces, as well as Naval-Infantry and Airborne Troops) and troops of the power ministries (MVD, FSB, Civil Defence and Border Guard Troops).[80] The main headquarters of the Joint Grouping of Forces was originally based in Mozdok, west of Chechnya, and then moved to Khankala, near Groznyy.[81]

In January 2001, the FSB took over command of operations in Chechnya. With regard to command and control, a Main Staff of Operations was formed, consisting of the Director of FSB, the heads of the power ministries, which had troops employed in Chechnya, such as the MVD, and of members of the Joint (military) Staff. The Joint Staff had until then been in command of the Chechen campaign. Furthermore, a Regional Staff of Operations was formed, led by a Deputy Director of the FSB, and made up of representatives of the power ministries and of the local authorities in the southern district of the RF. The Joint Staff continued to have command and control of the military units.[82]

Russian operational level: organization of air power

Command and control structure

All air assets, both MoD and power ministries, were under the unified command of Lieutenant-General Valery Gorbenko of the Joint Staff.[83] Just as in the Dagestani conflict, the air component of the Joint Grouping of Forces was made up of fixed-wing aircraft of VVS and rotary-wing aircraft, belonging to army aviation ASV. The VVS component comprised air regiments assigned to the 4th Air Army, and some separate units from the Moscow Air and Air Defence District.[84] Roughly half of the ASV helicopters were divided over the different groups of the

Joint Grouping of Forces; the other half was used as reserve for the Joint Grouping of Forces.[85]

The former bomber base of Mozdok, North-Ossetia, some 90 km northwest of Groznyy, was again the primary staging base for the fixed-wing part of the air component, as well as the main forward air base for supplies from elsewhere in Russia. Clearly, military operations in this region had been planned in advance. In spring the airbase had received an order, which stated that within two months, June and July, the runway had to be prepared for operational use.[86] Other bases used by the air component were Budënnovsk, on RF territory, and locations in the republics of Dagestan and Ingushetia.[87]

Force build-up

The aircraft of the air component in the second Chechen conflict were for the most part similar to those used in Dagestan. Rotary-wing aircraft employed by ASV were the Mi-24 *Hind* combat helicopter, the Mi-8 *Hip* transport helicopter and the Mi-26 *Halo* heavy lift helicopter. The latter was extensively used for the forward movement of troops. In September 1999 the contribution of ASV for the operation was 68 helicopters, consisting of 32 *Hinds*, 28 *Hips* and 8 *Halos*. Three years later, in September 2002, the number of helicopters was reduced to 40–22 *Hinds*, 17 *Hips* and 1 *Halo*.[88]

VVS fixed-wing aircraft were the Su-25 *Frogfoot* fighter-bomber, Su-27 and Su-30 *Flanker* fighters and Su-24M *Fencer-D* fighter-bomber aircraft. For air recce, Su-24 MR *Fencer-E* and MiG-25RBK *Foxbats-D* aircraft were utilized. At least a squadron each of *Fencers* and *Frogfoots* operated from Mozdok.

Intelligence gathering was conducted by AN-30B *Clanks* (photo surveillance), A-50 *Mainstays* (AWACS) and by Il-20 *Coots* (signal intelligence).[89] So again *Hip* and *Hind* helicopters and *Fencer-D* and *Frogfoot* fighter-bombers formed the core of the air component.

Russian tactical level: application of air power

Counter-Air Operations

At the outset of the conflict, the Chechens were reported to be using two helicopters for flying in supplies. In order to prevent this, the VVS carried out OCA missions, by keeping two *Flankers* and two *Frogfoots* on constant alert for conducting CAPs. In these missions *Mainstay* AWACS aircraft provided aerial radar cover. To secure RF airfields and cities against possible air attacks, DCA missions were conducted.[90]

Anti-Surface Force Air Operations

Fencers and *Frogfoots* undertook the main share of the number of strike sorties. Initially, the missions were conducted in support of the ground campaign and were targeted against bridges, major roads and buildings. Another task was to mine mountain roads and areas, in order to cut off supply routes and restrict freedom of movement. *Hinds* carried out missions of tactical suppression of suspected rebel positions. With the start of the fourth phase, missions were directed against camps and hardened shelters in the mountains and to cut Chechen supply routes from Georgia. Pairs of *Frogfoots* conducted 'free-hunt' missions, to suppress new strongholds in conquered territory.[91]

Strategic Air Operations

Although initially VVS authorities suggested that the strategic bomber force (*strategicheskaya aviatsiya*) DA might be employed, VVS Commander Kornukov later on repeatedly insisted that there was no need to do so. There is no evidence that the Russian strategic bomber force was ever used in the conflict. However, in addition to OAS missions, the ASV and VVS conducted offensive missions to destroy strategic targets. Thus the air component carried out missions against strategic targets, such as telecommunications (telephone, radio and TV) installations, command, control and communications networks, as well as against the oil refinery and the airport of Groznyy.[92]

Supporting Air Operations

Hips were extensively used to transport ground forces (for instance, *Spetnaz* units of MoD and MVD), to interdict communications and supply lines, to react to guerrilla raids, CSAR missions, as well as to transport supplies and ammunition into the mountains. In these missions *Hinds* or *Frogfoots* provided cover for the *Hips*.[93] In the second Chechen conflict more than in the first one, the emphasis was placed on effective recce and intelligence collection. *Clanks*, *Mainstays* and *Coots* were used to gather (electronic) intelligence and *Fencer-Es*, *Frogfoots and Foxbat-Ds* conducted air recce missions. However, on entering phase four of the conflict, intelligence gathering became complicated, because enemy bases in the mountains, without meaningful signals to intercept, were hard to detect.[94]

Tactics

As in the Dagestani conflict, the ASV operated in groups of two to four *Hinds* and one or two *Hips*. These formations were described as aviation tactical groups (ATGs). In an ATG *Hips* would direct *Hinds* to their targets. Another task of the *Hips* in the ATGs was CSAR, in support of downed *Hinds*. Two-thirds of the CAS missions of ASV were organized in this way. In addition to this tactic, without support of *Hips*, pairs of *Hinds* also carried out 'free hunt' missions, which comprised the remaining third of the total number of missions. Targets of these missions were similar to those of the aforementioned 'free-hunt' missions of *Frogfoots*. Helicopter strikes involved energetic manoeuvring, simultaneous attacks from opposing directions and dives from a formation outside anti-aircraft defence ranges. ATGs were assigned to regiments, together with an FAC in the regimental HQ. FACs were also posted at lower levels, at battalion and sometimes even at company level.[95]

VVS commander's appreciation of tasks and lessons learned

In July 2000, reviewing the operations in Dagestan and Chechnya, the VVS commander, Kornukov, gave an explanation of the tasks and lessons learned so far.[96] He defined the tasks of the air component as follows:

- air support for ground forces (Anti-Surface Force Air Operations);
- security against air attacks (Counter-Air Operations);
- psychological warfare: harassing the enemy (Strategic Air Operations);
- air recce of assigned areas (Supporting Air Operations);
- relay of command and control (Supporting Air Operations);
- transport of troops and supplies (Supporting Air Operations).

According to Kornukov, the effectiveness of air power had to be increased by improvements in the field of maintenance of aircraft and equipment, training and number of pilots and troops, upgrading of aircraft with state-of-the-art avionics, procurement of newly developed aircraft, combat readiness of units and airbases, command and control structure of air power as well as directives on the application of air power. However this 'shopping list' would not prove to be very realistic in the light of structural cuts in the defence budget.

Failures, problems and losses of air power

A number of failures arose in using air power. Although fewer than in the earlier conflicts, friendly fire now and then still occurred. For instance, in March 2000 an OMON (special police unit) detachment was wiped out by friendly fire from the VVS.[97] Although improvements had been made since the first Chechen conflict, coordination between forces/troops still was not optimal. Air power was mostly used as air support for ground troop operations. However, using aircraft as 'flying artillery', instead of platforms for precision weapons, caused collateral damage in the form of numerous civilian casualties, which subsequently left a negative impression on the public.[98]

In the fourth phase of the conflict, the lack of sophisticated equipment thwarted the effective application of air power against the mountain hideouts of the Chechens. Dispersed troops were hard to find targets and therefore difficult to detect and destroy. Air power was not an effective weapon against guerrilla warfare and urban terrorism.

Problems in the areas of finance, arms as well as personnel, owing to constant cuts in the defence budget, had affected the operational capabilities of the forces.

The air campaign in Chechnya influenced the combat readiness of the VVS as a whole; in February 2000 it had usurped up to 60 per cent of the annual budget of VVS. Deputy Prime Minister Klebanov stated that the VVS had not received any new aircraft since 1992, and was not likely to receive any in the coming year. The Federal forces, and especially the air component, were not capable of operating either in bad weather conditions or during the night.[99] Just as in Dagestan and in the first Chechen conflict, the absence of expensive PGMs, high-tech communications, navigation and targeting systems, as well as all-weather and day/night capabilities, made air power less effective than it could have been. According to the commander of the air component of the NCMD, another negative development influencing combat readiness was the fact that Federal forces lacked fuel, spare parts and maintenance. In official as well as independent newspapers, the VVS commander, Kornukov, openly admitted and discussed a number of these problems. The air component commander, Gorbenko, also confirmed these problems.[100]

As a result of the low funding levels pilot training and combat experience were insufficient. In 1999 average annual flying time for attack aviation were around 23 hours and for bombers around 25 hours, whereas during the Cold War average Soviet flying hours had been 150.[101] The lack of flying hours resulted not only in a higher rate of aircraft losses but also in less effective fulfilment of missions, for instance by dropping bombs too early.

The losses of the air component were as follows. Until March 2000 the air component had lost two *Frogfoots*, one *Fencer-E* and 18 helicopters. In addition to this, 24 aircraft had suffered combat damage. Only half of the helicopters were lost as a result of enemy fire. In June 2000, the number of helicopters lost amounted to 22, including 10 *Hinds*. In three years, from September 1999 to 2002, the ASV would lose no fewer than 36 helicopters, which was an average of one per month.[102] As mentioned earlier, this large number of rotary-wing losses was only partly caused by enemy fire, other causes could be found in insufficient pilot training and lack of maintenance, due to the reduced funding of the MoD.

Successes of air power

Air power (CAS) took care of a large share of the bombardments prior to the employment of ground forces. The VVS and ASV conducted 70–80 per cent of the fire missions, as opposed to 15–17 per cent carried out by artillery.[103] Between October 1999 and February 2000 air power was used for more than 4,000 combat sorties, of which the majority were strike sorties. The air strikes caused the destruction of a huge amount of armoured vehicles, ant-aircraft guns, armament-production facilities, weapon storage bunkers, oil refinery factories, fuel warehouses, as well as radar and relay stations.[104] Finally, air power, above all by providing air support to the operations of ground forces, formed a vital contribution to the successful Russian campaign during the first three phases of the conflict.

Chechen strategy and operations

To understand the political-strategic level, some background explanation on the Chechen resistance is necessary. Russian authorities have always portrayed all Chechen fighters as 'bandits and terrorists'. However, a distinction can be made between three different groups in Chechen armed resistance.[105] First, the official Chechen government, represented by President Aslan Maskhadov, a former Soviet army colonel.[106] The government was mainly made up of moderate, pro-Western people. The objective of the Chechen government was to maintain an independent Chechnya. Second, small locally orientated armed groups, whose main interest was to avenge dead relatives. They can best be described as unco-ordinated 'soldiers-of-fortune'. They lacked any specific political or military objective. The third group was the militarized and well-structured extremist Islamic organisation of the *Wahhabists*. The Chechen commanders in charge of the incursions into Dagestan, Basayev and Khattab belonged to this group. Their objective was not only to throw the Russians out of Chechnya, but also to install Islamic rule in Chechnya and in Muslim areas on RF territory.

At the operational and tactical level the personnel strength of the Chechen resistance was estimated at 20,000 men, of which some 3,000–6,000 fighters defended Groznyy.[107] When the overthrow of Groznyy was close, 2,000 Chechen fighters pulled out of their capital into the southern mountains, where around 8,000 fighters were believed to be based.[108] From the outset of the Russian ground campaign, Chechen fighters offered little resistance, apart from defending prepared strongholds, realizing that they were no match for the large and heavily armoured Russian forces. However, in December 1999 Chechen militants began counter attacks employing guerrilla tactics. From areas where they could not cope with the strength of the Russians, the Chechen fighters withdrew, with the intention of attacking the enemy in and from the southern mountains. The Chechen militants exploited the deteriorating weather conditions to step up attacks on Federal troops and made good use of the mountainous terrain. After the Russian recapture of Groznyy in February 2000, the Chechens continued their guerrilla warfare not only in the southern mountains, but throughout all of Chechnya and even in the neighbouring RF republics of Dagestan and Ingushetia. The guerrilla tactics employed by the Chechens were hit-and-run attacks, mining, ambushes, assassination of individual soldiers, urban terrorism in the occupied villages and cities, as well as sniper and (suicide) bomb attacks.

Next to countering the RF ground forces, the following can be said about Chechen (*anti-*) *air force warfare*. At the beginning of the conflict, the Chechen air component reportedly possessed two transport helicopters and one utility air-craft, an An-2 *Colt*, which was supposedly used for transport of arms and ammu-nition. At the end of September 1999, during the attack on the Groznyy airport the aircraft was destroyed.[109] Since the start of the conflict no further mention has been made of the two helicopters. So, again, the Russians had air supremacy in this conflict. The air defence capability of the Chechens was similar to that used in Dagestan. There was no organized air-defence system with radar and missiles. Man-portable SAMs, heavy machine-guns and ZSU-23/2 twin barrel anti-aircraft guns on trucks were the arms available for air defence.[110]

The Chechens were successful in disturbing the interface between Russian air and ground operations, by waging information/electronic warfare against the Russian FAC system. Chechens monitored FAC radio transitions and impersonated Russian FACs, in order to misdirect CAS missions, conducted by ATGs and other formations of the Russian air component. Furthermore, FACs were prime targets of Chechen snipers.[111]

Conclusions

Russian strategy and warfare

At the political-strategic level the emphasis was on influencing public opinion, which might also be described as information or psychological warfare. There were two objectives at the heart of information warfare in this conflict. The first objective was to convince the Russian nation of the inevitability of waging war against Chechnya. The second objective was to sustain public support during the conflict.

The bomb attacks of August/September 1999, as well as the Chechen raids into Dagestan and finally traditional dislike of Chechens, created a solid foundation in Russian society in favour of conducting a war against Chechnya for a second time. Putin's leading role in the campaign guaranteed popular support for his election as President in March 2000. To meet the second objective, tight control of the media was meant to create the impression of a smooth operation in Chechnya, and thus sustain support in society. The destruction of Chechen mass-media facilities (radio and TV) was also part of the information warfare, to prevent the broadcasting of other than the desired information. Furthermore, the Russians tried to copy NATO's media campaign in the Kosovo conflict. For instance, the VVS commander, Kornukov, showed pictures and videos to prove that targets were hit without causing any civilian casualties.[112] However, public support decreased as casualties mounted. The authorities were blamed for understating casualty figures and for making the same operational-tactical mistakes as in the first conflict. In addition to this, foreign non-governmental organizations and media reported on human rights abuses and disproportionate and indiscriminate use of force. So in spite of all efforts to control the media, eventually the Russian authorities were unable to maintain strict control of information.

Although the Russian political–military leadership achieved a military victory over Chechnya, they did not win the war politically. The Russians failed in combining military objectives with realistic political objectives. Occupation and oppression encouraged the Chechens to continue a protracted insurgency war against the Russians. As long as the Kremlin did not recognize that this conflict could only be ended by a political solution, the war continued.

At the military-strategic level, the change in command, from the military to the FSB, was a remarkable move. For two reasons this seems to have been the wrong decision. First, it was an error with regard to the difference in capabilities between the armed forces (MoD) and the troops of the power ministries. The Russians should have learned from the first Chechen conflict and the more recent Dagestani conflict that a sound command and control structure was of vital importance for a military campaign. In the aforementioned conflicts, command by the MVD had failed, mostly because of poor cooperation with MoD forces, especially with regard to calling in artillery and air support. This time another power ministry, the FSB, was ordered to take over command from the military. The choice of the FSB might have to do with Putin's background in the security services (his career in foreign intelligence and former Director FSB), and/or with his policy of appointing likeminded persons from the security services to vital positions. However, with the example of failed command in the MVD, it was not unlikely that the FSB would face similar problems, having no experience of conducting above all *military* operations. Second, changing the command to the FSB was a mistake regarding command and control. As a consequence of the FSB taking over command of the operation, new staffs were installed. This was another remarkable decision, which went against earlier experiences. The first Chechen conflict had shown that a divided chain of command had disastrous results. Now, once again staffs were created in addition to the unified (military) Joint Staff. It was not unlikely that the two staffs, led by the FSB, would compete with respectively the General Staff in Moscow and the Joint Staff in Chechnya. In this case, clearly no lesson had been learned.

Gradually, coordination between MoD forces and troops of the power ministries had improved, especially by the creation of a Joint Staff, consisting of all forces and troops involved, and by installing FACs as interface between ground and air operations. According to air component Commander Gorbenko, after the installation of a unified command no further problems had arisen between the MoD and MVD. Blue-on-blue incidents still occurred, but fewer than in the previous conflicts in Dagestan and Chechnya. Coordination and cooperation depended to a large extent on the desire for them. On several occasions criticism, especially from VVS Commander Kornukov on ASV, Ground Forces and MVD, revealed that a true desire for cooperation, shared by all commanders involved, had not yet been reached.[113] The 35th loss of a helicopter, a *Halo*, which was destroyed approaching Khankala airbase on 19 August 2002, was to create a watershed in air power command and control. A week later MoD sources announced that the ASV was to be resubordinated from Ground Forces to VVS, by the end of 2002.[114] The reason for this decision was probably the 'misuse' of helicopters by ground forces commanders; for instance, by overloading helicopters, as was the case with the *Halo*, shot down in August 2002. This decision meant a strengthening of the VVS in command and control of MoD air power, as well as a decline in military power of the Ground Forces. Opinions differed on whether this resubordination of ASV was an important lesson learned from the second Chechen conflict or an example of opportunistic decision-making.

In contrast to the command and control problems, Russian psychological warfare was quite successful. They used 'hearts-and-minds' tactics, by persuading residents to force the rebels out of their villages and thus save them from destruction. And before Groznyy was invaded VVS aircraft dropped leaflets urging residents to leave, warning them that people staying behind would be destroyed as 'bandits', as well as setting an ultimatum of five days.[115] Apparently the Russians had discovered that weapons are not the only way to wage a war.

Reviewing the operational and tactical levels it was atypical that the Russians started the invasion in autumn. This meant that Russian military leadership had to face deteriorating weather conditions. Heavy snow hampered the ground campaign, which encouraged the Chechens to increase their counter-attacks. Although politically opportune, commencing a military operation in the Caucasus in autumn was a risky endeavour from a military point of view. At first the Russian invasion gave the impression of being a smooth operation. The concepts of conducting heavy artillery and air barrages before sending in ground troops, as well as the 'go-slow' tactic were successful and preserved the Russian troops from the heavy casualties they suffered in the first Chechen conflict. Nonetheless, after recapturing the larger part of Chechnya, the Federal forces, in controlling the area, had to cope with guerrilla tactics. Unfortunately, since the first Chechen conflict the Russians still had not developed guidelines for a protracted insurgency conflict. Consequently, they still employed regular warfare tactics against the irregular tactics of the Chechens. Long-range air and artillery firepower, as used in the 'go-slow' approach, were no answer to guerrilla tactics. This asymmetric warfare made the conflict unsolvable. It seemed impossible for the Russians to achieve a final victory over the Chechens.

A clear lesson learned from the first Chechen conflict was to improve command over air support and subsequently, improve coordination between VVS, ASV and MVD. In the Joint Staff all air assets (of MoD and power ministries) were now under unified command. FACs were assigned to regimental levels and even further down to company level. In this way the tactical commander on the ground had direct access to air support, which meant more effective air power.

Yet, the effectiveness of air power could have been much higher if structural cuts in the defence budget had not affected the combat readiness of *matériel* as well as of personnel.

Chechen strategy and warfare

At the operational level the Chechen fighters followed an effective approach. Realizing that they could not overcome the overwhelming superiority in numbers as well as in *matériel* of the Russian forces, they offered little resistance at the beginning of the Russian invasion. Chechen fighters withdrew with the intention of attacking the enemy, at first, only in and from the southern mountains. The Chechen militants exploited the deteriorating weather conditions to step up attacks on Federal troops and made good use of the mountainous terrain. After the take-over of Groznyy in February 2000, the Chechens continued their guerrilla warfare, not only from the southern mountains, but throughout all of Chechnya and even into RF territory. Although the Chechen fighters were unable to defeat the strong Russian forces, by employing irregular warfare they were capable of damaging Russian control over Chechnya. Eventually this protracted insurgency conflict would result in the loss of public support and force the Russians to leave, as was the case in the first Chechen conflict. At the political-strategic level this would mean a Chechen victory, not just by military force but also by way of patient psychological warfare.

At the tactical level, the Chechens, in addition to employing guerrilla tactics, also waged a successful war against the Russian air component. They succeeded in disturbing the Russian FAC system, as well as in shooting down aircraft and helicopters.

Assessment: comparison of the use of air power in the Chechen conflicts

The development of RF air power in irregular warfare is now presented, based upon a comparison of the two Chechen conflicts (1994–96 and 1999–). The Dagestan conflict is not taken into account, because the operational use of air power in this conflict was very like that in the second Chechen war.

Structural problems

Four shortcomings are apparent, which occurred during the first Chechen conflict and which were not (entirely) solved in the second conflict.

Financial limitations

First, annual cuts in the defence budget resulted in limitations of *matériel* (aircraft) and personnel of air power in the conflict. The consequences of these reductions were:

- a low level of combat readiness, as a result of insufficient training of personnel (pilots) and inadequate maintenance of aircraft;
- limited use of air power during night and bad weather conditions, for lack of modern navigation and target acquisition equipment;
- about half of the losses of aircraft were caused by other reasons than enemy fire.

Joint performance of forces and troops

Second, coordination and cooperation among MoD forces and between defence forces and troops of the power ministries were improved but were still far from optimal. An important improvement was the establishment of a joint command for the air component. However, the rivalry among forces and troops had not come to an end when the second conflict started. One explanation for the continued competition, which harmed cooperation, was Putin's inconsistency. Apparently, because they had formed one of the vital segments that brought him into power, Putin wished to have good relations with all security organs. Consequently, he refrained from appointing one security organ in charge of the operation. In both Chechen conflicts overall command over the operation was transferred between the MoD and a power ministry (MVD and FSB). The changes in command did not contribute to the effectiveness of the operations. A second ground for continuation of the rivalry among security organs was the lack of willingness of the commanders of the various forces and troops to genuinely cooperate. One of the effects of insufficient cooperation was that friendly fire still occasionally occurred in the second conflict.

Public opinion

Third, in both conflicts civilian casualties and collateral damage caused by air power left a negative impression on the public. However, civilian casualties were not caused only by lack of flying experience among pilots, obsolete aircraft and lack of PGMs. The fact that Chechen fighters would often hide in and use air-defence weapons from urban areas also created innocent victims, for which the Russians were wrongly blamed. Although Kornukov tried to influence public opinion towards a more favourable stance for the VVS and ASV, the Chechens seemed to be more successful in propaganda techniques.

Irregular warfare

Finally, air power was effective as long as the ground forces were advancing. Air power was not an answer to a protracted guerrilla war. Two reasons can be found in support of this argument. First, as mentioned before, VVS and ASV lacked modern navigation and target acquisition equipment for effectively operating under conditions favourable for guerrillas and successfully detecting an opponent who was hard to find. Second, air power could support anti-guerrilla warfare but was not capable of controlling such a conflict. Not aircraft but land forces, because of their potential to control terrain, were designed to be in the lead in opposing guerrilla and urban terrorism.

Improvements

After the first Chechen conflict a number of improvements were successfully carried through.

Joint command of the air component

First of all, in the second Chechen conflict not only the establishment of a joint military staff but more importantly the formation of a unified air component of the VVS, ASV and MVD air assets improved coordination and cooperation and thus the effectiveness of air power. Furthermore, this formalized cooperation also diminished, though it did not fully remove, the occurrence of friendly fire.

Air support for land forces

Second, air support for ground force operations turned out to be more successful in the second Chechen conflict. I would perceive the following grounds for this improvement:

- by conducting air barrages prior to the advancement of troops, air power created favourable conditions for ground forces and diminished the possibility of friendly fire;
- FACs proved to be more effective than in the first conflict. It seemed that more FACs were available this time. Because of their greater number, FACs could be deployed in more units and at lower tactical levels, sometimes even at company level; and, finally, FACs were apparently better trained and perhaps better equipped with more sophisticated communications instruments;
- another ground for improved air support for ground forces operations was the formation of ATGs. By combining target-designation and attack helicopters, they proved to be highly effective tactical formations.

Contribution of rotary wing aircraft

A third improvement in the use of air power, related to the previous remark, was the return of rotary-wing aircraft as part of the combat force of air power. In the first Chechen conflict helicopters were used mainly for supporting tasks and usually were excluded from urban areas for fear of enemy air-defence. It was then thought that for combat tasks fixed-wing aircraft, such as the *Frogfoot*, would replace rotary wing. However, in the second Chechen conflict, most likely due to the introduction of the successful ATG concept, helicopters were 'back-in-business' for combat missions, which broadened the scope of air power.

Resubordination of ASV

Fourthly and finally, the resubordination of ASV from Ground Forces to VVS, although opinions differed on this in RF military circles, was likely to enforce central guidance of air power, which in turn should reinforce its effectiveness.

Conclusion

In conclusion, it is obvious that the most important structural problem for Russian air power was funding. Irregular warfare in Chechnya showed that lack or absence of expensive PGMs, high-tech communications, navigation and targeting systems, as well as all-weather and day/night capabilities, limited the effectiveness of air power. But in spite of the financial problems, Russian air power demonstrated that it was capable of enhancing its effectiveness without additional financial support, especially by innovations in command and control and by tactical improvements.

Notes

1 C.W. Blandy, *Chechnya: The Need to Negotiate*, OB88 (Camberley: Conflict Studies Research Centre, 2001), p. 9.

2 *Encyclopaedia of Conflicts, Disputes and Flashpoints in Eastern Europe, Russia and the Successor States* (Harlow: Longman, 1993), pp. 61–6.

3 Dzhokhar Musayevich Dudayev (1944–96) was a retired major-general of the Soviet VVS. One of his posts had been commander of a bomber division in Afghanistan. See G. Isenkov, 'VVS zadachu vypolnili', *Armeyskiy Sbornik*, 3, (1995), p. 42; A. Yavorskiy, 'Lëtchikam ne dali razvernut'sya', *Nezavisimoye Voyennoye Obozreniye*, 48 (171), 10 Dec. 1999, p. 5; and N.N. Novichkov, *Rossiyskiye Vooruzhënnyye Sily v Chechenskom Konflikte* (Moscow: Kholveg-Infoglob, and Paris: Trivola, 1995), p. 192.

4 *Encyclopaedia of Conflicts*, pp. 61–6.

5 G. Kosykh, 'Itogi Chechenskoy kampanii podvodit' eshchë rano', *Nezavisimoye Voyennoye Obozreniye*, 45 (72), 5 Dec. 1997, p. 2; I. Korotchenko, 'Voyennaya operatsiya v Chechene (Obzor)', *Nezavisimoye Voyennoye Obozreniye*, 1 (1), 11 Feb. 1995, p. 1.

6 Novichkov, *Rossiyskiye Vooruzhënnyye Sily v Chechenskom Konflikte*, p. 11.

7 For the geographical setting of attacks axes and locations in Chechnya, see Map 2, p. xxi. Novichkov, *Rossiyskiye Vooruzhënnyye Sily v Chechenskom Konflikte*, p. 28.

8 Korotchenko, 'Voyennaya operatsiya v Chechene', p. 1.

9 I. Safranchuk, 'Chechnya: Russia's Experience of Asymmetrical Warfare', in J. Olsen (ed.), *Asymmetric Warfare* (Oslo: Royal Norwegian Air Force Academy, 2002), p. 373; B. Lambeth, *Russia's Air Power in Crisis* (Washington, DC: Smithsonian Institution Press, 1999), p. 129; C. Gall and Th. de Waal, *Chechnya, Calamity in the Caucasus* (New York and London: New York University Press, 1998), p. 360; Kosykh, 'Itogi Chechenskoy kampanii podvodit' eshchë rano', p. 2.

10 Novichkov, *Rossiyskiye Vooruzhënnyye Sily v Chechenskom Konflikte*, pp. 10–11.

11 Ye. Moskvin, 'Zagovor chinovnikov protiv kontraktnika', *Nezavisimoye Voyennoye Obozreniye*, 15 (240), 25 April 2003, p. 1; Novichkov, *Rossiyskiye Vooruzhënnyye Sily v Chechenskom Konflikte*, pp. 178–9; Gall, *Chechnya, Calamity in the Caucasus*, p. 181.

12 P.K. Baev, 'Russia's Air power in the Chechen War: Denial, Punishment and Defeat', *Journal of Slavic Military Studies*, 10, (1997), p. 2.

13 Novichkov, *Rossiyskiye Vooruzhënnyye Sily v Chechenskom Konflikte*, p. 11. Under international law, Chechnya was arguably a constitutional entity of the Russian Federation. According to article 3.1 of the II Additional Protocol to the Geneva Conventions (1949), Russia was entitled to re-establish law and order in this republic: 'Nothing in this Protocol shall be invoked for the purpose of affecting the sovereignty of a State or the responsibility of the government, by all legitimate means, to maintain or re-establish law and order in the State or to defend the national unity and territorial integrity of the State'. See *Protocols Additional to the Geneva Conventions of 12 August 1949* (Geneva: International Committee of the Red Cross, 1996), p. 91.

This argument of international law would also be used by the RF authorities in the consecutive conflicts in Dagestan and Chechnya, which broke out in 1999.

14 The FSK was the predecessor of the FSB (*Federal'naya Sluzhba Bezopasnosti*), as internal security service of the RF. The change of name, which was accompanied by a broadening of responsibilities, took place on 3 April 1995. See Novichkov, *Rossiyskiye Vooruzhënnyye Sily v Chechenskom Konflikte*, p. 173.

15 For the exact boundaries of RF Military Districts, see Map 1: Military Districts of the Russian Federation (1997). Korotchenko, 'Voyennaya operatsiya v Chechene', p. 1; Novichkov, *Rossiyskiye Vooruzhënnyye Sily v Chechenskom Konflikte*, p. 29; Gall, *Chechnya, Calamity in the Caucasus*, p.180.

16 Novichkov, *Rossiyskiye Vooruzhënnyye Sily v Chechenskom Konflikte*, pp. 31, 38.

17 C.W. Blandy, *Chechnya: Two Federal interventions. An interim Comparison and Assessment* (Camberley: Conflict Studies Research Centre, 2000), pp. 16, 19; Lambeth, *Russia's Air Power in Crisis*, pp. 133, 141; O. Blotskiy and A. Nikol'skiy 'General-Major Vladimir Syamanov: "Mne opravdyvat'sya ne pered kem" ', *Nezavisimoye Voyennoye Obozreniye*, No. 10 (14), 30 May 1996, p. 1.

18 S. Babichev and V. Strugovets, 'Vozdushnyye izvozchiki', *Krasnaya Zvezda*, 25 Oct. 1995, p. 2; and S. Prokopenko and S. Babichev, 'Voyna v Chechne', *Aviatsiya i Kosmonavtika*, Nov. 1995, p. 15.

19 Novichkov, *Rossiyskiye Vooruzhënnyye Sily v Chechenskom Konflikte*, p. 107.

20 Yavorskiy, 'Lëtchikam ne dali razvernut'sya'; D.J. Marshall-Hasdell, *Russian Air power in Chechnya* P20 (Camberley: Conflict Studies Research Centre, 1996), p. 5; S. Prokopenko and B. Soldatenko, 'Vozdushnyye rabochiye voyny', *Krasnaya Zvezda*, 1 March 1995, p. 3.

21 T.L. Thomas, 'Air Operations in Low Intensity Conflict: the Case of Chechnya', *Air Power Journal*, Winter 1997, p. 53; Babichev, 'Vozdushnyye izvozchiki'.

22 Yavorskiy, 'Lëtchikam ne dali razvernut'sya'; Novichkov, *Rossiyskiye Vooruzhënnyye Sily v Chechenskom Konflikte*, pp. 107, 115.

23 An FAC or *avianavodchik* forms the link between the air and ground component. Instructed by the tactical ground commander he directs the pilots to their targets. In the years preceding the (first) Chechen conflict the allocation of resources for FAC was heavily reduced. The Chechen conflict necessitated the reinstatement of the FAC system and the founding of an emergency training course for FACs, in order to support pilots in their target tracing, which was hampered by mountainous and wooded terrain. Another reason for re-establishing the FAC system was to prevent friendly fire. See N. Baranov, 'Voyny diktuyut reorganizatsiyu', *Nezavisimoye Voyennoye Obozreniye*, 10 (183), 24 March 2000, p. 1; and A.M. Kornukov, 'Aviatsionnaya podderzhka voysk: gospodstvo v nebe – uspekh na zemle', *Krasnaya Zvezda*, 11 Nov. 1998, p. 2.

24 Isenkov, 'VVS zadachu vypolnili'; and S. Lefebvre, *The Reform of the Russian Air Force* B57 (Camberley: Conflict Studies Research Centre, 2002), p. 13.

25 In 1998 the VPVO amalgamated with the VVS.

26 Novichkov, *Rossiyskiye Vooruzhënnyye Sily v Chechenskom Konflikte*, p. 115.

27 Yavorskiy, 'Lëtchikam ne dali razvernut'sya'.

28 Ibid.; Thomas, 'The case of Chechnya', p. 52; and Novichkov, *Rossiyskiye Vooruzhënnyye Sily v Chechenskom Konflikte*, pp. 115, 120–1.

29 Novichkov, *Rossiyskiye Vooruzhënnyye Sily v Chechenskom Konflikte*, p. 114; and Isenkov, 'VVS zadachu vypolnili'.

30 Novichkov, *Rossiyskiye Vooruzhënnyye Sily v Chechenskom Konflikte*, pp. 112, 114.

31 Baev, 'Russia's Air power in the Chechen War', p. 3; Lambeth, *Russia's Air Power in Crisis*, p. 136; Novichkov, *Rossiyskiye Vooruzhënnyye Sily v Chechenskom Konflikte*, p. 112; and Yavorskiy, 'Lëtchikam ne dali razvernut'sya'.

32 Isenkov, 'VVS zadachu vypolnili'; Lambeth, *Russia's Air Power in Crisis*, pp. 122–3; Novichkov, *Rossiyskiye Vooruzhënnyye Sily v Chechenskom Konflikte*, pp. 114–16.

33 Novichkov, *Rossiyskiye Vooruzhënnyye Sily v Chechenskom Konflikte*, p. 116; Prokopenko, 'Voyna v Chechne'.

34 V.G. Rog, 'Vozdushnoye nastupleniye i vozdushnaya oborona', *Armeyskiy Sbornik*, 11 (1997), p. 4; Yavorskiy, 'Lëtchikam ne dali razvernut'sya'; Novichkov, *Rossiyskiye Vooruzhënnyye Sily v Chechenskom Konflikte*, pp. 119–20; Marshall-Hasdell, *Russian Air power in Chechnya*, p. 9.

35 P. d'Hamecourt, 'Russen protesteren tegen oorlog in Tsjetsjenië', *Algemeen Dagblad*, 4 Jan. 1995; S. Wynia, 'EU zet Rusland onder druk in Tsjetsjeense crisis', *Het Parool*, 5 Jan 1995.

36 Novichkov, *Rossiyskiye Vooruzhënnyye Sily v Chechenskom Konflikte*, p. 113; and Marshall-Hasdell, *Russian Air power in Chechnya*, p. 3.

37 Isenkov, 'VVS zadachu vypolnili'; Novichkov, *Rossiyskiye Vooruzhënnyye Sily v Chechenskom Konflikte*, pp. 107, 113.

38 Prokopenko, 'Voyna v Chechne'.

39 Ibid.; Lambeth, *Russia's Air Power in Crisis*, p. 124; Novichkov, *Rossiyskiye Vooruzhënnyye Sily v Chechenskom Konflikte*, pp. 107, 119; Thomas, 'The Case of Chechnya', pp. 54–5.

40 Novichkov, *Rossiyskiye Vooruzhënnyye Sily v Chechenskom Konflikte*, pp. 114, 118; Lefebvre, *The Reform of the Russian Air Force*, p. 13; Baev, 'Russia's air power in the Chechen War', p. 11; and Lambeth, *Russia's Air Power in Crisis*, p. 130.

41 Lefebvre, *The Reform of the Russian Air Force*, p. 12; and Yavorskiy, 'Lëtchikam ne dali razvernut'sya'.

42 Yavorskiy, 'Lëtchikam ne dali razvernut'sya'; Lambeth, *Russia's Air Power in Crisis*, p. 133.

43 Thomas, 'The Case of Chechnya', p. 54.

44 'First Chechnya War', 15 Jan. 2000, www.fas.org/man/dod-101/ops/war/ chechnya1.htm; Korotchenko, 'Voyennaya operatsiya v Chechene', p. 2; and Thomas, 'The Case of Chechnya', p. 58.

45 Yavorskiy, 'Lëtchikam ne dali razvernut'sya'; Novichkov, *Rossiyskiye Vooruzhënnyye Sily v Chechenskom Konflikte*, p. 108; and Prokopenko, 'Voyna v Chechne'.

46 Prokopenko, 'Voyna v Chechne'.

47 I.N. Vorobyev, 'Legko prognoziruyemyye resul'taty', *Nezavisimoye Voyennoye Obozreniye*, 2 (29), 18 Jan. 1997, p. 2.

48 Vorobyev, 'Legko prognoziruyemyye resul'taty'; Korotchenko, 'Voyennaya operatsiya v Chechene', p. 2; and Novichkov, *Rossiyskiye Vooruzhënnyye Sily v Chechenskom Konflikte*, p. 30.

49 Baev, 'Russia's Air power in the Chechen War', p. 10; and Marshall-Hasdell, *Russian Air power in Chechnya*, p. 3; Maksakov, I. 'Federal'naya gruppirovka ushla na peremiriye', *Nezavisimoye Voyennoye Obozreniye*, No. 17 (21), 12 September 1996; Lambeth, *Russia's Air Power in Crisis*, p. 134.

50 Novichkov, *Rossiyskiye Vooruzhënnyye Sily v Chechenskom Konflikte*, p. 30; Vorobyev, 'Legko prognoziruyemyye resul'taty'.

51 Thomas, 'The Case of Chechnya', p. 56.

52 Baev, 'Russia's Air power in the Chechen War', p. 12; Novichkov, *Rossiyskiye Vooruzhënnyye Sily v Chechenskom Konflikte*, pp. 117–19; Prokopenko, 'Voyna v Chechne'.

53 Blotskiy, 'General-Major Vladimir Syamanov: "Mne opravdyvat'sya ne pered kem"', p. 2.

54 J. Thomas, 'Dagestan: A New Center of Instability in the North Caucasus', 11 Oct. 1999, www.csis.org/ruseura/ex998.html

55 'Dagestan: khronika konflikta' (I), *Nezavisimoye Voyennoye Obozreniye*, 35 (158), 10 Sept. 1999, p. 2.
56 From 9 to 16 Aug. 1999 Putin was acting Prime Minister. On 9 Aug., in a television speech, Yeltsin announced Putin as his successor for the presidency. See www.peoples.ru/state/king/russia/putin/#bio. On 12 and 13 Aug. Putin made public statements on the fighting in Dagestan. See 'Dagestan: Khronika konflikta', *Nezavisimoye Voyennoye Obozreniye*, No. 32–36 (155–9), 20 Aug.–17 Sept. 1999, p. 2. The intensive involvement of Premier Putin in monitoring the operations in Dagestan was rather remarkable. According to Soviet/RF traditions of decision-making powers, the Prime Minister did not interfere with military or security matters, but was responsible for internal, social-economic affairs.
57 'Dagestan', p. 2. After his dominant role in the first Chechen conflict, Anatoly Kvashnin, who in the mean time was promoted to Chief of the General Staff, again fulfilled a key position in the operations in Dagestan. It became quite obvious that Kvashnin was more interested in commanding military operations than drafting security policy. Thus he apparently did not really interfere with the contents of the new military doctrine. He left these kinds of matters to his deputy, Colonel-General Valery Manilov.
58 P. Polkovnikov, 'Vtorzyeniye iz Chechni v Dagestan nachalos'', *Nezavisimoye Voyennoye Obozreniye*, 31 (154), 13 Aug. 1999, p. 1.
59 K. Tereenkov, 'Whirlwind over the Caucasus', *Air Forces Monthly*, Dec. 1999, p. 27.
60 Polkovnikov, 'Vtorzyeniye iz Chechni v Dagestan nachalos'', p. 1; 'Dagestan', p. 2.
61 The fact that initially the MVD received command and control over the operations in Dagestan corresponded with standard procedures, which stated that internal threats, such as revolt, riots and other forms of unrest were matters of the Other Troops of the power ministries, whereas the RF Armed Forces of the MoD were to counteract external threats, i.e. foreign aggressors. C.W. Blandy, *Dagestan: the storm*, P32, (Part II) (Camberley: Conflict Studies Research Centre, 2000), p. 27.
62 'Dagestan'.
63 'Dagestan: khronika konflikta' (II), *Nezavisimoye Voyennoye Obozreniye*, 32 (155), 20 Aug. 1999, p. 2.
64 Tereenkov, 'Whirlwind', p. 26; Polkovnikov, 'Vtorzyeniye iz Chechni v Dagestan nachalos'', p. 1.
65 Tereenkov, 'Whirlwind', p. 25; S. Sokut, 'Nevostrebovannyy potentsial', *Nezavisimoye Voyennoye Obozreniye*, 33 (156), 27 Aug. 1999, p. 2; A. Kornukov, 'Kontrterroristicheskaya operatsiya na Severnom Kavkaze: osnovnyye uroki i vyvody', *Voyennaya Mysl'*, 4 (2000), p. 6.
66 'Dagestan: khronika konflikta' (II), p. 2.
67 Blandy, *Chechnya: Two Federal Interventions*, pp. 34–5; 'Vozdushnaya voyna s banditami', *Nezavisimoye Voyennoye Obozreniye*, 37 (160), 24 Sept. 1999, p. 2; S. Babichev, 'Zyeleznyye argumenty VVS', *Krasnaya Zvezda*, 28 Sept. 1999, p. 1.
68 Blandy, *Dagestan*, Part II, p. 53.
69 'Vozdushnaya voyna s banditami', p. 2; Tereenkov, 'Whirlwind', p. 27; Blandy, *Dagestan*, Part III, p. 41.
70 'Dagestan: khronika konflikta' (III), *Nezavisimoye Voyennoye Obozreniye*, 34 (157), 3 Sept. 1999, p. 2.
71 Sokut, 'Nevostrebovannyy potentsial', p. 2.
72 C.W. Blandy, *Chechnya: A Beleaguered President*, OB61 (Camberley: Conflict Studies Research Centre, 1998); D. Billingsley, 'Chechnya seizes independence but unity still beyond its reach', *Jane's Intelligence Review*, Mar. 1999, pp. 14–18; and M. Galeotti, 'Chechen warlords still hold sway', *Jane's Intelligence Review*, Mar. 1999, pp. 8–9.

73 D. Balburov, 'Chechnya: just a little civil war', *Moskovskiye Novosti*, 30 July–5 August 1998, p. 3; Blandy, *Chechnya: a beleaguered president*, pp. 13–15; and M. Shevelyov, 'Chechnya: poor and dangerous again', *Moskovskiye Novosti*, 19–25 Feb. 1998.

74 S. Babichev, 'Bandity poluchat po zaslugam', *Krasnaya Zvezda*, 25 Sept. 1999, p. 1.

75 M. Khodarenok, 'Rukovodit' operatsiyey porucheno chekistam', *Nezavisimoye Voyennoye Obozreniye*, 3 (225), 26 Jan. 2001, p. 1.

76 'Diversii v Chechne', *Nezavisimoye Voyennoye Obozreniye*, 31 (301), 6 Sep. 2002, p. 2; *Military Balance 2000–2001*, p. 113.

77 Second Chechnya War, www.fas.org/man/dod-101/ops/war/chechnya2.htm

78 M.J. Orr, 'Russia's Chechen War Reaches Crisis Point', *Jane's Intelligence Review*, Oct. 2000, p. 17.

79 Khodarenok, 'Rukovodit' operatsiyey porucheno chekistam'; *Nezavisimaya Gazeta*, 5 Nov. 2002, p. 1.

80 M.J. Orr, 'Second time lucky?', *Jane's Defence Weekly*, 8 March 2000, pp. 34–5.

81 A. Aldis, *The Second Chechen War* P31 (Camberley: Conflict Studies Research Centre, 2000), p. 85.

82 Khodarenok, 'Rukovodit' operatsiyey porucheno chekistam'.

83 B. Nikolayev, 'V pylayushchem nebe Chechni', *Armeyskiy Sbornik*, 3 (2000), p. 32.

84 S. Sokut, 'Udary po banditam ne oslabeyut', *Nezavisimoye Voyennoye Obozreniye*, 45 (168), 19 Nov. 1999, p. 2.

85 Ye. Smyshlayev, 'Vertolety nad Chechney', *Nezavisimoye Voyennoye Obozreniye*, 38 (211), 13 Oct. 2000, p. 6.

86 S. Babichev, ' "Bazovyy" instinkt', *Krasnaya Zvezda*, 17 Nov. 1999, p. 2.

87 D. Fulghum, 'Air War in Chechnya Reveals Mix of Tactics', *Aviation Week & Technology*, 14 Feb. 2000, p. 77; J. Hedge, 'Air war over Chechnya', *World Air Power Journal*, 42 (2000), p. 18; A. Komarov, 'Chechen Conflict Drives Call for Air Force Modernization', *Aviation Week & Technology*, 14 Feb. 2000, p. 80; S. Babichev, 'V lyubykh usloviyakh, v lyuboye vremya sutok', *Krasnaya Zvezda*, 3 Nov. 1999, p. 3.

88 Smyshlayev, 'Vertolety nad Chechney'; Ye. Matveyev, 'Tridtsat' pyatyy: v srednem federal'nyye voyska terjayut v Chechne po vertoljotu v mesyats', *Nezavisimoye Voyennoye Obozreniye*, 30 (300), 30 Aug. 2002, p. 1.

89 Fulghum, 'Air War in Chechnya', p. 77; *Military Balance 2000–2001*, p. 114.

90 S. Babichev, 'Zyeleznyye argumenty VVS', *Krasnaya Zvezda*, 28 Sept. 1999, p. 1; Fulghum, 'Air War in Chechnya', p. 78.

91 Babichev, 'V lyubykh usloviyakh, v lyuboye vremya sutok', p. 1; S. Babichev, 'Razvedka s vozdukha', *Krasnaya Zvezda*, 6 Oct. 1999, p. 1.

92 Babichev, 'Bandity poluchat po zaslugam', Yu. Golotyuk, 'Groznyy bombili', *Izvestiya*, 24 Sept. 1999, p. 1; Babichev, 'Zyeleznyye argumenty VVS'.

93 V. Georgiyev, 'Rol' armeyskoy aviatsii vozrastayet', *Nezavisimoye Voyennoye Obozreniye*, 4 (177), 4 Feb. 2000, p. 2; Nikolayev, 'V pylayushchem nebe Chechni', p. 35.

94 Komarov, 'Chechen Conflict', p. 81; Fulghum, 'Air War in Chechnya'; p. 77; *Military Balance 2000–2001*, p. 114.

95 Georgiyev, 'Rol' armeyskoy aviatsii vozrastayet'. N.B.: MoD researchers had come to the conclusion that every lowest unit level (*zveno*, flight, four helicopters), should have an FAC at its disposal.

96 A. Kornukov, 'Kontrterroristicheskaya operatsiya na Severnom Kavkaze: osnovnyye uroki i vyvody', *Voyennaya Mysl'*, 4 (2000), pp. 5–10.

97 Sokut, 'Udary po banditam ne oslabeyut'; Aldis, *The Second Chechen War*, p. 86.

98 RF air component commanders, such as the VVS commander, Kornukov, repeatedly denied allegations regarding civilian casualties of air attacks: Babichev, 'Bandity poluchat po zaslugam'; Babichev, 'Zyeleznyye argumenty VVS'.

99 Sokut, 'Nevostrebovannyy potentsial', p. 2.
100 V. Aleksin and O. Finayev, 'V nebe nad Kavkazom', *Nezavisimoye Voyennoye Obozreniye*, 36 (159), 17 Sept. 1999, pp. 2; Babichev, 'V lyubykh usloviyakh, v lyuboye vremya sutok', pp. 1, 3; Sokut, 'Udary po banditam ne oslabeyut'; Nikolayev, 'V pylayushchem nebe Chechni', p. 33.
101 Fulghum, 'Air War in Chechnya', p. 76; Komarov, 'Chechen Conflict', p. 80.
102 Komarov, 'Chechen Conflict', p. 80; Hedge, 'Air War over Chechnya', p. 22; Smyshlayev, 'Vertolety nad Chechney'; Matveyev, 'Tridtsat' pyatyy: v srednem federal'nyye voyska terjayut v Chechne po vertoljotu v mesyats', p. 1.
103 Orr, 'Second time lucky?', p. 35; Babichev, 'V lyubykh usloviyakh, v lyuboye vremya sutok', p. 1.
104 Fulghum, 'Air War in Chechnya', p. 77; Komarov, 'Chechen Conflict', p. 80.
105 Blandy, *Chechnya: The Need to Negotiate*, pp. 10–12.
106 I. Safranchuk, 'Chechnya: Russia's Experience of Asymmetrical Warfare', p. 386.
107 A. Korbut, 'Ucheba v boyu', *Nezavisimoye Voyennoye Obozreniye*, 50 (173), 24 Dec. 1999, p. 2.
108 Second Chechnya War, www.fas.org/man/dod-101/ops/war/chechnya2.htm
109 Golotyuk, 'Groznyy bombili'.
110 Komarov, 'Chechen Conflict', p. 80; Babichev, 'Zyeleznyye argumenty VVS'; Babichev, 'V lyubykh usloviyakh, v lyuboye vremya sutok', p. 3.
111 Hedge, 'Air War over Chechnya', p. 22; Georgiyev, 'Rol' armeyskoy aviatsii vozrastayet'.
112 A. Zhilin, 'Udary po Chechne', *Moskovskiye Novosti*, 21 Sept. 1999, p. 5; Babichev, 'V lyubykh usloviyakh, v lyuboye vremya sutok', pp. 1, 3.
113 Nikolayev, 'V pylayushchem nebe Chechni', p. 34; Georgiyev, 'Rol' armeyskoy aviatsii vozrastayet'; Kornukov, 'Kontrterroristicheskaya operatsiya na Severnom Kavkaze', p. 5; S. Valchenko and K. Yuryev, 'Goryachiy vozdukh Kavkaza', *Armeyskiy Sbornik*, 2 (2001), p. 28.
114 'Peremeny v aviatsii', *Nezavisimoye Voyennoye Obozreniye*, 30 (300), 30 Aug. 2002, p. 3; Matveyev, 'Tridtsat' pyatyy', p. 1.
115 Second Chechnya War, www.fas.org/man/dod-101/ops/war/chechnya2.htm

5

CONCLUSIONS AND ASSESSMENT

In this final chapter the objectives and basic questions of this book will be answered. Next, the validity of the research will be discussed. Following this, I will expand on major developments after the year 2000 which influenced Russian foreign and security policies. In doing so, I shall analyse the consequences of the terrorist attacks against the United States of 11 September 2001, the dispute with Georgia on the Pankisi Valley and the 'Nord-Ost' stage-taking of October 2002, and assess the further development of Russia's security policy.

Conclusions

I have introduced the following objective to analyse the development of Russia's security policy: 'Acquiring insight into the development of Russian security policy. Subsequently, determining the realization and the contents of RF security policy. And, finally, analysing the effects of security policy for the use of air power, especially in irregular conflicts.' This objective was organized into four ordering principles:

1 What was the thought process of the Russian political–military leadership in formulating a security policy and establishing the armed forces?
2 Was Russian security policy characterized by a structural development or by opportunistic decisions?
3 What were the consequences of security policy for the build-up, tasks and status of the air forces?
4 What was the interaction between doctrinal thought and the experiences of the use of air power in and around Chechnya?

I have provided an overview of the decision-making process of Russian security policy from 1992 to 2002, and the security documents it generated, as well as the consequences of the policy for the air forces. On the *grand strategy* and *military-strategic* level I have discussed the development of the three leading security documents, i.e. the National Security Concept, the Foreign Policy Concept and the Military Doctrine. Subsequently, on the *operational and lower levels* of

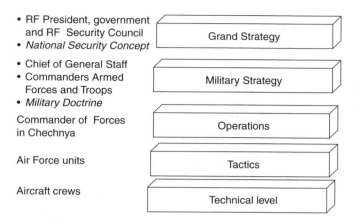

Figure 5.1 Levels of strategy of Russian security policy.

strategy I have concentrated on air power. I have described the consequences of Russian security policy for the organization and status of military aviation and for the RF Air Forces (VVS) especially. Next, in a case study on the conflicts in and around Chechnya, I have explained the practice of security policy in using air power in irregular conflicts.

Thought processes of the Russian political–military leadership in formulating a security policy and establishing the armed forces

General view on security thinking

For more than 70 years the Soviet citizen was raised in a world of Marxist–Leninist thought. In the USSR this ideology was the determining school of thought but also the theoretical basis of its grand strategy. In 1991 Marxist–Leninist ideology abruptly ceased to exist. As of 1992 this had consequences for the RF as the primary successor state to the USSR. In the field of security Russia was confronted with a two-fold vacuum, regarding its basic school of thought as well as a theoretical basis for its strategy. In due course the school of thought vacuum was filled by the dominant role of pragmatic thinking. This consisted of the perception that the RF was a great power with corresponding responsibilities, tasks and aspirations. The other vacuum, that of a theoretical basis for policy-making, also had to be filled. Leading Russian circles very soon came to the conclusion that a national security concept (NSC) would replace the annulled ideology. From the NSC, Russia's grand strategy, concepts of foreign and military policy would be derived. An important part of the RF military and political leadership is educated

173

in Soviet ideology. Taking this into account it is not remarkable that Russian security thinking in the 1990s still displayed features of the renounced ideology. The Soviet Union allotted itself a vanguard position in global class struggle. The three leading security documents show that Russia likes to fulfil a similar position, as a crucial actor in the international arena in general, and in the CIS especially. Another aspect is that the revolutionary nature of the Soviet state dictated the offensive as the leading form of combat. In the 1990s the Russian doctrinal development process unmistakably demonstrated that although its military doctrine from a political point of view was presented as defensive, in reality it increasingly emphasized the offensive as the leading form of combat. A final comparative aspect is threat perception. The USSR considered itself surrounded by the threat of hostile capitalist states. Russian doctrine also specified this 'encirclement syndrome'. Considering these comparative aspects I came to the conclusion that although Marxist–Leninist ideology was officially abandoned certain features of it remained vivid in Russian security thinking in the 1990s.

RF security policy was formally recorded in three documents, the NSC, the Foreign Policy Concept and the Military Doctrine. It would take until the end of the 1990s before a comprehensive security policy was reached in Russia. Not until December 1997 was the last but also the most important of the three documents, the NSC, published, which completed the theoretical basis of Russia's security policy. For a number of reasons it took six years before the whole spectrum of security policy was covered. The first reason was the hesitant approach of the executive and especially of President Yeltsin as to whether the security documents should be drafted for the CIS as a whole or exclusively for the RF, which was the choice in the end. Second, the Russian security elite debated heavily on which course to follow in foreign and security policies. Third, there was a struggle for power amongst the security organs, involving especially the MoD, the Ministry of Foreign Affairs and the Security Council of the RF (SCRF). For this reason the first Foreign Policy Concept as well as two Military Doctrines could be announced before the first NSC from which they were supposed to be drawn. Fourth, the period 1992–97 was characterized by instability, nationally (the 1993 conflict between the executive and the legislature and the first Chechen war), within the CIS (for instance, the civil wars in Tajikistan and Moldova) and in the Balkans. These circumstances delayed the further maturing of Russian security policy into an NSC. Only after consensus had been reached within the security elite and among the security organs and (inter)national circumstances had more or less stabilized, could a generally acceptable NSC be drafted.

National security concept

As mentioned earlier, initially President Yeltsin and his advisors had no clear view on the direction of Russia's security policy. For this reason there was no urgency in drafting a political strategy. In light of this it was peculiar that a proposal for a CIS Military Doctrine of February 1992 already specified an NSC as the leading security document. In May 1992 the choice was made. Yeltsin issued decrees which founded an RF MoD and RF Armed Forces, as well as the SCRF. This security structure opened the way for drafting an NSC. However, for the reasons mentioned, the first issue of this document would not appear until the end of 1997.

The NSC of 1997 in general provided a positive view of Russia in international developments and showed a realistic perception in considering the non-military, internal social-economic situation as the biggest threat. To improve these circumstances, Yeltsin's foreign and security policy was mainly oriented to the West, and consequently, Russia's policy was directed primarily at international cooperation, and the non-military means of RF international policy had received priority.

Within two years this outlook had changed radically. In the 1999 draft NSC the statement in the 1997 issue of the NSC that direct threats against the RF no longer existed, was declared out of date. Externally, the 1999 NSC documented an increase in number and strength of military threats, created in particular by NATO. Although internal threats were still listed as most important, external threats now prevailed in the NSC. This turning point had grown gradually in response to the progressively more leading role of this alliance in controlling international security, in which it did not refrain from using military force. The motives which gave rise to this new orientation in RF security policy were two-fold: NATO's new Strategic Concept of April 1999 and its military intervention in Kosovo of March–July in the same year. It should have come as no surprise to the West that Russia perceived NATO's security policy, which ignored the non-intervention principle of international law and Russia's position in the international arena, as a threat and felt itself forced to take action. Now the direction of RF security policy would change drastically and receive an anti-Western slant. Another aspect of change was the enlarged emphasis on economic, political and military cooperation within the CIS. This modification in foreign policy was not the result only of disappointment regarding cooperation with the West but also of a desire to restore its superpower status, which could best be realized within the CIS. This desire fitted into the framework of the thread of Russia's security policy which viewed itself as a great power. This perception was the result of pragmatism, which at the end of 1990s had become the leading trend in RF security thinking. The development of internal threats, such as the (first) conflict in Chechnya, had also necessitated adjustments in the NSC. Entries on internal policy in the (draft) NSCs of 1999 and 2000, aimed at reinforcing central authority, were a logical consequence of the assessment of the major internal difficulties. The chain of command of decisive organs of national security in the 2000 NSC unmistakably revealed that the President was the overall decision-maker in guaranteeing national security.

Foreign policy concept

At the time of the USSR overall responsibility in the areas of internal and external security were the prerogatives of the Politburo and the Secretary-General of the

CPSU. The RF Constitution of 1993 granted Russia's President similar responsibility. Hence it was the President rather than the Minister of Foreign Affairs who dominated RF foreign policy. Initially, Russian foreign policy, because of its unstable internal situation and subsequent economic dependence, proved to be outspokenly pro-Western. After 1993 as a result of discontent regarding lack of cooperation by the West, and the return of Russian 'imperial' thinking, the RF took a pragmatic nationalist course in its foreign policy, in which national interests dominated. In 2000 a revised edition of the Foreign Policy Concept was made public, replacing the 1993 one. In the introduction it stated that certain trends in international politics had compelled the RF to review its foreign and security policies. These negative trends were in contrast to the expectation, listed in the 1993 concept that multilateral cooperation would further intensify. In the 2000 issue major adjustments were listed, corresponding with those of the new NSC, specifying that the RF was a great power, that Russia's influence in international politics was to be strengthened, that cooperation and integration within the CIS would receive high priority; and that Western security policy was rejected.

The apparently contradictory views of a positive perception on international developments and a pro-Western course of 1993 on the one hand and the negative expectations and anti-Western sentiments of 2000 are manifestations of the dualistic nature of Russian foreign and security policy, which was dominant in the 1990s. Russian foreign policy put forward two different approaches. The first approach was characterized by accepting its declined post Cold War status, with emphasis on political and economic cooperation and integration in the international system, dominated by the West. The second approach emphasized sticking to (or regaining) great power status, which expressed itself in a desire for increased influence within the CIS and an emphasis on military and geopolitical instruments of policy. The danger of the first approach was that this could result in a position dependent on the West. The danger of the second approach was confrontation with the West, which could lead to isolation and a diminished international position. This dilemma of two sometimes contradictory policy directions, gave the impression that Russia's foreign policy was somewhat ambiguous in the 1990s. To correctly understand RF foreign and security policy it is therefore essential to bear in mind its dualistic nature.

Military doctrine

After the break-up of the Soviet Union, a number of CIS states created their own armed forces, independent of Moscow's wishes. Subsequently, Russia was forced to form separate RF Armed Forces. This also created the need for an RF military doctrine, which was published in May 1992. This draft Military Doctrine seemed to be the start of a movement towards a more assertive, confrontational Russian security policy, different from the above-all defensive and peaceful tone of the pervious Soviet doctrine. In the 1990s doctrinal development brought forward this assertive policy direction in entries on adopting a leading role for the RF in conflict resolution and military cooperation within the CIS; granting itself the right to protect Russian minorities in other CIS states, if necessary by using force; lowering of the nuclear threshold by abandoning 'no-first-use' statements; the return of terms such as 'opponents/enemies'; (forward) deployment of RF Armed Forces and Other Troops outside Russian territory; and a fierce anti-Western threat perception.

More specifically, doctrinal development in the 1990s included the following adjustments. The deteriorating relationship with the West was reflected in doctrinal entries on interference in internal Russian affairs; expansion of military blocs and alliances; attempts to ignore (or infringe on) RF interests in resolving international security problems and the feeling of being surrounded by enemies. Another illustration of the worsened relations was the development of doctrinal views on international military cooperation. Gradually cooperation with NATO disappeared from the doctrines.

As a residue of Soviet thinking that threats only came from abroad, internal threats were not recognized at first. However, experiences such as Yeltsin's clash with the legislature, armed conflicts within CIS states and, later on, the conflicts in Chechnya caused internal threats to be included in the doctrines since 1993. The growing importance of internal threats generated entries in other areas as well, for instance regarding the type of conflicts. During the 1990s the order of conflicts changed, from global and nuclear wars to local and internal armed conflicts being listed as the most important conflicts. The threat of global war had diminished. The Russian military–political leadership realized that the security apparatus would increasingly be faced with domestic and regional armed conflicts. This shift from external to internal conflicts was also reflected in the development of the perception of the use of military force. The emphasis changed from external large-scale warfare to operations within the CIS and joint operations of RF Armed Forces and Other Troops in internal conflicts. Another consequence of this change of warfare was expressed in doctrinal entries stating that the RF Armed Forces (of the MoD) could also be employed for internal operations and that cooperation between them and the Other Troops (of the power ministries) was essential.

The leadership of the security apparatus, as laid down in the command and control chain of the doctrine, has gradually been concentrated in the hands of the following institutions: the President, the Security Council, the Ministry of Defence and the General Staff of the RF Armed Forces. Clearly the consecutive doctrines gave evidence of power play by the military. Since drafting the doctrines was left mainly to the General Staff, the military leadership was to a great extent responsible for the assertive tone of the doctrines, as reflected in entries on the desire to control the former Soviet territory of the CIS and with regard to a fierce threat perception with a corresponding framework of tasks for the military. This forceful attitude was probably an attempt by the military to regain their strong influential position, which had shrunk under Gorbachev. Another example of their aspirations for power and influence was the fact that the SCRF, probably at the instigation of the military, was left out of the command and control chain in the doctrines of

1999/2000. Other entries were aimed at reducing the status and influence of the Other Troops. However, in doing so they found Putin in their way. After the Constitution of 1993 the President had a commanding position in doctrinal development, and the legislature no longer played a role in drafting or passing the doctrine. In the course of 2000, by moving responsibility for military reforms from the General Staff to the SCRF, Putin made it clear that he intended to strengthen the position of the SCRF at the expense of the MoD and the General Staff. It is likely that the reinforced position of the Security Council will be shown in future amendments to current security documents, such as the military doctrine.

Assessment

Summing up Russian security thinking in the 1990s the following can be said. The security discourse showed a development from an internationally orientated, pro-Western policy at the beginning of the 1990s, to a pragmatic and moderately nationalist policy in the following years. This pragmatic course combined power play with international cooperation. This two-fold or dual nature was characteristic of Russia's foreign and security policy. Externally two developments were of crucial importance for the contents of the RF security policy. The first major development was the Chechen conflict. The consequences of Russian interventions in Chechnya, such as bomb attacks in Russia, the high number of casualties on both sides, and (supposed) foreign support for the terrorists, led the Kremlin to believe that, once again, Russia was faced with internal as well as external military threats. This changed RF security policy to the extent that military means for conflict resolution and external threats now received the highest priority. A peaceful international outcome was no longer in prospect. Also, these conflicts demanded forces and troops to adjust their methods of warfare to these specific kinds of conflicts. Although the current military leadership was raised in large-scale warfare, doctrinal entries gave evidence to the fact that, perhaps reluctantly, at least a part of the military had come to realize that the spectrum of threats had changed from emphasis on external to internal threats. The second major development was the increasing role of NATO in international security. This role was demonstrated especially in the use of force in former Yugoslavia (Bosnia and Kosovo), its enlargement in an eastern direction and the adoption of a Strategic Concept granting itself the right to maintain international security in the Euro-Atlantic region, of which the boundaries were not specified. Both developments have promoted the introduction of anti-Western entries into the security documents of 2000. The solution to the internal threats of radicalization and separatism can to a large extent be found in the improvement of local and regional social-economic conditions by the RF government. Solving the second problem, anti-Western sentiments in Russia's security establishment and in the security documents it has produced, demands an active approach by the West. After '9/11' this insight has grown in the West. As of 2002, by increasing cooperation, NATO has made moves to improve its relationship with Russia.

The leading thread of Russian security thinking in the 1990s was that it perceived itself as a great power. This starting point has had consequences for its security policy, internally as well as externally. There was longing to regaining the status of superpower held by the former Soviet Union, possibly as a way out of Russia's internal and external difficulties. Lacking a sound economic base to support the status of superpower, military means, including the threat of using nuclear arms, became the best instrument to achieve this objective. Internally, a relationship was sought between domestic circumstances and Russia's international position by connecting the cohesion of the Russian state to the status of great power abroad. Externally, the principle of great power status led to a focus on the CIS politically, economically and militarily and to the entries in the security documents on the possibility of protecting Russian minorities abroad.

In the 1990s the pragmatic school of thought became dominant in Russia's security policy. This security policy originated from national interests, which in the case of threat, could be defended by every existing means of the state. Thus Russia conducted a firm course in international politics, in which international cooperation and power play could succeed each other.

Characterization of the development of Russia's security policy

Consequently, certainly until 1997, when the first NSC was made public, Russia's security policy was characterized by *ad hoc* decisions and opportunism.

After 1997 the RF security policy took shape. The majority of the policy-making elite had ranged themselves with pragmatic-nationalistic thinking. Furthermore, the policy scope for each of the security organs had been established. However, this overall consensus on security policy did not preclude continuing clashes among the security organs. There were also negative developments in Russia's security environment. In 1999 Russia clashed with NATO on the latter's intervention in Kosovo and domestically the second Chechen war was started.

By fulfilling consecutive positions such as Director of FSB, Secretary of the SCRF, Prime Minister and President, Putin clearly played a crucial role in the coordination and fine tuning of Russia's security policy. It is likely that his involvement and interest in security policy originated from his career in the security service. He conducted a resolute policy against the 'divide-and-rule' policy of his predecessor Yeltsin. Putin fulfilled his aim of controlling RF security policy by establishing a strongly centralized monopoly on security affairs combined with a strict personal command. He posted presidential plenipotentiary representatives to head regional power institutions, in order to strengthen central authority over the regions. Putin was well aware of clashes of opinion among the security organs, as had been the case throughout the decade. In order to prevent unilateral actions he realized that a consistent and strict supervision of these organs was essential. To accomplish this, he 'planted' individuals of his entourage, usually with a background in the forces, troops or security services, in the management of security organs and of other vital institutions and used the

179

SCRF as an overall institution by security policy. Although unilateral actions by security organs still occasionally occurred, these organs did not have the 'freedom of movement' which they had enjoyed under Yeltsin. Thus, as a result of these initiatives the power of the regions was reduced and control over the activities of the security organs was tightened. Abroad, Putin conducted a pragmatic and consistent policy in the tradition of the aforementioned dualistic policy, combining power play with international cooperation.

Shortly after the publication of the NSC in January 2000, subordinate documents such as the Military Doctrine and the Foreign Policy Concept were also reviewed. The order of publication and generally similar points of view of the different concepts gave proof of a well-coordinated and comprehensive approach to the foreign and security policies. Hence, 2000 can be considered as the year when the progress towards an integrated and comprehensive security policy was complete. It was especially to Putin's credit that a fairly stable and comprehensive foreign and security policy for the Russian Federation was accomplished.

The background to this achievement was two-fold. It was due in the first place to the individual; in contrast to Yeltsin, Putin was a healthy person with a steadfast view on what had to be done. The second part is found in the legalistic basis of Russian power. At the time of the Soviet Union the CPSU Politburo was the supreme power. Since the introduction of the Constitution of 1993 in the RF political constellation this position was held by the President. Although the President possessed all vital powers, it depended on the individual whether and how these were to be used. As mentioned earlier, Yeltsin acted by way of 'divide-and-rule'. Putin's presidential policy in contrast was dominated by a 'vertical' course, i.e. above all, authority dictated by the Kremlin. There was yet another similarity between the USSR Politburo and Russia's presidency. The executives of Soviet security policy, the Ministers of Defence, Foreign and Internal Affairs and the chief of the KGB, all of them members of the Politburo, reported directly to this institution instead of to the Council of Ministers. The political system of the RF resembled that of the USSR; the RF Ministers of Defence, Foreign and Internal Affairs and the directors of the various security services and other power ministries were in practice not subordinated to the government but to the President. Just like the Soviet Politburo, the RF President was able to control the security organs. However, Putin would make use of his presidential powers to a far greater extent than Yeltsin. Consequently, it was the combination of the nature of the individual and the legal background that brought about the consolidation of Russian security policy at the end of the 1990s.

Consequences of security policy for build-up, tasks and status of the air forces

Internal and external factors influencing air power

The development of Russian air power was influenced by internal as well as external factors. I would like to present four internal factors. The first internal factor was the end of the Cold War, which was accompanied by the annulment of the Warsaw Treaty Organization and the demise of the USSR. For Russian air power in the geostrategic field this resulted in the loss of buffer zones and forward air bases in Eastern Europe and the former Soviet republics. In the military field the consequences were first the end of an integrated military structure between Russia and the aforementioned states, for instance concerning air defence. Second, it demanded a restructuring of the order of battle (geographical distribution) of (air) units. Third, it resulted in the return to Russia of large numbers of personnel and *matériel* of dissolved air units of former Groups of Forces abroad and of former Soviet Military Districts. A second internal factor was the deteriorating economic situation of the country, which forced the RF government to drastically reduce the defence budget, including that of military aviation (Air [Defence] Forces and army aviation).

A third internal factor was the Chechen conflict. Warfare in both Chechen wars as well as in the Dagestani conflict had proved that RF military concepts, including that of air power, had to be changed from stress on large-scale conventional to internal, irregular warfare.

A fourth and final internal factor was the endeavour of the RF to regain superpower status, which had consequences for the allocation of resources to the different parts of military aviation.

Two external factors can be discerned regarding the development of Russian air power. The first factor was Western experience in using air power. The leadership of the RF Air Forces attached a lot of value to Western air power experiences in the Gulf War (1991), Bosnia (1995) and Kosovo (1999) and endeavoured to implement these lessons in procurement and doctrinal concepts of its own organization. A second external factor was the implementation of the CFE (Conventional Forces in Europe) Treaty, which also resulted in reductions and redeployments of aircraft, because of limited quotas on *matériel*.

I will elaborate on three aspects of the consequences: first, the influence of RF security policy on the priorities of air power; second, the policy of the Air Forces' generals in gaining power and influence and finally dualism in security policy as an obstacle for modern air power.

Consequences of RF security policy for air power priorities

Russia's security policy, which demanded annual cuts in the defence budget, affected the operational capabilities of military aviation, of *matériel* (aircraft) as well as of personnel. The Chechen conflicts proved that military aviation was not capable of operating either in bad weather or during the night, which the guerrilla type of warfare especially demanded. The shortage or absence of expensive precision-guided munitions, high-tech communications, navigation and targeting systems, as well as all-weather and day/night capabilities, reduced the combat readiness of military aviation. Another negative consequence of decreased defence budgets was the lack of fuel, spare parts and maintenance. As a result of the low funding levels pilot training and combat experience were insufficient as well. In 1999 average annual flying hours for attack aviation were around 23 and for bombers around 25, whereas Western (NATO) air force standards require 180 flying hours as a minimum for a skilled pilot. The lack of flying hours resulted not only in a higher rate of aircraft losses but also in less effective fulfilment of missions, for instance by dropping bombs too early. Although reorganizations such as the amalgamation of Air Defence and Air Forces produced cuts in personnel as well as in *matériel*, they did not bring about a structural improvement in combat readiness.

Another aspect of security policy was the preferential status of the strategic bomber force of the RF Air Forces. The desire of the political–military leadership to regain a superpower status gave rise to a focus on nuclear forces and power projection in the leading security documents. In turn this led to a special status for the strategic bomber force, because of its nuclear and long-distance capabilities. As a result of this privileged position the combat readiness level of this element became much higher than for the other parts of the Air Forces. Since the end of the 1990s the military–political leadership has regularly used the strategic bomber force in exercises for demonstrations of force, for instance by carrying out missions up to the US coastline. In June 1999 strategic bombers participated in the command-staff exercise *Zapad-99*, which was clearly Russia's reply to NATO's use of force in Kosovo. The renewed attention to the capabilities of the strategic bomber force for power projection corresponded very well with Russia's latest security concepts. This was a clear example of how the opportunistic views of the leadership were able to affect the build-up of the armed forces, at the expense of a long-term perspective on its structure.

Centralized control over air power: Air Forces' method of gaining power

In the 1990s, just as the other MoD services and troops of the power ministries, the Air Forces had to face structural cuts in their budget. Every force tried to make the best of these bad times, usually at the expense of the others. The Navy did so by introducing a naval doctrine including a powerful position for the Navy. The Ground Forces managed to create a situation in which all forces and troops within the Military Districts would be under their operational command, instead of being subordinated to their own staffs.

The Air Forces pursued a different course to strengthen their position. They did so by emphasizing the generally accepted principle of centralized command and control and decentralized execution of air power. Naturally this centralized command of air power would have to be placed in the hands of the Commander-in-Chief of the Air Forces. At the beginning of the 1990s Russian military aviation was divided among Air Forces, Air Defence Forces, Ground Forces (army aviation), Navy (naval aviation), Border Troops (aviation section) and Internal Troops (aviation section). Having promoted this reorganization since 1994, the

Commander-in-Chief of the Air Forces saw the merger of Air Defence and Air Forces implemented in 1998. In August 2002 the shooting down in Chechnya of an overloaded helicopter made the MoD decide to resubordinate army aviation from the Ground Forces to the Air Forces by the end of that year. Following this, in January 2003 the MoD announced that it would examine the pros and cons of resubordinating all other elements of military aviation to the Air Forces. Undoubtedly this statement was whole-heartedly welcomed by the Air Forces.

With the prospect of acquiring all military aviation, the position of the Air Forces among the other services and troops would be substantially consolidated. Consequently, the principle of centralized command and control of air power not only served the effectiveness of air warfare but was also beneficial for the status of the Air Forces.

Dualistic security policy as an obstacle for modern air power

One of the main characteristics of Russian security policy was its dualism. On the grand strategy level this was expressed by, on the one hand, accepting the post Cold War situation with internal threats outweighing external ones and cooperating with the West, for instance within NATO. The objective of this policy was to enhance the social-economic development of the RF, which prevailed over (military) political power play. On the other hand, Russia's security policy promoted 'imperial' views of power and influence. This was evident in efforts to regain superpower status and in stressing the threat of encirclement by hostile Western countries. The latter was included in the 2000 issues of the National Security Concept and the Military Doctrine, expressed in entries regarding an assertive attitude towards the West, reinforcement of Russia's position in the international arena and military solution of problems as the dominating instrument of security policy.

On the military-strategic level this dualism was implemented as follows. A realistic approach was demonstrated in the conclusion of some policy-makers that as a result of the end of the Cold War and the rise of internal conflicts, the armed forces should change their concepts accordingly, from large-scale to local, irregular warfare. However, conservative policy-makers, on the other hand, retained their focus on large-scale, conventional conflicts which was translated into emphasis on nuclear forces and on maintaining massive ground forces. These conservatives considered local, irregular conflicts such as Chechnya, and modern warfare with a leading role for air power, such as the Western air power experiences of recent years, as of minor importance.

The dualistic security policy was also reflected in the status and tasks of the Air Forces. On the positive side the convictions of the generals of the Air Forces, derived from Chechen and Western experiences, concerning the dominant position of air power in internal, irregular conflicts were adopted in the Military Doctrine. For dealing with these kinds of conflicts this security document demanded the formation of a unified air component subordinated to a joint military staff, which would be in command of the aviation units of all services and troops. Other entries covered intensified cooperation among MoD services and troops of power ministries, as well as a clear description of the dominating role of air power, in the form of air campaigns, air operations and air support for ground forces. This was a realistic view of developments with positive consequences for the Air Forces.

On the other hand, the stress on power projection and the enforcement of Russia's international position implied concentration of resources on large-scale warfare and nuclear capabilities. Except for the strategic bomber force, which benefited from this policy, the rest of the Air Forces suffered from structural cuts in manpower and *matériel* causing a diminishing combat readiness. Irregular warfare in Chechnya showed that the shortage or absence of sophisticated weaponry and avionic instruments limited the effectiveness of air power. However, these conservative views of an important part of the security establishment prevented the necessary improvements that might realize concepts of modern warfare, including a dominating position for air power.

In conclusion, it is evident that the most important structural problem for Russian air power was funding, due to the economic situation as well as to other priorities of the political–military leadership. But in spite of the financial problems, the RF Air Forces demonstrated that they were capable of enhancing effectiveness even without additional financial support. By promoting the principle of centralized command and control, the RF Air Forces managed to strengthen their control over air power. However, at the end of the 1990s as a result of priorities of the military–political leadership other than reinforcing air power, the combat readiness of the Air Forces was increasingly declining. This neglected position of the Air Forces was rightly characterized as a status of tailspin.

Interaction between doctrinal thought and the use of air power in and around Chechnya

This analysis of the interaction between doctrinal thinking and air power experiences is based upon data on doctrinal development, as mentioned in Chapter 2 (implementation of security policy), as well as on information provided on the Chechen air wars in Chapter 4 (implementation of air power, war around Chechnya). With respect to the interaction between doctrine and air power it is worth noting that the 1993 Military Doctrine was drafted before the first Chechen conflict started, at the end of 1994. Therefore, combat experiences had not yet been included in this doctrine. The 2000 Military Doctrine was published six months after the second Russian invasion of Chechnya, in autumn 1999. The Dagestan conflict is not separately taken into account in this assessment, because the operational use of air power in this conflict was very like that in the second Chechen war. Command and control, cooperation among the RF Armed Forces (MoD) and Other Troops (power ministries), as well as the employment of military force in internal conflicts come to the fore as the main aspects of interaction between doctrine and air power.

Command and Control

At the political and military strategic level the Military Doctrine of 1993 made a clear distinction between command of the RF Armed Forces and that of the Other Troops. This was put into practice in the first Chechen conflict when forces and troops, including the different air assets of the MoD and of the Internal Troops, acted on their own. The result was a disaster and frustrated the effective course of the operation. Keeping this experience in mind the Military Doctrine of 2000 took a different approach. According to the provisions in this doctrine the General Staff of the MoD, apart from commanding its own forces, was now also in charge of the joint (MoD and power ministries) employment of the military forces as a whole. In the second Chechen conflict these doctrinal entries were put into practice. Overall command and control was carried out by the Staff of the Joint Grouping of Forces, on behalf of the General Staff. However, at the beginning of 2001 this constructive move was hampered by transferring authority over the operation from the MoD to FSB, which was in fact 'window-dressing', aimed at proving that the military operation had ended and could be replaced by an anti-terror operation. Consequently FSB-led headquarters were formed in addition to Joint Staff HQ, thus damaging the 'unity of command' principle which, incorporated in the latest doctrine as a lesson learned. Hence, doctrinal insights were set aside by politically opportunistic decision-making. Although politics has primacy over doctrines, in this case the decision of the political leadership to overrule the doctrine was wrong.

Russian military doctrines usually aim at the highest levels of strategy and only modestly at the operational level. Thus it is not really surprising that the 1993 and 2000 doctrines make no mention of the (desired) command and control structure at this level of strategy. Nonetheless, the emphasis on joint performance of forces and troops in the 2000 Military Doctrine, as stated in entries on the political and military strategic levels, was echoed in practice at lower strategic levels as well: by creating a joint air component, at the operational or campaign level, this doctrinal demand was implemented in the second conflict. In the air component all elements of military aviation of MoD forces and Other Troops were unified under a single command, which strengthened command and control. In this way improvements in command and control were also reflected in a justified growing attention to the operational level of strategy.

Cooperation among armed forces and Other Troops

In the Military Doctrine of 1993 little attention was given to cooperation, among forces and troops. Pertaining to cooperation, this doctrine merely stated that military assignments were to be conducted by forces together with troops and that MoD forces could be used in support of Other Troops for internal operations, if these were not capable of handling the situation. The first Chechen conflict showed shortcomings in cooperation in air operations between VVS, ASV and aviation sections of the Internal Troops. Joint performances between air and land forces, in which FACs played a crucial role, also showed up deficiencies. Both developments demonstrated that ignoring provisions on a structured approach to cooperation between forces and troops proved to be a serious inadequacy of the 1993 Military Doctrine. As stated earlier, the 2000 Doctrine by demanding the formation of joint forces in resolving internal conflicts incorporated these lessons learned. In the second Chechen war, apart from the formation of a unified joint air component, cooperation between military aviation and ground forces was also improved. By conducting air barrages prior to the advance of troops, air power created favourable conditions for ground forces and lessened the possibility of friendly fire. Because FACs were deployed in more units and at lower tactical levels of the ground forces, they contributed to improved air–ground cooperation. Thus, in this case, the lessons learned, as written down in the doctrine, were well applied.

Employing military force in internal conflicts

Since the Russian–Chechen conflict had not yet started, it was not surprising, although perhaps somewhat short sighted, of the Military Doctrine of 1993 not to elaborate on solving internal conflicts. The absence of internal conflicts made the doctrine concentrate on external threats. Therefore the use of air power in the first conflict was not based upon doctrinal guidelines, which led to the aforementioned shortcomings, for instance in command and control. The lessons learned having been incorporated, the 2000 Doctrine not only extensively mentioned warfare in internal conflicts, but for the first time also dealt with levels lower than those of grand strategy and military strategy. Regarding air power, in this doctrine provisions on air campaigns, air operations, joint operations by (special) forces, as well as regarding air power missions of psychological and information warfare were set out. In the second conflict these doctrinal guidelines were applied by starting the hostilities with an intensive air campaign, providing air support for ground forces in the form of CAS, AI and transporting special units in anti-terror operations, as well as by providing air support for psychological operations. Thus air power was employed in line with the Doctrine.

Assessment

'Chechnya' made it clear to the political and military leadership that the threat of internal conflicts could no longer be ignored. In the Soviet Union, according to official statements, internal conflicts did not exist, simply because this would go against the ideology of one state, united by its socialist principles. Probably due to the fact that the majority of Russia's leading circles had only recently 'liberated' themselves from this ideological foundation, initially they found it difficult to accept the fact that internal armed conflict could break out in the RF. Thus, it was some time before these new perceptions were included in doctrinal documents.

Likewise, air power, as part of the armed forces, was left without doctrinal guidelines until the second Chechen conflict. The doctrinal guidance of forces and troops clearly improved between the first and second Chechen conflicts as a result of lessons learned. The growing emphasis on internal, irregular conflicts as well as the increased doctrinal attention to warfare at the lower levels of strategy was evidence of a more realistic approach of the General Staff towards current security threats. As a result, in the second Chechen conflict air power was supported by and used in accordance with doctrinal provisions, in (joint) command and control as well as in the actual use of force.

Clearly doctrine and the use of air power have influenced each other. The deficiencies of the 1993 Military Doctrine with regard to (joint) warfare in internal conflicts and the use of air power had disappeared in the 2000 Military Doctrine because of the inclusion of entries on these subjects. It is to be expected that future military doctrines will continue to give evidence of a development towards a further deepening of the interaction between (air) warfare experiences and doctrinal thought.

Validity

In order to present solutions to the basic questions posed earlier (p. 172) I have applied the following three methods: an analysis of development of and relationship among actors of security policy; a detailed comparison of security documents; and a case study in which the data and theoretical approaches are applied.

Development of and relationships among personnel

In analysing the development of RF security policy, alongside other methods, I have studied the involvement of some 40 individuals, most of whom belonged to one or more of the aforementioned institutions.[1] My choice of this specific group of security actors was determined by the sources. In the roughly 340 Russian sources I used, these individuals time and again were mentioned with regard to the drafting or explanation of particular elements of security policy. These persons belonged to the legislature or the executive, to departments or other central state agencies, law-enforcing organs, RF Armed Forces and Other Troops, academic circles, lobby organizations and the media. I was forced to make a selection in analysing individual actors, since it simply was not possible to study all persons involved in the decision-making processes of security policy. Multiple sources can underline the fact that the actors selected have made a vital contribution to the development of RF security policy. The great variety of individual and institutional actors analysed should preclude bias.

Comparison of security documents

Another method of analysing the development of RF security policy was a comparison in depth of the texts of the primary security documents, i.e. the

National Security Concept, the Foreign Policy Concept and the Military Doctrine. I am conscious of the risks involved in leaning heavily on official, probably biased texts. With regard to this method at least two critical remarks can be made. The value attached by Russian society and the military to these official documents as well as the influence of these documents on effecting security policy can be questioned. I will elaborate on these two points.

Views of public opinion and military on security documents

In meetings with journalists of independent Russian media I discovered that they did not take these documents seriously. However, when I asked them on what other foundation a judgement of Russian security policy could be based, I got no reply. A critical attitude of the independent media towards government policy is laudable but should be based upon facts, not on sentiments. Although the contents might be subjective, these documents remain the basis for and guide to RF security policy. Between the sometimes pompous entries they do show the development of views of the military–political leadership. I will go into further detail on this aspect below. Ignoring the official documents means that the independent media have less chance of understanding Russia's security policy.

During arms control inspections in Russia I have asked accompanying Russian officers what their opinion was of the latest edition of the Military Doctrine. They showed an obvious lack of interest in this document and usually replied that doctrine was an issue for the generals in Moscow and not for the common soldier in the field. In explaining this lack of interest in vital government documents I will not only focus on the military but include Russian society in general as well. Taking into account the deplorable status of the military apparatus it is well known to insiders that the average Russian officer has to put a lot of effort into his own survival and that of his family. The pay is bad and the social-economic conditions of the military are awful. Therefore, the military have matters to attend to other than discussing doctrine. Another aspect of the lack of interest in policy documents has to do with the contents. Russian military doctrines as well as the other leading security documents show a high degree of abstractness. This is in contrast to Western military doctrines, which are in fact operational concepts, dealing with the realities of warfare, and therefore are very down to earth for the soldiers in the field. Russian military doctrines are geared mainly to the military–political level, important for a general, but not for a commanding officer of a unit that is struggling to survive in the irregular Chechen conflict. This officer is interested primarily in successfully fulfilling his assignment with a minimum of casualties. Doctrines do not provide him with the required solutions, because they restrict themselves to the higher levels of strategy. Hence the lack of interest of the average officer, as well as of the average Russian citizen, who each day are involved in a struggle to survive, makes sense.

Influence of security documents on effecting security policy

A tradition which the RF inherited from the USSR is its legalistic approach; the state has a strong desire to record or base its policies in law. This also applies to security policy. The three main security documents provide a detailed description of issues, such as destabilizing factors, national interests, threats and military, political as well as social-economic measures for guaranteeing national security. I acknowledge that some of the entries in the documents can only be qualified as 'wishful thinking'. Examples of these are statements on Russia's status of a great power and control over the high seas. Russia still cannot cope with the fact that its position in the world is less than the superpower status which the USSR possessed. So, to a certain extent this is in line with opinions of doubt about the value of specific elements of the security documents. However, the policy intentions which are expressed should not be ignored. It is important to include these intentions in an assessment of the future development of RF security policy.

The analytical method of comparing texts can also contribute to establishing an accurate review of the present and future directions of security policy. The comparison of documents produces insight in two aspects: in the *evolution of the policy* itself and in the *position of the actors* in this policy. Regarding the *evolution of policy* three examples will underline the importance of this method of analysis. Comparison of texts on *security policy* shows for instance an augmentation of anti-Western sentiments and a gradual disappearance of conventional and nuclear 'no-first-use' statements. This suggests a move towards a more assertive stand in the international system. Not surprisingly, this tendency also appears in the implementation of policy. The raid of Russian forces on Pristina and the suspension of cooperation with NATO, as a consequence of NATO's intervention in Kosovo in 1999, can be considered as examples of this tougher attitude in foreign and security policy. A second example, dealing with *foreign policy*, has to do with the protection of Russian minorities outside of Russian territory. The wording used for describing 'in a foreign country', indicating the former Soviet republics, varies from the connotation of 'our legitimate sphere of influence' to 'abroad in general'. A final example of development, in this case of *military policy*, is the joint employment of RF Armed Forces (MoD) and Other Troops (power ministries) and the use of MoD forces in internal conflicts. Both of these policy adjustments, as shown in the development of military doctrine, were lessons learned in the Chechen wars. This raises the value of the doctrine, since these alterations are likely to be included in operational concepts, which enlarges the understanding and assessment of RF military policy. This knowledge is valuable, for instance for NATO's military cooperation with Russia. Therefore, it is worth studying the texts of security documents to gain insight into policy intentions. Of course, opinions might differ on whether the adjustments in policy were caused by changed circumstances or by the revised documents.

Concerning the *position of security actors* I have explained that predominantly in the first half of the 1990s the security organs were engaged in a struggle among themselves in order to gain supremacy over specific security documents. This rivalry among security organs regarding security documents and the assignment of duties presented a clear indication of their position in the field of security policy. That the relationship between security actors and security documents remained of essential importance, for instance was shown in autumn 1999, when the military put aside the SCRF in announcing a new military doctrine before the revised NSC was made public. This effort in overruling the SCRF corresponded with the proposed text of the new doctrine, in which the entry on the SCRF, as one of the vital organs in the chain of command of security policy, was deleted. I also mentioned that in 2000 Putin transferred responsibility for military reforms from the General Staff to the SCRF. Thus it would seem logical to expect that the SCRF to turn up again in the text as one of the organs in charge of security policy after the next revision of the doctrine. Consequently an interaction exists between security documents and policy.

Having discussed the influence of security documents on policy it is clear that an analysis of the documents provides a well-founded assessment of the present and future trends of RF security policy.

Case study: war around Chechnya

I have discussed the implementation of RF security policy in general and the use of air power, in particular, on the basis of a case study of the Chechen conflicts. This case study, comprising the first (1994–96) and second (1999–) Chechen conflicts as well as the Dagestani conflict (autumn 1999), offers adequate grounds for examining the national security policy and the use of air power. In contrast to Russian military intervention in conflicts in the CIS, in this case MoD forces as well as Other Troops were involved. Thus it was possible to see a connection between the development of security policy in Moscow and actual warfare in the Chechnya region.

A complication in using Russian sources for analysis could be reliability, especially when it comes to describing successes and setbacks of the implementation of security policy. This applies especially to the case of Chechnya. In this instance, the official RF sources have a tendency to overvalue the performance of their own forces and troops while disparaging the actions of the Chechen opponents. In order to provide an objective, factual account of the conflict situations, I described the operation of security policy around Chechnya by using a combination of official and independent Russian sources, supplemented by Western publications.

Further developments and outlook

The year 2000 showed the completion of the development process towards a comprehensive RF security policy in the form of revised versions of the three leading security documents. Of course internal as well as external developments in the field of security did not end that year. I wish now to look at developments after the year 2000 that had a major impact on Russian security policy. First, the consequences of the terrorist attacks against the United States of 11 September 2001[2] and the dispute with Georgia concerning the Pankisi Valley and finally the 'Nord-Ost' hostage-taking in Moscow in October 2002. These three developments had consequences for Russia, regarding its position in the world as well as the direction of its foreign and security policies, domestically as well as abroad.

'9/11': the influence of the 'War on terrorism'

I will now describe the way '9/11' affected foreign policy objectives, as laid down in the Foreign Policy Concept of June 2000.[3]

Supporting the principles of Russian foreign policy

On the positive side, Putin's support for the United States' war against terrorism during his visit to Germay, shortly after the attacks of '9/11', in its turn brought about Western agreement for Putin's fight against Chechen terrorism.[4] This support for Russia's struggle in Chechnya meant a break-through in the longstanding Western criticism of Russian violations of the law of armed conflict and human rights, especially by the Council of Europe and the European Union. Time and again Putin and representatives of his security establishment had stated in the media that the case of Chechnya was not only an internal issue for Russia, making foreign criticism irrelevant, but also that it had to be regarded as part of international extreme Islamic terrorism, as was the case with '9/11'. This admission by the West provided Putin with a justification to solve the conflict according to his own view, without foreign interference, by forcefully re-establishing RF law and order in Chechnya. The invasion of US and other Western forces in Afghanistan also supported Russian viewpoints regarding the fight against international terrorism and concerning the threat of border-crossing instability, which arose from the Taliban regime in this country. After '9/11' the RF cooperated closely with the United States to end the Taliban regime as well as the terror network of Osama bin Laden. This teamwork strengthened Russia's desired status of great power. Putin felt that Russia finally was taken seriously by the West. This had to result in an increase of Russian influence on international politics. The outcome of the reconsideration of NATO–Russia cooperation was to be the evidence of this strengthened position of the RF: Russia's input in NATO's decision-making process in the field of international security would increase.[5]

Counteracting principles of Russian foreign policy

Russia consistently attached great value to the United Nations and its Security Council (UNSC), among other reasons because of its veto right as one of its permanent members. Therefore, it was not surprising that the RF strongly rejected

Table 5.1 Developments after '9/11' in relation to the RF Foreign Policy Concept

	Corresponding or opposing principles in the RF Foreign Policy Concept
Positive developments for the RF	
The West recognizes 'Chechnya' as part of the war on terrorism	• to ensure reliable security of the country, to preserve and strengthen its sovereignty and territorial integrity
	• growth of separatism, ethnic-nationalist and religious extremism
International fight against islamic-extremist terrorism	• Russia regards as its most important foreign policy task to combat international terrorism which is capable of destabilizing the situation not only in individual states, but in entire regions
	• the protracted conflict in Afghanistan creates a real threat to security of the southern CIS borders and directly affects Russian interests
	• to promote elimination of the existing and prevent the emergence of potential hotbeds of tension and conflicts in regions adjacent to the Russian Federation
Strengthening of the ties between Russia and the West	• to achieve firm and prestigious positions in the world community, most fully consistent with the interests of the Russian Federation as a great power, as one of the most influential centres of the modern world
	• Russia has managed to strengthen its positions in a number of principal areas in the world arena
	• Russia shall seek to achieve a multi-polar system of international relations that really reflects the diversity of the modern world with its great variety of interests
	• Russian–US interaction is the necessary condition for the amelioration of the international situation and achievement of global strategic stability
	• relations with European states is Russia's traditional foreign policy priority
Strengthening of the cooperation between the RF and NATO	• Russia proceeds from the importance of cooperation with NATO in the interests of maintaining security and stability on the continent and is open to constructive interaction
	• substantive and constructive cooperation between Russia and NATO is only possible if it is based on the foundation of a due respect for the interests of the sides and an unconditional fulfilment of mutual obligations assumed
Negative developments for the RF	
Military action or presence of the USA and other Western powers in Afghanistan, in CIS	• Russia proceeds from the premise that the use of force in violation of the UN Charter is unlawful and poses a threat to the stabilization of the entire system of international relations
	• the United Nations must remain the main centre for regulating international relations in the twenty-first century. The Russian Federation shall resolutely oppose attempts to belittle the role of the United Nations and its Security Council in world affairs

countries (Central-Asia and Georgia) and in Iraq (as of 2003)	• strict observance of the fundamental principles in the UN Charter, including the preservation of the status of the permanent members of the UN Security Council
Annulment of the AMB treaty and further development of NMD by the USA	• Russia shall seek preservation and observance of the 1972 Treaty on the Limitation of Anti-Ballistic Missile (ABM) Systems – the cornerstone of strategic stability • the implementation of the plans of the United States to create a national missile defence (NMD) system will inevitably compel the Russian Federation to adopt adequate measures for maintaining its national security at a proper level • there is a growing trend towards the establishment of a unipolar structure of the world with the economic and power domination of the United States • the strategy of unilateral actions can destabilize the international situation
Infringements by the West of the traditional strong influence of the RF on CIS member states	• a priority area in Russia's foreign policy is ensuring conformity of cooperation with the member states of the CIS to national security tasks of the country • Russia attaches a priority importance to joint efforts towards settling conflicts in CIS member states, and to the development of cooperation in the military–political area and in the sphere of security, particularly in combating international terrorism and extremism • the Russian Federation will make efforts to ensure fulfilment of mutual obligations on the preservation and augmentation of the joint cultural heritage in the CIS member states • Practical relations with CIS member states should take into account the interests of the Russian Federation, including in terms of guarantees of rights of Russian compatriots
NATO's policy in international security	• in solving principal questions of international security, the stakes are being placed on Western institutions and forums of limited composition, and on weakening the role of the UN Security Council • attempts to introduce into the international parlance such concepts as 'humanitarian intervention' and 'limited sovereignty' in order to justify unilateral power actions bypassing the UN Security Council are not acceptable • NATO's present-day political and military guidelines do not coincide with security interests of the Russian Federation and occasionally directly contradict them. This primarily concerns the provisions of NATO's new strategic concept, which do not exclude the conduct of use-of-force operations outside of the zone of application of the Washington Treaty without the sanction of the UN Security Council • Russia retains its negative attitude towards the expansion of NATO

Source: 'Kontseptsiya vneshney politiki Rossiyskoy Federatsii', *Nezavisimoye Voyennoye Obozreniye*, 25, 14 July 2000, p. 4.

unilateral (military) interventions by states or international organizations, such as NATO's invasion in Kosovo in 1999 and the US–British invasion of Iraq in 2003. The US/Western intervention in Afghanistan, although backed by a UNSC resolution, was therefore also considered to be in breach of the corresponding guiding principles of RF foreign policy. Putin did not speak out against the deployment of US and other Western forces in Central Asian states of the CIS and in Georgia, although the RF regards them as part of its traditional sphere of influence. Putin's attitude differed from RF foreign policy fundamentals such as the threat of Western dominance over international security and the RF national interest of the CIS area as its exclusive 'back garden'. Not surprisingly other actors in Russia's security discourse fiercely resisted this interference by the West.[6] Even more remarkable was the fact that Putin withdrew his opposition to other Western policy plans, such as the unilateral cancellation of the Anti-Ballistic Missile (ABM) Treaty in December 2001 and the further development of National Missile Defense (NMD) by the United States, as well as NATO's intention of further enlarging its membership. The RF President's attitude did not agree with the guiding principles of the Foreign Policy Concept, which called for an opposite response.

Assessment

Since 11 September 2001, when the terror attacks in New York and Washington, DC caused the United States to start its 'War on Terrorism', Russia's international position has weakened, *physically* as well as *psychologically*. *Physically*, in the sense that the West has lodged itself in the traditionally Russian 'backyard' of the CIS. Already before '9/11' the West had gradually strengthened its position in this region. NATO achieved this through its cooperation programme 'Partnership for Peace' and the United States by conducting military exercises with some of the CIS states in Central Asia. Since '9/11' a remarkable turning point in positions has occurred. Many CIS states previously had been tied to the RF because of economic and/or military dependency. However, the growing Western presence in this area could very well end this dependency. The involvement of the West in the CIS is slowly appearing to be of the long-lasting kind. The United States has been investing hundreds of millions of dollars in airbases in Uzbekistan, Kyrgyzstan and Tajikistan.[7] It is not likely that these costly investments were made for stationing troops in that area for a limited period of time. Another aspect of these investments is that they lead to an economic impulse for the CIS states in question. It is said that the United States has to pay $7,000–7,500 for every air movement from and to Manas airbase in Kyrgyzstan. This Western, or better US, policy towards the CIS improves the economic as well as the security situation of a number of CIS states and subsequently diminishes their dependency on Moscow. This, then, leads to the conclusion that Russia has 'physically' lost ground in the CIS.

In a *psychological* sense Putin has also suffered defeat, from a national as well as from a CIS point of view; nationally after '9/11' Putin dropped his resistance to Western initiatives such as the annulment of the ABM treaty, the development of America's NMD and further enlargement of NATO. Russia's security and foreign affairs elite, including the two Ivanovs (Ministers of Defence, Sergey and Foreign Affairs, Igor) voiced a great deal of criticism of Putin, for giving in to the West. Putin's aspired status as a 'strong leader' might have been at stake, although his position does not seem to be threatened as yet. Putin has been 'psychologically' damaged also in the eyes of other CIS states, who have noticed that he was forced by the West to give way on a number of occasions. This has affected Russia's status within the CIS.

'9/11' was beneficial for the realization of Russian objectives in domestic as well as in foreign affairs, even though a number of these benefits have already faded away. After '9/11' the West recognized Russia's use of force in Chechnya to be a legal instrument against terrorism. Yet in the spring of 2002 Western criticism of Russia's actions in Chechnya revived, both from official circles and from the media and public opinion. Western support in fighting international terrorism indeed helped defeat the Taliban regime in Afghanistan, whose destabilizing capacity also threatened the RF. Nevertheless, these Western anti-terrorist actions in Central Asia have resulted in a long-lasting presence of the West in Russia's 'backyard'.

In May 2002 US President Bush and RF President Putin signed in Moscow a treaty with the intention of reducing mutual stocks of nuclear arms by two-thirds to an amount of 2,200 warheads per state in 2010.[8] On first sight this was a positive development, because the RF actually could not afford the huge costs of maintaining the stockpile of nuclear arms. On the other hand, the current editions of the NSC and Military Doctrine mentioned an important role for nuclear arms in preventing or solving armed conflicts. According to the need to uphold deterrence against aggression, as mentioned in these documents, a reduction of nuclear arms would demand an equal increase of conventional forces. However, this option would require financial resources. Therefore, the intention to reduce nuclear weapons did not agree with the corresponding entries in the security documents. Apart from this, the intended reduction no doubt would be met by a negative response from the proponents of a strong nuclear potential, in the military leadership and in the military–industrial complex. This could endanger the consensus within the decision-making elite on RF security policy.

One last important effect of '9/11' was the benefit of closer cooperation between Russia and NATO. Long negotiations led to meagre results. Not unexpectedly, the RF Chief of the General Staff (CGS) General Kvashnin was convinced that NATO still considered Russia its opponent.[9] At the NATO summit in Rome, on 28 May 2002, concerning the revised cooperation between NATO and Russia, it became clear that Russia still did not have a direct say in NATO's operational decision-making. On the other hand, in the new NATO–Russia Council issues were discussed by NATO's 19 member states and the RF together, in contrast to its predecessor, the Permanent Joint Council of 1997, in which NATO members only after reaching consensus discussed matters with the RF. However, although the meeting procedure had been improved, the rise in substantial involvement of the RF in NATO's decision-making process did not come up to Russia's expectations. In the NATO–Russia Council the RF was only allowed to have an equal say on a limited number of matters, such as the fight against terrorism, disarmament and non-proliferation of weapons of mass destruction. Russia did not receive a right of veto against unwelcome resolutions, nor was it invited to join the North Atlantic Council, which remained the decision-making body of the alliance.[10] The RF's anticipated 'structural deepening' of relations with NATO clearly was not yet the case. Cooperation between NATO and Russia had only improved to a limited extent. This being the final outcome of the negotiations, Minister of Foreign Affairs Igor Ivanov came to the conclusion that Russia should continue to reject further enlargement of the alliance.[11] Although Putin tried to present things differently, the reactions of Kvashnin and Ivanov were evidence of the fact that prominent representatives of Russia's security establishment persisted in their aversion to NATO as well as against the West in general. Hence the overall result of '9/11' has been mostly negative for Russia, in that it weakened its position both within the CIS and internationally, and has affected the earlier national consensus on security and foreign policy.

Dispute with Georgia on the Pankisi Valley

At the beginning of 2002 a conflict arose between Russia and Georgia regarding the Pankisi Valley, on Georgian territory. For more than one reason this example of foreign policy in practice is an interesting case. The dispute over the Pankisi Valley is an illustration of the transformed geostrategic relations in the region of the CIS, an extension of the Chechen conflict, as well as an expression of the dualistic nature of RF foreign and security policy.

Setting of the dispute

The dispute began early in 2002 when President Putin and both Ivanovs (Defence and Foreign Affairs Ministers) repeatedly voiced their disquiet regarding the presence of Chechen fighters in Georgia's Pankisi Valley. Their expressions of concern were accompanied by a warning that if Georgia did not neutralize these rebels, then Russia reserved to itself the right to prevent attacks on Russian territory, by pre-emptive RF military action into the Pankisi Valley. In September 2002 Putin allegedly instructed the General Staff to draft an operation plan to invade the Pankisi Valley. These threats in the direction of Georgia were repeated for months.[12] The allegations that Georgia offered shelter to Chechen rebels were not new. In autumn 1999, around the start of the second Chechen conflict, they had been made public for the first time.

Another point that made 'Pankisi' an interesting case for analysis of RF foreign policy was its relationship to '9/11'. After Western deployment of forces in Central Asia, related to the conflict in Afghanistan, in February 2002 the

United States and Georgia reached an agreement to deploy US military advisors in this Caucasian CIS state. In addition to this, the United States provided military equipment: 10 combat helicopters. US military assistance was meant to support Georgia in the fight against terrorism. In contrast to both Ivanovs, who protested against this US move, Putin, again, as in the case of Central Asia, did not oppose Western interference in the CIS.[13]

A third point had to do with the second Chechen conflict, which in 2002 had already entered its fourth year. In spite of frequent statements by RF authorities that Chechnya was 'pacified', the bloodshed on both sides continued. According to the highest levels of the RF Armed Forces an important reason for continuation of this conflict was found in the fact that Georgia was a free haven for Chechen fighters.[14]

'Pankisi' as a model of RF foreign policy

As mentioned, Russia's influence in the CIS had been diminished as a result of '9/11'. The international geostrategic relations had changed since Western forces had been deployed in parts of the CIS for an enduring period. Relations of CIS states with Western powers were strengthened, whereas relations with the RF were weakened. Thus, although probably reluctantly, Putin was forced to accept US military assistance to Georgia. In this respect it was painful that Georgian President Shevardnadze repeatedly declined Russia's offer to jointly fight terrorism. In addition to this, it was a thorn in Russia's side that Georgia at the same time showed much interest in joining NATO. Russia's political leadership, especially personified in both Ivanovs, as well as its military leadership, perceived these developments as a humiliation for Russia's position in this region.

In Chechnya the war carried on in the form of anti-terrorist actions of Russian MoD forces and Other Troops. With regard to Pankisi the RF military leadership distinguished three options to enhance Russia's (international) status. First, by diverting attention from the Chechen conflict. Second, to use Georgia as a scapegoat for the prolongation of the fighting in Chechnya;[15] and third, by carrying out an invasion, to possibly punish Georgia for its pro-Western stance and its unwillingness to cooperate with Russia. To justify a possible invasion against Chechen rebels, Putin appealed to the right of self-defence, as stated in the UN Charter.[16] Another foundation for the possible use of military force on Georgian soil came from CGS Kvashnin. He claimed that Russia, with the example of the new US doctrine of pre-emptive use of force, was entitled to do the same.[17] In comparing Russia with the United States Kvashnin personified the heartfelt wish of the RF political and military leadership to achieve a status similar to that of the United States, acting as a superpower without any restrictions. The security establishment refused to accept Russia's lower international status. By using force against Georgia it wanted to demonstrate to the international community that Russia's military power and international influence were still valid.

Assessment

In explaining RF foreign policy I stated that the nature of this policy was dualistic. On the one hand, it strove towards the maintenance or strengthening of Russia's international power and influence, in which military capabilities played an essential role. On the other hand, a part of Russia's security elite acknowledged that the important point in the international arena had changed from military to economic potential, in which international cooperation received a high priority. In the case of Pankisi this dualism in RF foreign policy was also displayed. The former direction in foreign policy, of sabre rattling with regard to the Western presence in the CIS and Chechen rebels sheltering in Georgia, was emphasized by both Ivanovs and General Kvashnin. In addition to them, Deputy Minister of Defence General Kosovan as well as the Duma expressed their feelings of concern regarding the deployment of the US military in Georgia. According to Kosovan this US involvement should upset every Russian soldier.[18] On some occasions even Putin threatened to use force against Georgia, but at the same time he also followed the other direction of RF foreign policy, aiming at international cooperation. He did not disapprove of the US military presence in Georgia and in October 2002 reached an agreement with Shevardnadze, in which measures were announced to lower tensions between their two countries.[19] Thus 'Pankisi' was a typical example of Russia's dualistic policy: on the one hand, expressing power play, by threatening to use force and striving to regain the status of superpower, whilst, on the other hand, simultaneously demonstrating international teamwork, by negotiating a peaceful settlement of the dispute and accepting the US presence in Georgia, in order not to damage (economic) cooperation with the West.

'Nord-Ost' hostage-taking: watershed for Russia's security policy?

In October 2002 Chechen fighters took hostages in a theatre in Moscow, in which the musical 'Nord-Ost' was being performed. Special forces (*spetsnaz*) units of the power ministries violently made an end to this act of terror. 'Nord-Ost' had brought the Chechen conflict into Russia's capital. As a result of this hostage-taking there was a broad feeling amongst Russian military–political decision makers as well as in Russian society that this terrorist attack meant a turning point in RF security policy, which was illustrated by the Russian press by describing 'Nord-Ost' as Russia's '9/11'.[20] On 29 October 2002, President Putin affirmed this defining moment by ordering his security ministers and chiefs to draft a revision of the NSC.

The case of 'Nord-Ost' had an impact on a number of elements of RF security policy. Three aspects in particular came to the fore: its influence on the Chechen conflict, on military reforms and on the legal foundation of security policy.

Intensification of the Chechen conflict

'Nord-Ost' forced Putin to prove that his firm commitment to breaking Chechen resistance and thus ending the conflict would now be put into practice. His reputation was at stake. Putin must have been well aware of the fact that to maintain his strong support in Russian society, he simply could not afford to loose this battle.

In the first Chechen conflict the Chechen resistance had demonstrated that hostage-taking was an excellent tactical weapon with political-strategic consequences. The total failure of RF Armed Forces and Other Troops to cope with hostage taking in Budënnovsk in June 1995, in which some 200 citizens and soldiers were killed, and in Pervomayskoye in January 1996, in which tens of *spetsnaz* officers as well as 90 citizens died, had been an important factor in the decision to withdraw Russian forces and troops from Chechnya at the end of 1996. The reputation of the military as well as that of President Yeltsin had suffered deeply from this defeat.

Putin was determined to prevent a recurrence of this failure and probably for this reason granted the anti-terror units great freedom of movement in solving the hostage situation of 'Nord-Ost'. This time the hostage-taking was brought to an end in favour of RF authorities. The fact that the solution of 'Nord-Ost' caused a large number of casualties among the hostages was probably due to the interests of the political and military leadership, who were resolute in winning this time. In order to deal with the Chechens once and for all, straight away after the end of the hostage-taking MoD Minister Sergey Ivanov intensified military action in Chechnya, fully supported by public opinion.[21] Taking into account the fact that *spetnaz* units conducted around 90 per cent of the operations of the Internal Troops, Putin decided to give them a high priority in finishing the Chechen conflict.[22]

'Nord-Ost' turned out to be a victory for Putin. It strengthened his conviction that the 'Chechen problem' could be solved by military means. His position and reputation, as well as that of the military leadership were secured. However, this triumph was a short-term one. In the long run intensifying military action in Chechnya as a result of 'Nord-Ost' would not lead to a peaceful settlement of the conflict. Not only critics from the West but Russian scientists also deplored the fact that Putin did not pay any attention to the dreadful socio-economic situation in Chechnya, which was a major cause of Chechen separatism.[23] A political resolution, making an end to the bloodshed of Chechen citizens as well as of Russian soldiers, remained a distant prospect.

Military reforms led by opportunism

For Putin, 'Nord-Ost' was a test case also in another way: his response to this terror attack would prove to what extent he controlled the security apparatus. As described earlier, power struggles among security organs (MoD and power ministries) had been a constant factor in Russian security policy of the last decade, which had consequences for military build-up and reforms. In the hostage taking of 'Nord-Ost', apart from back-up support by the military intelligence service GRU of the MoD, it was the special forces of the power ministries, the Ministry of Internal Affairs MVD (SOBR unit) and the Federal Security Service FSB

(*Alfa* and *Vympel* units), which took the lead and carried out the operation against the hostage takers.[24] In the recent past the MVD had been 'punished', by having its budget and personnel strength reduced, for its failures in the first Chechen conflict. Now, for killing the terrorists (and more than 100 hostages as well) the MVD, as well as the FSB, not only received a budget increase, but the intention to reform the MVD's Internal Troops into a Presidential National Guard and strengthen the FSB's command over the operation in Chechnya raised the status of both power ministries at the expense of other security organs, such as the MoD.[25] Hence in the aftermath of 'Nord-Ost' Putin decided to form a National Guard, consisting exclusively of professional soldiers and directly subordinated to the RF President. The commander of the Internal Troops was convinced of the fact that this proposed structure for his troops, closely related to the President, would be beneficial for the allocation of funds into their hands.[26] In addition to this, Putin decided to unite the different *spetnaz* units of the MVD into a rapid reaction force, directed at improving the fight against guerrilla warfare in Chechnya, as well as against terrorist attacks elsewhere in Russia.[27] Even Sergey Ivanov, although most likely reluctantly, had to acknowledge that it was not his department but the FSB that was in the forefront of the fight against terrorism, supported by MoD forces.[28]

These policy decisions expressed a constant factor of RF security policy in the 1990s: competition among security organs encouraged by a presidential military reform policy which rewarded security organs for successful operations while cutting budgets of departments whose troops had failed. This constant factor had two negative consequences. The aforementioned statement by the commander of the Internal Troops (see above) gave evidence of the fact that this opportunistic approach damaged the joint use of military force and was thus in contrast with a unified and harmonious military policy. Second, this structural feature of security policy demonstrated short-term thinking, which had a negative effect on a well-thought plan of military reforms. It seemed that Putin, just like the chiefs of the security organs, showed a tendency to support 'conjuncture' policy in the field of military reforms, which went against the solid build-up of the security apparatus.

Revision of the legal foundation of security policy

Shortly after 'Nord-Ost', parliamentarians such as Aleksey Arbatov and Andrey Nikolayev, as well as academic security specialists, declared in public that this hostage taking had demonstrated that the current legal system lacked a normative basis for an effective fight against acts of terror.[29] The existing legal system did not live up to the demands of the necessary anti-terrorist operations; for the structure of these operations provisions concerning a joint approach (MoD forces together with troops of the power ministries) were absent, and for the actual conduct of operations legal grounds for the use of *spetsnaz* units were needed. For that reason, current legislation, such as the Constitution, the NSC, the Military Doctrine, the laws on anti-terrorism, defence as well as on a state of emergency was to be revised. In addition to this, new legislation was to be passed on the joint use of forces, troops and security organs in internal conflicts, on the deployment of RF Armed Forces, an anti-terror concept and a law on fighting terrorism. The plea for adaptation of current legislation and the introduction of dedicated additional legislation, concerning operations against terrorism, not only touched upon laws and security documents, but included operational directives of forces and troops, which to a large extent were still directed at large-scale warfare.[30] Apart from legislation, another essential aspect of an effective fight against terrorism came to the fore: command and control of anti-terror operations. Politicians and scientists demanded that one security organ be put in command of anti-terror policy, which as a principle and coordinating security institution would head all security organs involved. Arbatov, Nikolayev and other security experts also pleaded for one person to be responsible for anti-terror operations.[31]

As mentioned before, on 29 October 2002 President Putin instructed his security ministers and chiefs to draft a revision of the NSC. According to MoD Minister Ivanov the adjustments to current legislation would include the following provisions: intensifying the involvement of the RF Armed Forces in fighting terrorism, assessing the increased threats against national security and the readiness of the RF to act against terrorists but also against their sponsors abroad. After revising the NSC, the Military Doctrine was to be altered, followed by other security documents subordinated to the NSC.[32]

Assessment

The anticipated revision of security policy was ambivalent. On the one hand, recognizing the growing importance of internal threats and conflicts seemed to be a realistic approach by Putin. This was in contrast to the focus on large-scale warfare, which conservative circles in the General Staff, by emphasizing nuclear instead of conventional forces, still considered to be the primary conflict. If the repeated conflicts in Chechnya and Dagestan did not make this clear, then surely 'Nord-Ost' proved that the primary threats to Russia's national security were of an internal nature. Therefore it would make sense that the revised Military Doctrine as well as other security documents took account of the increased importance of non-nuclear military resources, which would correspond with the current threat perception.

Another positive effect was the conviction that power struggles among security departments definitely should make place for overall command and control by one security organ. The conflicts in and around Chechnya made perfectly clear that, in particular, shortcomings in command and control had resulted in the failures of the military. The latest edition of the Military Doctrine (2000), as well as the way warfare was conducted in the second Chechen conflict, emphasizing joint performance of operations by forces and troops, showed that the military leadership had learned from its failures in the past. The fact that this policy was now extended to anti-terror operations in Russia as a whole was justified and logical.

On the subject of appointing a principal and coordinating security institution in charge of anti-terror action, and taking into account Putin's demand for centralized control of security policy, Russia's Security Council (SCRF), consisting of the President and the chiefs of all security departments and services, was likely to be selected for this capacity.

On the other hand, the ambivalence came to the fore with regard to the trend of the proposed revision in security policy, stressing military solutions and not social-economic ones. The vast number of policy concepts and laws, which were to be drafted in the aftermath of 'Nord-Ost', unmistakeably highlighted stress on military and political solutions to the problem of terrorism. However, not violence and oppression but social-economic support by providing housing, food and medical care could take away the grounds for internal conflict, which were expressed in poverty, unemployment and lack of education. Another feature of ambivalence was the fact that Russian authorities repeatedly made it clear that the RF granted itself the right to attack terrorists abroad. This option to use force abroad was not to be conducted by an invasion of troops, but by employing precision-guided munitions in operations against terrorist training camps or against other targets out of the country, which were related to international terrorism.[33] By doing so, the RF permitted itself to violate norms of international law, such as the prohibition on using force and the non-intervention principle, as laid down in the UN Charter.

The aforementioned policy intentions of using military force against internal (terrorist) threats and if necessary against targets abroad as well were not new concepts. These entries were already included in the existing security documents but were now to be stepped up. The emphasis in security policy remained on military instead of social-economic solutions, although a swift change from external to internal threats was rightly included. This gave the impression that current policy principles would continue. Consequently, 'Nord-Ost' did not result in a watershed for Russian security policy.

Outlook

After the terrorist attacks of '9/11' President Putin took a pro-Western course. In the long run, Putin desired to strengthen Russia's international position, not excluding the use of military means to achieve this. However, Putin realized quite well, in contrast to many Soviet leaders, that nowadays influence on a global level is more than ever based on economic leverage. Taking this into account, his rapprochement towards the West, and especially towards Europe, did not seem strange. Closer cooperation with the EU could serve more than one objective of Russian policy. First, economic cooperation with Europe would most likely bring about growth in the Russian economy, which in turn would enhance Russia's international position. Second, closer ties with the EU might also weaken the relationship between Europe and the United States, even more so if Russia supported, or participated in, the further development of an independent European security policy with its own military power, which possibly could be in contrast with US interests. From a weakening or even split in the Trans-Atlantic camp Russia naturally could benefit in the international arena, by promoting its foreign policy principle of multipolarity in international politics and Russia's status as a great power. At the start of the second Gulf War, in March 2003, Putin was well aware of this policy option of splitting the Trans-Atlantic, Western camp. In their plea in the UNSC for military intervention against Iraq, the United States and the UK were diametrically opposed to Germany and France. Putin supported the latter in their rejection of the use of force by, just like France, threatening to use the right of veto, and, after 'Operation Iraqi Freedom' was launched, by strongly worded condemning the use of force.[34] Once again the RF reaction demonstrated the dualistic nature of its policy. On the one hand, Putin used the division in the Western camp to strengthen Russia's status in the international community. At the same time, he apparently had instructed Foreign Affairs Minister Igor Ivanov to use more measured words towards the United States, thus serving the other side of Russia's dualistic policy: cooperation with the West in order to improve the RF economy.[35] Putin's policy regarding the war against Iraq was definitely also intended for domestic consumption. His firm stand against the United States created goodwill among the conservative representatives of the RF security elite, who had rebuked Putin for his pro-American attitude since '9/11'. Hence, in the case of the second Gulf War, by adhering to the customary dualistic approach, Putin managed to accomplish the national as well as international objectives of RF foreign and security policy.

Russia's present and future foreign and security policy is laid down in three documents: the NSC, the Foreign Policy Concept and the Military Doctrine. Major points of view in the 2000 editions of these documents were an assertive attitude towards the West, a strengthening of Russia's position within the CIS as well as on a global level, and lastly an emphasis on military means as an instrument of security policy. The leading security documents have originated in the Russian security establishment, consisting of generals, politicians, diplomats and scientists. Judging from their criticism of Putin's gestures towards the West, the state of mind of this elite did not change after '9/11'. Putin's positive policy towards the West since '9/11' had only manifested itself in public statements. Thus Putin's rapprochement with the West did not imply a structural change of Russian foreign and security policy. After 'Nord-Ost' Putin ordered a revision of security documents, to make them more applicable to (Russia's) fight against terrorism. The extent to which anti-Western rhetoric was removed from these documents was to show the depth of Putin's positive stance towards the West as well as his control over his hard-line opponents. However, the following account shows little hope of a turning point in the anti-Western course.

In January 2003 the Academy of Military Sciences of the RF General Staff held its annual conference.[36] The tone of this conference, at which speeches were delivered not only by military scientists but also by the CGS and the Minister of Defence, revealed that Russia's security establishment had not freed itself from its conservative views. The lectures of Army-General Makhmut Gareyev, President of the Academy of Military Sciences, and other representatives of this institute, evidently expressed a continuation of anti-Western tendencies. For example, NATO allegedly was using the fight against terrorism to weaken Russia's military power. Furthermore, MoD Minister Sergey Ivanov stated that maintenance of a nuclear potential of deterrence was the highest priority of military policy. And CGS Kvashnin pointed at the threat of a large-scale conflict and emphasized the importance of Russia's position as a key player in the international arena. Only rarely at this conference was attention paid to Putin's order to set the fight against terrorism as the primary task of forces and troops. Clearly this conference revealed that the political as well as the military leadership of the MoD stuck to the basics of the 2000 issues of the security documents, underlining an anti-Western stance, reinforcing Russia's international stature and military means as the primary policy instrument.

The United States' '9/11' and Russia's 'Nord-Ost' made a big impression on international security thinking, also on Russian policy-makers in this field. Putin's policy was one of pragmatism. After '9/11' it was opportune to support the West. However, if so demanded by RF interests, Putin would turn the helm, especially if the pressure of his security elite forced him to do so. This was the case with the 2003 war against Iraq. 'Nord-Ost' reinforced already taken steps in improving unified control over military and anti-terrorist actions, which had been the outcome of lessons learned from the Chechen conflicts. This did not mean a new course in security policy. Other evidence of prolongation of existing tendencies in security thinking were the stress on military means in solving 'Chechnya' and the prominence of Russia's great power status at the conference of the Academy of Military Sciences. This then leads to the conclusion that '9/11' and 'Nord-Ost' had some bearing on Russia's thought processes on security, but did not result in a turning point for RF security policy.

RF President Putin had to balance the pressures of his security establishment with reinforcing Russia's economic capacity. Putin's policy was symbolic for the dualistic nature of RF foreign and security policy. On the one hand, international (economic) cooperation was continued and internal conflicts received a higher priority in security thinking. On the other hand, Russia continued to claim a great power status in the international arena. And a large part of the RF security establishment remained on putting the accent on preparation for large-scale conflicts, on sabre-rattling with nuclear arms and in its feeling of encirclement by the hostile West. RF security policy is characterized by manoeuvring between traditional Russian imperial thinking, in terms of power and influence, and in recognizing Russia's new post Cold War status, resulting in cooperation with the West. Prolongation of this dualism is likely to be the future of the foreign and security of the Russian Federation.

Notes

1 See Appendix I: Biographies of security policy actors.
2 I will refer to the terrorist attacks of 11 Sept. 2001 as '9/11'.

3 'Kontseptsiya vneshney politiki Rossiyskoy Federatsii', *Nezavisimoye Voyennoye Obozreniye*, 25, 14 July 2000, p. 4.

4 'Poetin krijgt ovatie in Bondsdag', *NRC–Handelsblad*, 26 Sept. 2001.

5 A.A.C. de Rooij, 'Nieuwe start in relatie met Rusland', *Reformatorisch Dagblad*, 6 Oct. 2001.

6 M. Khodarenok, 'Ozherelye iz Amerikanskikh baz', *Nezavisimoye Voyennoye Obozreniye*, 10, 29 March 2002, p. 4.

7 Khodarenok, 'Ozherelye iz Amerikanskikh baz', and ' "Starshego brata" sdali za milliard dollarov', *Nezavisimoye Voyennoye Obozreniye*, 4, 8 Feb. 2002, p. 3.

8 'Amerikaanse veiligheidsinspanningen', *Atlantisch Perspectief*, 26, 4 (2002), p. 28.

9 'Russia-NATO Talks on New Form of Partnership Hit Stalemate', *Radio Free Europe/Radio Liberty Security Watch*, 3, 9, 8 March 2002.

10 'NAVO-Rusland Raad nieuwe stijl', *Atlantisch Perspectief*, 26, 4, 2002, pp. 27–8.

11 'With No Right of Veto for Kremlin', *Radio Free Europe/Radio Liberty Security Watch*, 3, 14, 23 April 2002.

12 *Radio Free Europe/Radio Liberty Security Watch*, 3, Feb.–Oct. 2002.

13 *Radio Free Europe/Radio Liberty Security Watch*, 3, 8, 1 March 2002, and 9, 8 March 2002.

14 V. Solovyev, 'Doktrina uprezdayushchikh deystviy po-Moskovski', *Nezavisimoye Voyennoye Obozreniye*, 33, 20 Sept. 2002, pp. 1–2.

15 In autumn 2000 and again in September 2001 there were already indications that the Russian military leadership had intentions to seize Chechen fighters in the Pankisi Valley. See M.J. Orr, 'Russia's Chechen War Reaches Crisis Point', *Jane's Intelligence Review*, October 2000, p. 18; Blandy, *Chechnya: The Need to Negotiate*, p. 3.

16 'Putin Warns Georgia over Toleration of Chechen "terrorism" ', *Radio Free Europe/Radio Liberty Security Watch*, 3, 32, 19 Sept. 2002.

17 Solovyev, 'Doktrina uprezdayushchikh deystviy po-Moskovski'.

18 'Russian Defense Official Expresses Concern over US Military Role in Georgia', *Radio Free Europe/Radio Liberty Security Watch*, 3, 14, 23 April 2002.

19 'Putin, Shevardnadze Soften Russia–Georgia Discrepancies', *Radio Free Europe/ Radio Liberty Security Watch*, 3, 35, 8 Oct. 2002.

20 V. Solovyev, 'I vsë-taki my pobedim', *Nezavisimoye Voyennoye Obozreniye*, 39 (309), 1 Nov. 2002, p. 1.

21 'New Military Offensive in Chechnya', *Radio Free Europe/Radio Liberty Security and Terrorism Watch*, 3, 39, 5 Nov. 2002; 'Backs Harsh Reaction', *Radio Free Europe/ Radio Liberty Security Watch*, 3, 39, 5 Nov. 2002.

22 Solovyev, 'I vsë-taki my pobedim'; V. Udmantsev, 'My gotovim universal'nykh soldat', *Nezavisimoye Voyennoye Obozreniye*, 39 (309), 1 Nov. 2002, p. 3.

23 A. Sudoplatov, 'Voyna tol'ko nachinayetsya', *Nezavisimoye Voyennoye Obozreniye*, 39 (309), 1 Nov. 2002, p. 1.

24 'Nord-Ost', dossier *Nezavisimaya Gazeta*, 2002, www.ng.ru/special/NordOst; A. Khokhlov, 'We Did Not Injure a Single Hostage', *Izvestiya*, 28 Oct. 2002, p. 1.

25 Solovyev, 'I vsë-taki my pobedim'; 'Duma Allocates More Funds for Fighting Terrorism', *Radio Free Europe/Radio Liberty Security Watch*, 3, 41, 19 Nov. 2002.

26 'Nord-Ost'.

27 Udmantsev, 'My gotovim universal'nykh soldat'.

28 'Defence Minister says Russia Is at War', *Radio Free Europe/Radio Liberty Security Watch*, 3, 40, 12 Nov. 2002.

29 S. Sokolov, 'Poslesloviye k "Nord-Ostu" ', *Nezavisimoye Voyennoye Obozreniye*, 39 (309), 1 Nov. 2002, p. 8, and 'Neobkhodima reorganizatsiya spetssluzhb Rossii', *Nezavisimoye Voyennoye Obozreniye*, 40 (310), 15 Nov. 2002, p. 1; S. Bogdanov, 'Voyna vne zakona', *Nezavisimoye Voyennoye Obozreniye*, 38 (308), 25 Oct. 2002, p. 4; 'Orders

revision of national security concept', *Radio Free Europe/Radio Liberty Security and Terrorism Watch*, 3, 39, 5 Nov. 2002; A.I. Nikolayev, 'U nas – terroristicheskaya voyna', *Nezavisimoye Voyennoye Obozreniye*, 40 (310), 26 Nov. 2002, p. 1.

30 Bogdanov, 'Voyna vne zakona'.

31 Sokolov, 'Poslesloviye k "Nord-Ostu" ', and 'Neobkhodima reorganizatsiya spetssluzhb Rossii'; Nikolayev, 'U nas – terroristicheskaya voyna'.

32 V. Solovyev, 'Zvezdoy po terrorismu', *Nezavisimoye Voyennoye Obozreniye*, 42 (312), 29 Nov. 2002, p. 1.

33 'Defence Minister says Russia Is at War'.

34 'Putin Says Iraq Crisis Most Serious Conflict since End of Cold War', *Radio Free Europe/Radio Liberty Security Watch*, 4, 13, 1 April 2003.

35 'Foreign Minister Concerned by US Efforts to Seize Iraqi Assets', *Radio Free Europe/Radio Liberty Security Watch*, 4, 12, 26 March 2003; 'Putin Stresses Need to Avoid Conflict with US', *Radio Free Europe/Radio Liberty Security Watch*, 4, 14, 9 April 2003.

36 V. Solovyev, 'Nash Genshtab otvetchayet NATO', *Nezavisimoye Voyennoye Obozreniye*, 2 (317), 24 Jan. 2003, pp. 1, 3.

APPENDIX I

Biographies of security policy actors

Adamishin,
Anatoly Leonidovich
(1934)

Former First Deputy Minister of Foreign Affairs
(1992–94); expert on European politics.

Member of SVOP; career in MID, among others
ambassador in Italy and Britain (1957–97); Soviet
Deputy Minister of Foreign Affairs (1986–90);
Duma member on behalf of *Yabloko* (1993–94);
Minister for Cooperation with CIS states
(appointed August 1997).

Arbatov,
Aleksey Georgiyevich
(1951)

Deputy Chairman Duma defence committee
(since 1994); defence expert and proponent of
genuine and structural military reforms.

Duma member of *Yabloko* (1993–); member of
SVOP, scientific researcher for RAS (1976–94):
analyst for ISK(R)AN; head of the centre for
international security of IMEMO.

Baluyevsky,
Yuri Nikolayevich
(1947)

First Deputy Chief of the General Staff (since
27 July 2001); Colonel-General; in August
2000 nominated by the Russian press as
candidate CGS.

Military career as officer of operations; functions
in the GS main directorate of operations
(1982–88); Chief-of-Staff of RF forces in
Trans-Caucasus (1993–95); posts at and chief of
GS main directorate of operations (1995–2001);
succeeded Manilov as First Deputy CGS.

Baturin,
Yuri Michaylovich
(1949)

Former Secretary Defence Council RF
(July 1996–August 1997); cosmonaut; in August
2000 nominated by the Russian press as
candidate Minister of Defence.

Associated with the Gagarin training centre for cosmonauts; participated in space flights in 1998 and 2001; member of SVOP; studied aero physics, law and journalism; functionary of space agency *Energiya* (1973–80); member of the RAS Institute of State and Law (1980–93); different posts in the presidential apparatus in legal and security matters (1993–97); presidential assistant for national security (January 1994–June 1996); chairman interdepartmental commission on disarmament of chemical weapons (appointed November 1995); passed the General Staff Academy course as civilian.

Bordyuzha,
Nikolai Nikolayevich
(1949)

Former Secretary SCRF (September 1998–March 1999).

Career in KGB, FAPSI and Border Troops (1976–95); Deputy Director Federal Border Guard Service (1995–98); Director Federal Border Guard Service (until September 1998).

Deynekin,
Pëtr Stepanovich
(1937)

Former commander-in-chief of the Air Forces VVS (September 1992–January 1998); army general (retd.); December 1994 allegedly personally instructed the air assault on Chechnya to destroy the Chechen air force; air power expert and publicist.

Career in the strategic air force DA; commander DA (1988–90); first deputy commander-in-chief of the Soviet Air Forces (1990–91); commander-in-chief of the Soviet Air Forces and Deputy Soviet Minister of Defence (appointed September 1991); commander-in-chief of CIS Air Forces (appointed February 1992); promoted to army general (June 1996).

Dmitriyev,
Mikhail Arkadyevich

Deputy Minister of Defence for equipment and chairman committee for military–technical cooperation with other states (appointed March 2001); Lieutenant-General (retd.).

Career in the foreign intelligence service SVR; Deputy Minister for Industry, Science and Technology (spring 2000–March 2001).

Fradkov,
Mikhail Yefimovich
(1950)

Ambassador to the European Union
(appointed 11 March 2003); as Minister of
Trade associated with arms export; August 2000
nominated by the Russian press as candidate
Minister of Defence.

Career in the Soviet Ministry for Foreign
Economic Relations (as of 1984); First Deputy
Minister for Foreign Economic Relations
(appointed October 1993); Minister for
Foreign Economic Relations and Trade
(appointed April 1997); Minister for Trade
(appointed May 1999); First Deputy Secretary
SCRF (appointed May 2000); Director Federal
Tax Police (March 2001–03).

Gareyev,
Makhmut Akhmetovich
(1923)

President of the Academy of Military Sciences
(1993–); army general; prominent military
scientist (over 250 publications); in the 1990s
frequently changed his views from anti- to
pro-Western.

Veteran of the Second World War; member
scientific council SCRF; military career with
postings such as Soviet military advisor in
Egypt and Afghanistan (1989–91), commander
Frunze Military Academy, chief GS directorate
military science and Deputy Chief of the
Soviet General Staff for operational training
and military science (1980s).

Gorbachev,
Mikhail Sergeyevich
(1931)

Former President of the USSR (1990–91).

Member of the CPSU Central Committee
(as of 1971); member Presidium Supreme
Soviet (1985–90); Secretary-General CPSU
(1985–91); since 1992 active in civic
organizations such as the International Green
Cross and Civil Forum.

Grachev,
Pavel Sergeyevich
(1948)

Former Minister of Defence (May 1992–June
1996); army general (retd.); chose Yeltsin's side
in the *coup d'état* of August 1991; outspoken
proponent of strong armed forces.

Career in the Airborne Troops; served for five
years in Afghanistan; commander Airborne
Troops (December 1990–September 1991);

first Deputy Soviet Minister of Defence and chairman Defence Committee RSFSR (appointed September 1991); first RF Deputy Minister of Defence (March–May 1992).

Gryzlov,
Boris Vyacheslavovich
(1950)

Minister of Internal Affairs MVD (appointed March 2001); expert of defence in space.

Engineer, career in private enterprises in the field of (space) communications systems; member of Duma for Putin's party *Yedinstvo* (appointed December 1999); chairman Duma group of *Yedinstvo* (appointed January 2000).

Ivanov,
Igor Sergeyevich
(1945)

Minister of Foreign Affairs MID (appointed 11 September 1998).

Scientific researcher IMEMO (1969–73); career in Soviet and RF MID (1973–93); First Deputy Minister of Foreign Affairs under Kozyrev and Primakov (December 1993–September 1998).

Ivanov,
Sergey Borisovich
(1953)

Minister of Defence *Minoborony* (appointed 28 March 2001); Lieutenant-General SVR (retd.); friend of Vladimir Putin.

Studied English and Swedish; career in the KGB in foreign intelligence; was posted in Leningrad together with Putin; SVR General (appointed mid-1990s); Deputy Director FSB (appointed August 1998); Secretary SCRF (November 1999–March 2001); resigned as general when he was appointed to the SCRF.

Ivashov,
Leonid Grigoryevich
(1943)

Vice-President of the RAS Academy for Geo-Politics (as of 2001); reserve Colonel-General; hawkish attitude towards the West; fierce opponent of NATO's campaign in Kosovo in spring 1999.

Career as political officer; staff member MoD (as of 1976); Secretary CIS Council of Defence Ministers (1992–96); head of the MoD main directorate for international military cooperation (1996–July 2001).

Karaganov,
Sergey Aleksanderovich
(1952)

Chairman presidium Council on Foreign and Defence Policy SVOP (as of 1994); liberal adherent of Gorbachev's 'new thinking' (1980s);

frequently mentioned in the press as foreign and security expert.

Deputy director RAS Europe Institute (appointed 1989); member scientific council SCRF (since 1993); member MID council for foreign policy (as of 1991); started career at ISKAN RAS (1978–88); subsequently joined the Europe Institute.

Klebanov,
Ilya Yosifovich
(1951)

Minister for Industry, Science and Technology (appointed 18 February 2002); associated with the military–industrial complex (MIC) and arms trade; in August 2000 and March 2001 nominated by the Russian press as candidate Minister of Defence.

Engineer; career in St. Petersburg enterprise for optical instruments (1977–97); first Vice-Governor of St. Petersburg for economic and industrial affairs (appointed December 1997); Deputy Prime Minister (as of May 1998); Deputy Prime Minister and Minister for Industry, Science and Technology (appointed October 2001).

Klimenko,
Anatoly Filippovich

Former head of the GS centre for military-strategic research TsVSI (1999–mid-2001); reserve Lieutenant-General; member of the RAS Far East Institute (since mid-2001); expert on doctrine and strategy.

Member scientific council SCRF; career started at the Tank academy; postings at the GS (1986–2001); published a proposal for a CIS doctrine, which subsequently became the foundation of the first RF Military Doctrine (February 1992); involved in the drafting of NSC and Military Doctrine documents (second half 1990s).

Kokoshin,
Andrei Afanashevich
(1945)

Deputy chairman of the Duma committee on industry and technology; fulfilled a broad variety of posts in defence and security; civilian defence expert and publicist of military–political works; proponent of military reforms. In August 2000 nominated by the Russian press as candidate Minister of Defence.

211

Member of the Duma party 'Fatherland is Entire Russia', led by Primakov; member scientific council SCRF; member of SVOP; former deputy director of ISKAN (appointed 1984); first Deputy Minister of Defence (1992–96); Secretary Defence Council (1997–98); Secretary SCRF (March–September 1998); acting vice-president of RAS (1999).

Kornukov, Anatoly Michaylovich (1942)

Former commander-in-chief of the Air Forces VVS (January 1998–2002); army general (retd.); complained frequently about the deplorable combat readiness of VVS, which allegedly was the reason Putin refrained from further delaying his retirement from the military.

Career in the Air Defence Forces VPVO up to the level of commander of a VPVO army; commanded the military action in which a Korean airliner was shot down (September 1983); commander PVO District Moscow (appointed September 1991).

Kozyrev, Andrei Vladimirovich (1951)

Former RSFSR and RF Minister of Foreign Affairs (October 1990–January 1996); had to cope with fierce criticism for his pro-Western course.

Career followed in the Soviet MID (1974–90 allegedly was nominated for the post of MID Minister of the RSFSR by Eduard Shevardnadze (1990); during the *coup d'état* of August 1991 sought support of the international community on behalf of Yeltsin; member of SCRF (October 1993–December 1995); involved in the formation of the party Vybor-Rossii, led by Gaydar (1993); member of Duma, first for the party Vybor-Rossii and next as an independent representative (December 1993–99).

Kudelina, Lyubov Kondratyevna (1955)

Deputy Minister of Defence for financial and economic affairs (appointed 28 March 2001); first female functionary in the management of MoD; financial expert; aimed at optimal efficiency of the defence budget.

Economist; career with the Ministry of Finance, in which she was responsible for financial

supervision over the power ministries as well as
for military–industrial questions; Deputy Minister
of Finance (as of July 1999).

Kvashnin, Anatoly Vasilyevich (1946)	Chief of the General Staff and first Deputy Minister of Defence (appointed 19 June 1997); army general; had a public dispute with Minister of Defence Sergeyev on the primacy of conventional or nuclear forces (summer 2000); allegedly undermined the position of the next minister, Ivanov, with the intention of being appointed as successor.

Member of SCRF (as of June 2000); Military
career as tank officer; postings at GS
(since 1992); commander first campaign in
Chechnya (December 1994–February 1995);
commander Military District North-Caucasus
NCMD (February 1995–May 1997).

Lebed, Aleksandr Ivanovich (1950–2002)	Former Governor of the region Krasnoyarsk (until 2002); supported Yeltsin in the *coup d'état* of August 1991; led the negotiations with the Chechens which ended the first Chechen war (August 1996).

Military career in the Airborne Troops up to the
rank of Lieutenant-General; Afghanistan veteran;
commander RF 14th Army in Moldova
(1992–95); reached third position in the RF
presidential elections (summer 1996);
Secretary SCRF (June–October 1996); died in
a helicopter crash (28 April 2002).

Lobov, Oleg Ivanovich (1937)	Former Secretary SCRF (1993–96). First Deputy Prime Minister and Minister of Economy (appointed 1993), Deputy Prime Minister (mid-1996–March 1997).

Manilov, Valery Leonidovich (1939)	Former First Deputy Chief of the General Staff (September 1996–July 2001); Colonel-General (retd.); 'founding father' of editions of NSC and Military Doctrine; August 2000 nominated by the Russian press as candidate CGS.

Member of the Federation Council of the RF
Parliament (appointed August 2001); first
deputy chairman of the Federation Council

committee on defence and security; member of
SVOP; military career as political officer;
military journalist, no operational experience;
staff member of the MoD (as of 1978);
postings in information services of MoD and
CIS (until 1993); Deputy Secretary SCRF
(1993–96); chairman SCRF interdepartmental
commission on drafting the NSC (as of 1994);
acting chairman interdepartmental commission
on drafting the military doctrine (as of 1998);
military retirement (July 2001).

Mikhaylov,
Vladimir Sergeyevich
(1943)

Commander-in-chief of the Air Forces VVS
(appointed 21 January 2002); Colonel-General;
was aware of the deplorable status of VVS
but at the same time convinced of Russia's
leading role in the world, to which VVS would
have to make a vital contribution.

Military career in the VVS; among others in
command posts in the Military Districts of
Moscow (MOMD) and North-Caucasus
(NCMD) and as commander of an air army
(1985–mid-1990s); deputy commander-in-chief
VVS (1998–2002); considering his age, close to
the retirement age of 60 years, as commander-
in-chief VVS he was not likely to have much
influence on essential reforms in the VVS.

Moskovsky,
Aleksey Michaylovich
(1947)

Deputy Minister of Defence for armament of the
Armed Forces (appointed 28 March 2001);
Colonel-General; fulfilled vital posts in MIC
and in arms export; in August 2000 and March
2001 nominated by the Russian press as
candidate Minister of Defence.

Appointed by First Deputy Minister of Defence
Kokoshin as first deputy chief of MoD
armaments (mid-1990s); Deputy Secretary
Defence Council as assistant of Kokoshin
(1997–98); Deputy Secretary SCRF, responsible
for military reforms (May 1998–March 2001);
protégé of Minister of Defence Ivanov.

Nikolayev,
Andrei Ivanovich
(1949)

Chairman Duma defence committee; army
general (retired December 1997); in March 2001
nominated by the Russian press as candidate

Minister of Defence; was a proponent of civil control on military affairs but also adhered to Russia's desired status of a great power, supported by military power.

Independent member of Duma on behalf of a district in Moscow; specialist on military–social matters; military career leading up to the post of First Deputy CGS (1992); Deputy Minister of Security (August–December 1993); Commander Border Troops (1993–94), Director Federal Border Guard Service (December 1994–97); member Defence Council and SCRF (1994–97).

Primakov,
Yevgeni Maksimovich
(1929)

Chairman of the Duma party 'Fatherland is Entire Russia'; fulfilled a broad scope of state functions on foreign and security affairs.

Member of the Duma committees on CIS and on relations with compatriots abroad; member of SVOP; started career as director IMEMO (appointed April 1985); member of the Presidential Council of Gorbachev (as of March 1990); Chief of SVR (October 1991–January 1996); Minister of Foreign Affairs (January 1996–September 1998); Prime Minister (September 1998–12 May 1999).

Putin,
Vladimir Vladimirovich
(1952)

President Russian Federation (as of 31 December 1999); strong proponent of centralized control over the state at the expense of the regions; generated synchronized security documents (2000), exercised more control over security organs as well as over foreign and security policy than his predecessor.

Lawyer; career in the KGB in its first main directorate (foreign intelligence) (1975–90); served as such five years in the DDR; resigned from the KGB (20 August 1991); posts at the university and municipality of Leningrad/St. Petersburg (1991–96); functions in the presidential apparatus (August 1996–June 1998); Director FSB (July 1998–August 1999); Secretary SCRF (March–August 1999); Prime Minister (as of August 1999); as *protégé* of

Yeltsin nominated for the presidency by the
latter in a television speech (9 August 1999);
appointed by Yeltsin as acting President RF
(31 December 1999); elected as President RF by
52 per cent of the voters (26 March 2000);
inaugurated as second President RF
(7 May 2000).

Rodionov,
Igor Nikolajevich
(1936)

Former Minister of Defence (17 July 1996–
23 May 1997); army general (retd.); tried to
subject national security policy to military
doctrine (May 1992); held hard-line conservative
views on security policy in favour of a strong
and unified RF and rejected Putin's policies.

Duma member for the communist party KPRF
(as of 1999); member of the Duma committee
for veterans' matters; military career with the
tank troops; commander 40th Army in
Afghanistan (1985–86); commander Military
District Trans-Caucasus (1986–89);
responsible for forcefully breaking down revolt
in Tbilisi, Georgia (April 1989); commander
General Staff Academy (1989–96); first
'civilian' Minister of Defence; because of his
military retirement (December 1996); adhered
as Minister of Defence to progressive ideas
regarding military reforms; chairman of the new
radical left-wing People's Patriotic Party
(23 February 2002).

Rog,
Valentin Grigoryevich
(1924)

Prominent air power expert and publicist;
Major-General VVS (retd.); convinced of a
decisive role for air power in modern warfare;
fervent proponent of a strong air force as
guarantee for Russia's national security.

Member of the GS Academy of Military Sciences
and of the RAS Academy of Natural Sciences;
advisor to the Federation Council committee
on defence and security; military career in the
VVS, among others for 14 years as professor
at the General Staff Academy; frequently
published air power and military build-up
related articles together with former VVS
commander-in-chief, Deynekin.

Rogov,
Sergey Michaylovich
(1948)

Director of the RAS Institute on the United States and Canada ISKRAN (as of 1995); has taken an influential position in the realization of RF security policy since 1992, when he pleaded for a national security strategy.

Member scientific council SCRF; member of the consultative council of MID; advisor to the foreign affairs committees of Duma and Federation Council; well-known publicist on foreign and security affairs, published over 300 articles and 16 books; career at ISK(R)AN (as of 1976); deputy director ISK(R)AN (1991–95).

Rushaylo,
Vladimir Borisovich
(1953)

Secretary SCRF (appointed March 2001); MVD Colonel-General; would allegedly in this position concentrate on restoration of law and order in Chechnya as well as on the fight against corruption.

Career in the militia-police of the MVD; specialised in fighting organized crime; First Deputy Minister of Internal Affairs (March 1998–May 1999); Minister of Internal Affairs (May 1999–March 2001).

Sergeyev,
Igor Dmitriyevich
(1938)

Former Minister of Defence (23 May 1997–28 March 2001); marshal RF (retd.); advisor of the RF President on strategic stability (as of March 2001); proponent of strong nuclear capabilities.

Military career in the Strategic Missile Forces RVSN; commander RVSN (August 1992–May 1997); promoted to marshal (1998); had a public dispute with CGS Kvashnin on his attempt to prolong the primacy of nuclear forces over conventional forces (summer 2000).

Shaposhnikov,
Yevgeni Ivanovich
(1942)

Advisor of the RF President on air and space research (as of 1997); VVS marshal (retd.); supported Yeltsin in the *coup d'état* of August 1991; was proponent of continuation of the former Soviet army as integrated CIS Armed Forces.

Military career in the Soviet Air Forces VVS; commander-in-chief Soviet VVS and

Deputy Soviet Minister of Defence
(July 1990–91); Soviet Minister of Defence
(August–December 1991); commander-in-chief
CIS Unified Armed Forces (January 1992–June
1993); Secretary SCRF (June–September 1993);
functions in military industry and as director
Aeroflot (1994–97).

Yeltsin,
Boris Nikolayevich
(1931)

Former President RF (June 1991–December
1999); led the resistance against the *coup d'état*
of August 1991 but subsequently deprived
Gorbachev and the USSR of their powers in
favour of the RSFSR/RF, which resulted in the
collapse of the USSR (August–December 1991).

Career in the CPSU (1968–90); Secretary Central
Committee CPSU (1985); candidate-member
Politburo CPSU (1986–87); because of a
critical attitude removed from the Politburo
(October 1987); member of RSFSR Parliament
(1990); gave up CPSU membership at its 28th
Congress (1990); Chairman Supreme Soviet
RSFSR (1990–91); elected as first President
RSFSR/RF (June 1991); co-founder of the
CIS (December 1991); acting RF Minister of
Defence (March–May 1992); ordered military
action to disband the Supreme Soviet and
subsequently introduced a Constitution with
dominating powers for the President
(October/December 1993); elected for a
second term as President (summer 1996);
appointed Vladimir Putin as his successor
(31 December 1999).

Sources: www.mil.ru; www.days.peoples.ru; www.nns.ru/ssi/persons.cgi; www.whoiswho.ru; www.ras.ru; www.svop.ru; www.duma.gov.ru; www.council.gov.ru; www.mil.ru; www.mn.ru; www.atlcom.nl; www.ng.ru; www.nvo.ng.ru; www.rian.ru; www.president.kremlin.ru; www.gov.ru; www.scrf.gov.ru.

APPENDIX II

Main Russian aircraft types used in the Chechen conflicts

NATO code name	Russian designation	Type/task	VVS component
Backfire	Tu-22M3	Strategic bomber	DA
Candid	Il-76	Transport	VTA
Clank	An-30	Photo reconnaissance	FA
Cock	An-22	Transport	VTA
Condor	An-124	Transport	VTA
Coot	Il-20	Signal intelligence/EW	FA
Cub	An-12	Transport	VTA
Curl	An-26	Transport	VTA
Fencer-D	Su-24M	Fighter-bomber	FA
Fencer-E	Su-24 MR	Reconnaissance	FA
Fitter	Su-17/22M	Fighter-bomber	FA
Flanker	Su-27/30	Interceptor	PVO
Foxbat-D	MiG-25RBK	Reconnaissance	FA
Foxhound	MiG-31	Interceptor	PVO
Frogfoot	Su-25 *Grach* (rook)	Ground-attack	FA
Halo	Mi-26	Heavy transport helicopter	ASV
Hind	Mi-24	Combat helicopter	ASV
Hip	Mi-8	Transport helicopter	ASV
Hip	Mi-9	Command and control helicopter	ASV
Mainstay	A-50	Air warning; command and control	FA/PVO

BIBLIOGRAPHY

Adamishin, A.L. 'Naskol'ko bezopasna nyneshnyaya Yevropa?', *Nezavisimaya Gazeta*, 2 Nov. 2000, p. 3.

Agapova, Ye. 'Rossiya bez kryl'ev – ne Rossiya', *Krasnaya Zvezda*, 15 Aug. 1992, pp. 1–2.

Akhromeyev, S.F. *Voyennyy Entsiklopedicheskiy Slovar'* (Moscow: Voyenizdat, 1986).

Aldis, A. *The Second Chechen War* (Camberley: Conflict Studies Research Centre, 2000).

Aleksin, V. 'Aviatsiya v "shtopore" ', *Nezavisimoye Voyennoye Obozreniye*, 4 (164), 22 Oct. 1999, p. 6.

Aleksin, V. and Finayev, O. 'V nebe nad Kavkazom', *Nezavisimoye Voyennoye Obozreniye*, 36 (159), 17 Sept. 1999, p. 2.

The Alliance's Strategic Concept (Brussels: NATO Office of Information and Press, 1999).

'Amerikaanse veiligheidsinspanningen', *Atlantisch Perspectief*, 26, 4 (2002), p. 28.

Antoshkin, N.T. 'Speech at the RNLAF Base Leeuwarden on 20.4.93', in R.W. Dellow, *Organization and Equipment: Priorities for the Russian Air Force*, B52 (Camberley: Conflict Studies Research Centre, 1993).

'Aviatsiya poiznosilas'', *Nezavisimoye Voyennoye Obozreniye*, 38 (308), 25 Oct. 2002, p. 3.

Babichev, S. 'I prikrytiye, i karayushchiy mech', *Krasnaya Zvezda*, 25 June 1999, p. 1.

Babichev, S. 'Bandity poluchat po zaslugam', *Krasnaya Zvezda*, 25 Sept. 1999, p. 1.

Babichev, S. 'Zyeleznyye argumenty VVS', *Krasnaya Zvezda*, 28 Sept. 1999, p. 1.

Babichev, S. 'Razvedka s vozdukha', *Krasnaya Zvezda*, 6 Oct. 1999, p. 1.

Babichev, S. 'V lyubykh usloviyakh, v lyuboye vremya sutok', *Krasnaya Zvezda*, 3 Nov. 1999, pp. 1, 3.

Babichev, S. ' "Bazovyy" ' instinkt', *Krasnaya Zvezda*, 17 Nov. 1999, p. 2.

Babichev, S. and Strugovets, V. 'Vozdushnyye izvozchiki', *Krasnaya Zvezda*, 25 Oct. 1995, p. 2.

'Backs Harsh Reaction', *Radio Free Europe/Radio Liberty Security Watch*, 3, 39, 5 (Nov. 2002).

Baev, P.K. 'Russia's Airpower in the Chechen War: Denial, Punishment and Defeat', *Journal of Slavic Military Studies*, 10, 2 (1997), pp. 1–18.

Balburov, D. 'Chechnya: Just a Little Civil War', *Moskovskiye Novosti*, 30 July–5 Aug. 1998, p. 3.

Baranov, N. 'Voyny diktuyut reorganizatsiyu', *Nezavisimoye Voyennoye Obozreniye*, 10 (183), 24 March 2000, p. 1.

Billingsley, D. 'Chechnya Seizes Independence But Unity Still Beyond Its Reach', *Jane's Intelligence Review*, March 1999, pp. 14–18.

Blandy, C.W. *Chechnya: A Beleaguered President*, OB61 (Camberley: Conflict Studies Research Centre, 1998).

Blandy, C.W. *Chechnya: Two Federal Interventions. An Interim Comparison and Assessment* (Camberley: Conflict Studies Research Centre, 2000).

Blandy, C.W. *Dagestan: The Storm*, P30 (Part I), P32 (Part II) and P33 (Part III) (Camberley: Conflict Studies Research Centre, 2000).

Blandy, C.W. *Chechnya: The Need to Negotiate*, OB88 (Camberley: Conflict Studies Research Centre, 2001).

Blotskiy, O. and Nikol'skiy, A. 'General-Major Vladimir Syamanov: "Mne opravdyvat'sya ne pered kem"', *Nezavisimoye Voyennoye Obozreniye*, 10 (14), 30 May 1996, pp. 1–2.

Bogdanov, S. 'Voyna vne zakona', *Nezavisimoye Voyennoye Obozreniye*, 38 (308), 25 Oct. 2002, p. 4.

Butowski, P. 'Air Force Must Look Up as Training Hits a Low', *Jane's Defence Weekly*, 2 Aug. 2000, p. 22.

CFE (Treaty on Conventional Forces in Europe) *Dogovor ob obychnykh vooruzhënnykh silakh v Yevrope: informachiya ob obychnykh vooruzhënnykh silakh Rossiyskoy Federatsii* (Moscow: MoD, 1992–2002).

Chel'tsov, B. 'VVS ishchut svoyë mesto v trëkhvidovoy strukture vooruzhënnykh sil', *Nezavisimoye Voyennoye Obozreniye*, 29 (202), 11 Aug. 2000, p. 1.

Chernorechenskiy, A. and Sokut, S. 'Vykhod iz shtopora otkladyvayetsya', *Nezavisimoye Voyennoye Obozreniye*, 2 (175), 21 Jan. 2000, p. 3.

Chernov, V. 'Natsional'nyye interesy Rossii i ugrozy dlya ego bezopasnosti, Boris Yel'tsin utverdil kontseptsiyu vneshney politiki RF', *Nezavisimaya Gazeta*, 29 April 1993, pp. 1, 3.

Council on Foreign and Defence Policy (CFDP), List of members, provided at Wilton Park Conference, Steyning, June 1998. Current list of members: www.svop.ru

Covault, C. 'Russian Air Force Faces Deepening Crisis', *Aviation Week & Space Technology*, 5 March 2001, pp. 60–3.

d'Hamecourt, P. 'Russen protesteren tegen oorlog in Tsjetsjenië', *Algemeen Dagblad*, 4 Jan. 1995.

'Dagestan: khronika konflikta', *Nezavisimoye Voyennoye Obozreniye*, No. 32–36 (155–9), 20 Aug.–17 Sept. 1999, p. 2.

'Defence Minister Says Russia is at War', *Radio Free Europe/Radio Liberty Security Watch*, 3, 40, 12 Nov. 2002.

Deynekin, P.S. 'Vremya reshitel'nykh deystviy', *Aviatsiya i Kosmonavtika*, Jan. 1993, pp. 2–4.

Deynekin, P.S. 'U rossiyskikh VVS budut tol'ko noveyshiye samolëty', *Izvestiya*, 24 March 1993, p. 6.

Deynekin, P.S. 'Basic Directions of Air Force Organizational Developments and Training under Present Conditions', *Voyennaya Mysl'*, 7, July 1993, pp. 2–8.

Deynekin, P.S. 'Problemnyye voprosy stroitel'stva i primeneniya voyenno-vozdushnykh sil Rossii', *Aviatsiya i Kosmonavtika*, May 1996, pp. 2–11.

Deynekin, P.S. 'Reform of the Air Force is a Must', *Military News Bulletin*, 8, Aug. (1996), pp. 6–9.

Dick, C.J. *The Military Doctrine of the Russian Federation*, Occasional Brief 25 (Camberley: Conflict Studies Research Centre, 1993).

Dick, C.J. 'The military doctrine of the Russian Federation', *Journal of Slavic Military Studies*, 7, 3, Sept. 1994, pp. 481–506.

Dick, C.J. *If Democracy Fails in Russia*, Occasional Brief 49 (Camberley: Conflict Studies Research Centre, 1996).

Dick, C.J. 'Military Reform and the Russian Air Force 1999', *Journal of Slavic Military Studies*, 13, 1 (2000), pp. 1–12.

Dick, C.J. 'Down, but Not Out', *Jane's Defence Weekly*, 2 Aug. 2000, pp. 19–20.

'Diversii v Chechne', *Nezavisimoye Voyennoye Obozreniye*, 31 (301), 6 Sept. 2002, p. 2.

Dobrovol'skiy, A. 'VVS budut spasat' svoyu tekhniku', *Nezavisimoye Voyennoye Obozreniye*, 18 (141), 14 May 1999, p. 6.

'Doklad o perekhode', *Nezavisimoye Voyennoye Obozreniye*, 1 (316), 17 Jan. 2003, p. 3.

'Doktrina budet utochnyat'sya', *Nezavisimoye Voyennoye Obozreniye*, 13, 13 April 2001, p. 1.

Drobyshevshkiy, A. and Babichev, S. 'Boyegotovnost' trebuyet raskhodov', *Krasnaya Zvezda*, 17 July 1999, pp. 1–2.

'Duma Allocates More Funds for Fighting Terrorism', *Radio Free Europe/Radio Liberty Security Watch*, 3, 41, 19 Nov. 2002.

Encyclopaedia of Conflicts, Disputes and Flashpoints in Eastern Europe, Russia and the Successor States (Harlow: Longman, 1993).

Fel'gengauer, P. 'Armii obeshchayut perestroyku', *Moskovskiye Novosti*, 45, 14 Nov. 2000, pp. 2–3.

Fel'gengauer, P. 'Kakov mozg, takova i armiya', *Moskovskiye Novosti*, 3, 16 Jan. 2001, p. 14.

'First Chechnya War', 15 Jan. 2000, www.fas.org/man/dod-101/ops/war/chechnya1.htm

'Foreign Minister Concerned by US Efforts to Seize Iraqi Assets', *Radio Free Europe/Radio Liberty Security Watch*, 4, 12, 26 March 2003.

Fulghum, D. 'Air War in Chechnya Reveals Mix of tactics', *Aviation Week & Technology*, 14 Feb. 2000, pp. 76–8.

Galeotti, M. 'Chechen Warlords Still Hold Sway', *Jane's Intelligence Review*, March 1999, pp. 8–9.

Gall, C. and Waal, Th. de. *Chechnya, Calamity in the Caucasus* (New York and London: New York University Press, 1998).

Gareyev, M.A. 'Yadernym oruzhiyem problem ne reshit'', *Krasnaya Zvezda*, 5 Aug. 1994, p. 2.

Gavrilov, Yu. and Babichev, S. 'Ne teryat' temp, zavershit' nachatoye', *Krasnaya Zvezda*, 12 Aug. 1998, pp. 1–2.

Geibel, A. 'Caucasus Nightmare', *Armor*, March–April 1995, pp. 10–15.

Georgiyev, V. 'Rol' armeyskoy aviatsii vozrastayet', *Nezavisimoye Voyennoye Obozreniye*, 4 (177), 4 Feb. 2000, p. 2.

Glantz, M.E. 'The Origins and Development of Soviet and Russian Military Doctrine', *Journal of Slavic Military Studies*, 7, 3, Sept. (1994), pp. 443–80.

Godzimirski, J.M. 'Russian National Security Concepts 1997 and 2000: a Comparative Analysis', *European Security*, 9, 4 (2000), pp. 73–91.

Golotyuk, Yu. 'Groznyy bombili', *Izvestiya*, 24 Sept. 1999, p. 1.

Haas, M. de. 'Tsjetsjenië, keerpunt voor het Russische doctrinaire denken?', *Militaire Spectator*, 168, 10 (1999), pp. 550–9.

Haas, M. de. 'An analysis of Soviet, CIS and Russian military doctrines 1990–2000', *Journal of Slavic Military Studies*, 14, 4, Dec. 2001, pp. 1–34.

Haas, M. de. *The Use of Russian Air Power in the Second Chechen War*, B59 (Camberley: Conflict Studies Research Centre, 2003).

Haas, M. de. 'The Development of Russian Security Policy 1992–2002', in A.C. Aldis and R.N. McDermott (eds), *Russian Military Reform 1992–2002* (London: Frank Cass, 2003).

Hedge, J. 'Air War over Chechnya', *World Air Power Journal*, 42 (2000), pp. 18–23.

'Intelligence Community Celebrates its Soviet Origins', *Radio Free Europe/Radio Liberty Security Watch*, 3, 45, 24 Dec. 2002.

Isenkov, G. 'VVS zadachu vypolnili', *Armeyskiy Sbornik*, 3 (1995), p. 42.

Kamalov, N. 'Komandiry otdeleniy bezgramotnoy armii', *Nezavisimoye Voyennoye Obozreniye*, 24, 19 July 2002, p. 3.

Kassianova, A. 'Russia: Still Open to the West? Evolution of the State Identity in the Foreign Policy and Security Discourse', *Europe–Asia Studies*, 53, 6 (2001), pp. 821–39.

Kedrov, I. 'Staryye vertolety resyayut novyye zadachi', *Nezavisimoye Voyennoye Obozreniye*, 40 (163), 15 Oct. 1999, pp. 1, 3.

Khodarenok, M. 'Zadumano radikal'noye usileniye Sovet Bezopasnosti', *Nezavisimaya Gazeta*, 28 Sept. 2000, pp. 1, 3.

Khodarenok, M. 'Vremya sobirat' kamni', *Nezavisimoye Voyennoye Obozreniye*, 19 Jan. 2001, pp. 1, 4.

Khodarenok, M. 'Rukovodit' operatsiyey porucheno chekistam', *Nezavisimoye Voyennoye Obozreniye*, 3 (225), 26 Jan. 2001, p. 1.

Khodarenok, M. '"Starshego brata" sdali za milliard dollarov', *Nezavisimoye Voyennoye Obozreniye*, 4, 8 Feb. 2002, p. 3.

Khodarenok, M. 'Zatyanuvsheesya pike', *Nezavisimoye Voyennoye Obozreniye*, 8 (278), 15 March 2002, p. 4.

Khodarenok, M. 'Ozherelye iz Amerikanskikh baz', *Nezavisimoye Voyennoye Obozreniye*, 10, 29 March 2002, p. 4.

Khokhlov, A. 'We Did Not Injure a Single Hostage', *Izvestiya*, 28 Oct. 2002, p. 1.

Khrolenko, A. 'Bez platy za strakh', *Nezavisimoye Voyennoye Obozreniye*, 1 (316), 17 Jan. 2003, p. 6.

Klimenko, A.F. 'O role i meste voyennoy doktriny v sisteme bezopasnosti Sodruzhestva nezavisimykh gosudarstv', *Voyennaya Mysl'*, 2, Feb. 1992, pp. 11–21.

Klimenko, A.F. 'Osobennosti novoy Voyennoy doktriny', *Voyennaya Mysl'*, 5 (2000), pp. 22–34.

Klimenko, A.F. 'TsVSI issleduyet, prognoziruyet, rekomenduyet...', *Krasnaya Zvezda*, 10 Aug. 2000, p. 2.

KLu Airpower Doctrine (The Hague: Royal Netherlands Air Force, 1996 and 2001).

Komarov, A. 'Chechen Conflict Drives Call for Air Force Modernization', *Aviation Week & Technology*, 14 Feb. 2000, pp. 80–1.

'Konstitutsiya Rossiyskoy Federatsii', *Rossiyskaya Gazeta*, 25 Dec. 1993; www.gov.ru:8104/main/konst/konst0.html

'Kontseptsiya natsional'noy bezopasnosti Rossiyskoy Federatsii', *Krasnaya Zvezda*, 27 Dec. 1997, pp. 1, 3–4; *Sobraniye Zakonodatel'stva RF* (1997), item 5909, p. 10418.

'Kontseptsiya vneshney politiki Rossiyskoy Federatsii', *Nezavisimoye Voyennoye Obozreniye*, 25, 14 July 2000, p. 4.

Korbut, A. 'Rossiya utochnyayet Voyennuyu doktrinu', *Nezavisimoye Voyennoye Obozreniye*, 40, 15 Oct. 1999, p. 1.

Korbut, A. 'Ucheba v boyu', *Nezavisimoye Voyennoye Obozreniye*, 50 (173), 24 Dec. 1999, p. 2.

Korbut, A., 'Genshtab berët upravleniye na sebya', *Nezavisimaya Gazeta*, 17 Nov. 2000, p. 1.

Kornukov, A.M. 'To Preserve and Build Up Combat Capabilities', *Military News Bulletin*, 3 (1998), pp. 8–9.

Kornukov, A.M. 'Teoriya stroitel'stva novykh VVS', *Nezavisimoye Voyennoye Obozreniye*, 10 (84), 13 March 1998, pp. 1–3.

Kornukov, A.M., 'Aviatsionnaya podderzhka voysk: gospodstvo v nebe – uspekh na zemle', *Krasnaya Zvezda*, 11 Nov. 1998, pp. 1–2.

Kornukov, A.M. 'Zavoyevat', uderzhat', podderzhat'', *Armeyskiy Sbornik*, 12 (1998), pp. 27–33.

Kornukov, A.M. 'Voyenno-Vozdushnyye Sily – eto i shchit, i mech', *Vestnik Vozdushnogo Flota*, 7–8 (1999), pp. 8–9.

Kornukov, A.M. 'VVS kak faktor natsional'noy bezopasnosti', *Krasnaya Zvezda*, 12 Nov. 1999, pp. 1–2.

Kornukov, A.M. 'Kontrterroristicheskaya operatsiya na Severnom Kavkaze: osnovnyye uroki i vyvody', *Voyennaya Mysl'*, 4 (2000), pp. 5–10.

Korotchenko, I. 'Voyennaya operatsiya v Chechene (Obzor)', *Nezavisimoye Voyennoye Obozreniye*, 1 (1), 11 Feb. 1995, pp. 1–2.

Korotchenko, I. 'Novyy pretendent na post ministra oborony', *Nezavisimoye Voyennoye Obozreniye*, 9, 22 March 2002, p. 1.

Kosykh, G. 'Itogi Chechenskoy kampanii podvodit' eshchë rano', *Nezavisimoye Voyennoye Obozreniye*, 45 (72), 5 Dec. 1997, p. 2.

Krasnov, A. 'Nash argument protiv MAU', *Vestnik Vozdushnogo Flota*, Nov.–Dec. 1998, pp. 16–18.

Lake, J. 'Order of Battle: Russia's Air Forces Today', *Combat Aircraft*, Oct.–Nov. 1998, pp. 702–12.

Lambeth, B. *Russia's Air Power in Crisis* (Washington, DC: Smithsonian Institution Press, 1999).

Lefebvre, S. *The Reform of the Russian Air Force* (Camberley: Conflict Studies Research Centre, 2002).

'Lichnyy kontrol' nachal'nika GSh', *Nezavisimoye Voyennoye Obozreniye*, 32 (302), 13 Sept. 2002, p. 1.

Lough, J.B.K. *Years in Big Politics – Ye. M. Primakov*, F70 (Camberley: Conflict Studies Research Centre, 2000).

Luttwak, E.N. *Strategy, the Logic of War and Peace* (Cambridge, MA, and London: Belknap, 1987).

Lynch, A.C. 'The Realism of Russia's Foreign Policy', *Europe–Asia Studies*, 53, 1 (2001), pp. 7–31.

Main, S.J. *Russia's Military Doctrine*, Occasional Brief 77 (Camberley: Conflict Studies Research Centre, 2000).

Maksakov, I. 'Federal'naya gruppirovka ushla na peremiriye', *Nezavisimoye Voyennoye Obozreniye*, 17 (21), 12 Sept. 1996.

Malcolm, N., Pravda, A., *et al. Internal Factors in Russian Foreign Policy* (Oxford: Oxford University Press, 1996).

Manilov, V.L. *Voyennaya Bezopasnost' Rossii* (Moscow: Probel, 2000).

Marshall-Hasdell, D.J. *Russian Airpower in Chechnya* (Camberley: Conflict Studies Research Centre, 1996).

Matveyev, Ye. 'Tridtsat' pyatyy: v srednem federal'nyye voyska terjayut v Chechne po ver-toljotu v mesyats', *Nezavisimoye Voyennoye Obozreniye*, 30 (300), 30 Aug. 2002, pp. 1, 6.

Matyash, V. 'S trevogoy i nadezhdoy', *Krasnaya Zvezda*, 3 Dec. 1996, pp. 1, 3.

Mezhdunarodnoye Pravo, sbornik dokumentov (Moscow: Yuridicheskaya Literatura, 2000).

Mezhvedomstvennyye komissii Sovet Bezopasnosti Rossiyskoy Federatsii, 2002, www.scrf.gov.ru/Documents/Commissions.html

Militaire Doctrine, LDP-I (The Hague: Royal Netherlands Army, 1996).

Military Balance (London: Brassey's, and Oxford: Oxford University Press: International Institute for Strategic Studies, 1990–2002).

'Military Chief Says Army in Critical Condition', *Radio Free Europe/Radio Liberty Security and Terrorism Watch*, 3, 20, 4 June 2002.

Miranovich, G. 'Geopolitika i bezopasnost' Rossii', *Krasnaya Zvezda*, 30 July 1999, p. 2, and 31 July 1999, p. 2.

'Morskaya doktrina Rossiyskoy Federatsii na period do 2020 goda', *Nezavisimoye Voyennoye Obozreniye*, 28, 3 Aug. 2001, p. 4.

Moskvin, Ye. 'Zagovor chinovnikov protiv kontraktnika', *Nezavisimoye Voyennoye Obozreniye*, 15 (240), 25 April 2003, p. 1.

Mukhin, V. 'Voyennaya strategiya dlya novogo presidenta', *Nezavisimoye Voyennoye Obozreniye*, 8 (181), 3 March 2000, p. 3.

Mukhin, V. 'The Army: One Year with Sergei Ivanov', *Former Soviet Union Fifteen Nations: Policy and Security*, 3 (March 2002), pp. 1–2.

Mukhin, V. 'Sergei Ivanov Quoted the President as Saying that the Mi-26 Catastrophe was Another *Kursk*', *Nezavisimaya Gazeta*, 9 Sept. 2002, pp. 1–2.

NATO Handbook (Brussels: NATO Office of Information and Press, 1995, 2001).

'NAVO-Rusland Raad nieuwe stijl', *Atlantisch Perspectief*, 26, No. 4, 2002, pp. 27–8.

Nederlof, K.A. *Lexicon politiek-militair-strategische termen* (Alphen aan den Rijn (NL)/Brussels: Samson, 1984).

'New Military Offensive in Chechnya', *Radio Free Europe/Radio Liberty Security and Terrorism Watch*, 3, 39, 5 Nov. 2002.

Nikolayev, A.I. 'U nas – terroristicheskaya voyna', *Nezavisimoye Voyennoye Obozreniye*, 40 (310), 26 Nov. 2002, p. 1.

Nikolayev, B. 'V pylayushchem nebe Chechni', *Armeyskiy Sbornik*, 3 (2000), pp. 32–6.

Nikunen, H. *The Current State of the Russian Air Force*, 28 Nov. 2001, www.sci.fi/~fta/ruaf.htm

'Nord-Ost', dossier *Nezavisimaya Gazeta*, 2002, www.ng.ru/special/NordOst

'Novaya Voyennaya doktrina Rossii – adekvatnyy otvet na vyzov vremeni', *Krasnaya Zvezda*, 8 Oct. 1999, p. 1.

Novichkov, N.N. *Rossiyskiye Vooruzhënnyye Sily v Chechenskom Konflikte* (Moscow: Kholveg-Infoglob, and Paris: Trivola, 1995).

Novikov 'The Russian Helicopter Fleet – What will it be?', *Krasnaya Zvezda*, 3 Feb. 1993, p. 2.

Odom, W.E. *The Collapse of the Soviet Military* (New Haven, CT, and London: Yale University Press, 1998).

Oparin, M.M. 'Dal'nyaya aviatsiya i bezopasnost' Rossii', *Armeyskiy Sbornik*, 10 (1999), pp. 25–30.

Oparin, M.M. 'Ot "Ilyi Muromtsa" do Tu-160', *Nezavisimoye Voyennoye Obozreniye*, 50 (173), 24 Dec. 1999, p. 1.

'Orders Revision of National Security Concept', *Radio Free Europe/Radio Liberty Security and Terrorism Watch*, Vol. 3, No. 39, 5 Nov. 2002.

Orr, M.J. 'Second time lucky?', *Jane's Defence Weekly*, 8 March 2000, pp. 32–6.

Orr, M.J. 'Russia's Chechen War Reaches Crisis Point', *Jane's Intelligence Review*, Oct. 2000, pp. 15–18.

Orr, M.J. *Manpower Problems of the Russian Armed Forces*, D62 (Camberley: Conflict Studies Research Centre, 2002).

'Osnovy voyennoy doktriny Rossii (Proyekt)', *Voyennaya Mysl'*, special issue, 19 May 1992.

Parchomenko, W. 'The Russian Military in the Wake of the Kursk Tragedy', *Journal of Slavic Military Studies*, 14, 4, Dec. 2001, pp. 35–56.

'Park VVS stareyet', *Nezavisimoye Voyennoye Obozreniye*, 26 (199), 21 July 2000, p. 1.

Pel'ts, A. 'Nuzhna novaya voyennaya doktrina', *Krasnaya Zvezda*, 6 Nov. 1996, p. 1.

'Peremeny v aviatsii', *Nezavisimoye Voyennoye Obozreniye*, 30 (300), 30 Aug. 2002, p. 3.

'Poetin krijgt ovatie in Bondsdag', *NRC – Handelsblad*, 26 Sept. 2001.

Polkovnikov, P. 'Vtorzheniye iz Chechni v Dagestan nachalos' ', *Nezavisimoye Voyennoye Obozreniye*, 31 (154), 13 Aug. 1999, p. 1.

Polozheniye ob apparate Soveta Bezopasnosti Rossiyskoy Federatsiya, 1998, www.scrf.gov.ru/Documents/Decree/1998/294-1.html

Posen, B.R. *The Sources of Military Doctrine – France, Britain, and Germany between the World Wars* (Ithaca, NY: Cornell University Press, 1984).

Powell, S.M. 'Russia's Military Retrenchment', *Air Force Magazine*, Aug. 2001, pp. 71–4.

'President Consolidates Security Agencies', *Radio Free Europe/Radio Liberty Security Watch*, 4, 10, 11 March 2003.

'Pri ob"yedinenii VVS i PVO budet sokrashcheno 40% boyevogo sostava', *Interfaks*, 29, 11 Feb. 1998, p. 3.

'Principles of RF Naval policy, as Confirmed by Presidential Decree, 4 March 2000', *Nezavisimoye Voyennoye Obozreniye*, 11, 31 March 2000, pp. 1, 4.

Prokopenko, S. and Babichev, S. 'Voyna v Chechne', *Aviatsiya i Kosmonavtika*, Nov. 1995, p. 15.

Prokopenko, S. and Soldatenko, B. 'Vozdushnyye rabochiye voyny', *Krasnaya Zvezda*, 1 March 1995, p. 3.

Protocols Additional to the Geneva Conventions of 12 August 1949 (Geneva: International Committee of the Red Cross, 1996).

'Putin Says Iraq Crisis Most Serious Conflict since End of Cold War', *Radio Free Europe/Radio Liberty Security Watch*, 4, 13, 1 April 2003.

'Putin Stresses Need to Avoid Conflict with US', *Radio Free Europe/Radio Liberty Security Watch*, 4, 14, 9 April 2003.

'Putin Warns Georgia over Toleration of Chechen "Terrorism" ', *Radio Free Europe/Radio Liberty Security Watch*, 3, 32, 19 Sept. 2002.

'Putin, Shevardnadze Soften Russia–Georgia discrepancies', *Radio Free Europe/Radio Liberty Security Watch*, 3, 35, 8 Oct. 2002.

Rog, V.G. 'Vozdushnoye nastupleniye i vozdushnaya oborona', *Armeyskiy Sbornik*, 11 (1997), p. 4.

Rog, V.G. 'Vozdushniye operatsii uprazdnit' nel'zya', *Nezavisimoye Voyennoye Obozreniye*, 38 (211), 13 Oct. 2000, p. 1.

Rog, V.G. 'Bor'ba za gospodstvo v vozdukhe', *Nezavisimoye Voyennoye Obozreniye*, 3 (225), 26 Jan. 2001, p. 4.

Rog, V.G. 'Oriyentir – neyadernoye sderzhivaniye', *Nezavisimoye Voyennoye Obozreniye*, 38 (260), 12 Oct. 2001, p. 4.

Rog, V.G. 'Put' Rossiyskoy voyennoy aviatsii', *Nezavisimoye Voyennoye Obozreniye*, 26 (296), 2 Aug. 2002, p. 1.

Rog, V.G. 'Zlovrednaya kon"yunkturshchina', *Nezavisimoye Voyennoye Obozreniye*, 43 (313), 6 Dec. 2002, p. 4.

Rog, V.G. and Drobyshevskiy, A. 'Improvizatsiy ne bylo', *Nezavisimoye Voyennoye Obozreniye*, 47 (220), 15 Dec. 2000, p. 4.

Rogov, S. 'Nuzhna li Rossii svoya politika natsional'noy bezopasnosti?', *Nezavisimaya Gazeta*, 45, 6 March 1992, p. 2.

Rooij, A.A.C. de. 'Nieuwe start in relatie met Rusland', *Reformatorisch Dagblad*, 6 Oct. 2001.

'Rossiya gotova otstaivat' svoi interesy', *Krasnaya Zvezda*, 27 Dec. 1997, p. 1.

Rukavishnikov, V. 'The Military and Society in Post-communist Russia at the Threshold of the 21st century', in J. Kuhlmann and J. Callaghan, *Military and Society in 21st Century Europe* (Garmisch-Partenkirchen, Germany: George C. Marshall European Center for Security Studies, 2000), pp. 161–82.

Rukovodstvo apparata Soveta Bezopasnosti Rossiyskoy Federatsiya, 2001, www.scrf.gov.ru/Personnels/Staff.htm

'Russian Army Suffers from Mass Exodus of Officers', *Radio Free Europe/Radio Liberty Security Watch*, 3, 6, 15 Feb. 2002.

'Russian Defense Official Expresses Concern over US Military Role in Georgia', *Radio Free Europe/Radio Liberty Security Watch*, 3, 14, 23 April 2002.

'Russia–NATO Talks on New Form of Partnership Hit Stalemate', *Radio Free Europe/Radio Liberty Security Watch*, 3, 9, 8 March 2002.

Safranchuk, I. 'Chechnya: Russia's Experience of Asymmetrical Warfare', in J. Olsen (ed.), *Asymmetric Warfare* (Oslo: Royal Norwegian Air Force Academy, 2002).

Saranov, V. 'Critical Mass: There Are Too Many Armed Formations in Russia', *Versiya*, 47, 11 Dec. 2001.

Second Chechnya War, www.fas.org/man/dod-101/ops/war/chechnya2.htm

Shevelyov, M. 'Chechnya: Poor and Dangerous Again', *Moskovskiye Novosti*, 19–25 Feb. 1998.

Slonov, L. 'War in Chechnya continues', *Former Soviet Union Fifteen Nations: Policy and Security*, 8, Aug. 2002, pp. 4–5.

Smith, M.A. *The Security Council*, C94 (Camberley: Conflict Studies Research Centre, 1997).

Smith, M.A. *Putin's Regime: Administered Democracy*, E108 (Camberley: Conflict Studies Research Centre, 2000).

Smith, M.A. *Russia and the Far Abroad 2000*, F72 (Camberley: Conflict Studies Research Centre, 2000).

Smith, M.A. *Putin's Power Bases*, E109 (Camberley: Conflict Studies Research Centre, 2001).

Smyshlayev, Ye. 'Vertolety nad Chechney', *Nezavisimoye Voyennoye Obozreniye*, 38 (211), 13 Oct. 2000, p. 6.

Snel, G. *From the Atlantic to the Urals, the Reorientation of Soviet Military Strategy, 1981–1990* (Amsterdam: VU University Press, 1996).

Sokolov, S. 'Poslesloviye k "Nord-Ostu"', *Nezavisimoye Voyennoye Obozreniye*, 39 (309), 1 Nov. 2002, p. 8.

Sokolov, S. 'Neobkhodima reorganizatsiya spetssluzhb Rossii', *Nezavisimoye Voyennoye Obozreniye*, 40 (310), 15 Nov. 2002, p. 1.

Sokut, S. 'Dal'she sokrashchat' VVS nel'zya', *Nezavisimoye Voyennoye Obozreniye*, 31 (154), 13 Aug. 1999, pp. 1, 3.

Sokut, S. 'Nevostrebovannyy potentsial', *Nezavisimoye Voyennoye Obozreniye*, 33 (156), 27 Aug. 1999, p. 2.

Sokut, S. 'Udary po banditam ne oslabeyut', *Nezavisimoye Voyennoye Obozreniye*, 45 (168), 19 Nov. 1999, p. 2.

Sokut, S. 'Kurs na lokal'nyye konflikty', *Nezavisimoye Voyennoye Obozreniye*, 4 (226), 2 Feb. 2001, p. 3.

Sokut, S. 'Osmysleniye Chechenskogo opyta', *Nezavisimoye Voyennoye Obozreniye*, 29 (251), 10 Aug. 2001, p. 3.

Sokut, S. 'Perspektivy razvitiya boyevoy aviatsii', *Nezavisimoye Voyennoye Obozreniye*, 29 (251), 10 Aug. 2001, p. 1.

Solovyev, V. 'Voyenachal'niki usilivayut davleniye na Kreml'', *Nezavisimoye Voyennoye Obozreniye*, 42, 16 Nov. 2001, p. 1.

Solovyev, V. 'V Minoborony gryadet chistka', *Nezavisimoye Voyennoye Obozreniye*, 7, 1 March 2002, p. 1.

Solovyev, V. 'Doktrina uprezdayushchikh deystviy po-Moskovski', *Nezavisimoye Voyennoye Obozreniye*, 33, 20 Sept. 2002, pp. 1–2.

Solovyev, V. 'I vsë-taki my pobedim', *Nezavisimoye Voyennoye Obozreniye*, 39 (309), 1 Nov. 2002, p. 1.

Solovyev, V. 'Zvezdoy po terrorismu', *Nezavisimoye Voyennoye Obozreniye*, 42 (312), 29 Nov. 2002, p. 1.

Solovyev, V. 'Nash Genshtab otvetchayet NATO', *Nezavisimoye Voyennoye Obozreniye*, 2 (317), 24 Jan. 2003, pp. 1, 3.

Sostav nauchnogo soveta pri Soveta Bezopasnosti Rossiyskoy Federatsiya, 1999, www.scrf.gov.ru/Documents/Decree/1999/1317-2.html.

Sovet Bezopasnosti Rossiyskoy Federatsii, istoriya, sozdaniya, pravovoy status, struktura i osnovnyye napravleneyiya deyatel'nosti, 2002, www.scrf.gov.ru/Documents/History.html

Strategic Survey (Oxford: Oxford University Press International Institute for Strategic Studies, 1990–2001).

'Struktura federal'nykh organov ispolnitel'noy vlasti', *Sobraniye Zakonodatel'stva RF*, 39, item 4886, 1998.

Sudoplatov, A. 'Voyna tol'ko nachinayetsya', *Nezavisimoye Voyennoye Obozreniye*, 39 (309), 1 Nov. 2002, p. 1.

Suleymanov, S. 'Sluzhba – delo desyatoye', *Nezavisimoye Voyennoye Obozreniye*, 11, 5 April 2002, p. 3.

Suleymanov, S. '23-ya otsrochka ot prisyva', *Nezavisimoye Voyennoye Obozreniye*, 27, 9 Aug. 2002, p. 4.

Suleymanov, S. 'V poiskakh vinovnykh', *Nezavisimoye Voyennoye Obozreniye*, 31 (301), 6 Sept. 2002, p. 3.

Suvorov, V. *Inside the Soviet Army* (London: Hamish Hamilton, 1982).

Teitler, G., Bosch, J.M.J., Klinkert, W., *et al. Inleiding Militaire Strategie* (Den Haag: KIK, 1999).

Teitler, G., Bosch, J.M.J., Klinkert, W., *et al. Militaire Strategie* (Amsterdam: Mets & Schilt, 2002).

Tereenkov, K. 'Whirlwind over the Caucasus', *Air Forces Monthly*, Dec. 1999, pp. 24–7.

'The Special Forces are More than Special Forces in Russia', *Vek*, 9 Aug. 2002, p. 5.

Thomas, J. 'Dagestan: A New Center of Instability in the North Caucasus', 11 Oct. 1999, www.csis.org/ruseura/ex998.html

Thomas, T.L. 'Air Operations in Low Intensity Conflict: the Case of Chechnya', *Air Power Journal*, Winter 1997, pp. 51–9.

'U ofitserov net deneg i zhil'ya', *Nezavisimoye Voyennoye Obozreniye*, 11 (233), 30 March 2001, p. 1.

Udmantsev, V. 'My gotovim universal'nykh soldat', *Nezavisimoye Voyennoye Obozreniye*, 39 (309), 1 Nov. 2002, p. 3.

'Ukaz Prezidenta Rossiyskoy Federatsii o sozdanii Vooruzhënnykh sil Rossiyskoy Federatsii', *Armiya*, 11–12 (June 1992), p. 2; *Vedomosti RF* (1992), item 1077, p. 1401.

'Ukaz Prezidenta Rossiyskoy Federatsii ob utverzdenii Voyennoy doktriny Rossiyskoy Federatsii', *Krasnaya Zvezda*, 25 April 2000, p. 1.

'V VVS ne khvatayet ofitserov', *Nezavisimoye Voyennoye Obozreniye*, 37 (210), 6 Oct. 2000, p. 1.

'V VVS nekomu letat'?', *Nezavisimoye Voyennoye Obozreniye*, 38 (211), 13 Oct. 2000, p. 1.

Valchenko, S. and Yuryev, K. 'Goryachiy vozdukh Kavkaza', *Armeyskiy Sbornik*, 2 Feb. 2001, pp. 24–32.

Volten, P.M.E. *Brezhnev's Peace Program: a Study of Soviet Domestic Political Process and Power* (Boulder, CO: Westview Press, 1982).

Volten, P.M.E. 'Burgers in het offensief: het debat over het defensief in de militaire strategie van de Sovjet-Unie', *Transaktie*, 26, 1 (1997), pp. 134–49.

Vorobyev, I.N. 'Legko prognoziruyemyye resul'taty', *Nezavisimoye Voyennoye Obozreniye*, 2 (29), 18 Jan. 1997, p. 2.

'Voyennaya doktrina Rossiyskoy Federatsii', *Nezavisimoye Voyennoye Obozreniye*, 15, 28 April 2000, pp. 1, 4–5; *Sobraniye Zakonodatel'stva RF* (2000), item 1852, p. 3843.

'Vozdushnaya voyna s banditami', *Nezavisimoye Voyennoye Obozreniye*, 37 (160), 24 Sept. 1999, p. 2.

'VVS ne boyegotovy?', *Nezavisimoye Voyennoye Obozreniye*, 49 (222), 29 Dec. 2000, p. 1.

'With No Right of Veto for Kremlin', *Radio Free Europe/Radio Liberty Security Watch*, 3, 14, 23 April 2002.

Wynia, S. 'EU zet Rusland onder druk in Tsjetsjeense crisis', *Het Parool*, 5 Jan. 1995.

Yavorskiy, A. 'Lëtchikam ne dali razvernut'sya', *Nezavisimoye Voyennoye Obozreniye*, 48 (171), 10 Dec. 1999, p. 5.

Yuzbasyev, V. 'A Show of Punishment Instead of a True Investigation of the Mi-26 Crash', *Moskovskiye Novosti*, 10 Sept. 2002, p. 3.

Zabolotin, V.D. *Slovar' voyennykh terminov* (Moscow: Kosmo, 2000).

'Zakon Rossiyskoy Federatsii o Bezopasnosti', *Vedomosti RF*, No. 15, 9 April 1992, item 769; *Rossiyskaya Gazeta*, 103, 6 May 1992; www.scrf.gov.ru/Documents/2646-1.html#sb

'Zakon Rossiyskoy Federatsii ob Oborone', *Vedomosti RF* (1992), item 2331, p. 3026; or 'Law of the Russian Federation on Defence', *Military News Bulletin*, 10 (Oct. 1992), pp. 1–7.

Zhilin, A. 'Udary po Chechne', *Moskovskiye Novosti*, 21 Sept. 1999, p. 5.

Websites

Academy of Sciences RF (RAS)	www.ras.ru
Biographies of security actors	www.days.peoples.ru
	www.nns.ru/ssi/persons.cgi
	www.whoiswho.ru
Chechen Republic	www.amina.com

Commonwealth of Independent States (CIS)	www.cis.int
Conflict Studies Research Centre (CSRC)	www.csrc.ac.uk
Council on Foreign and Defence Policy (SVOP)	www.svop.ru
Duma RF	www.duma.gov.ru
Federation Council RF	www.council.gov.ru
Federation of American Scientists (FAS)	www.fas.org
Government RF (RF)	www.gov.ru
GUUAM regional cooperation within CIS (GUUAM)	www.guuam.org
Krasnaya Zvezda	www.redstar.ru
Military Doctrine Joint Staff USA	www.dtic.mil/doctrine
Ministry of Defence RF	www.mil.ru
Moscow News/Moskovskiye Novosti (MN)	www.mn.ru
Netherlands Atlantic Commission	www.atlcom.nl
Nezavisimaya Gazeta (NG)	www.ng.ru
Nezavisimoye Voyennoye Obozreniye (NVO)	www.nvo.ng.ru
Novosti, Russian Information Agency (RIAN)	www.rian.ru
President RF	www.president.kremlin.ru
Radio Free Europe/Radio Liberty (RFE/RL)	www.rferl.org
Russian air forces (non-governmental site)	www.airforce.ru
Security Council RF (SCRF)	www.scrf.gov.ru

AUTHOR'S CURRICULUM VITAE

Marcel de Haas was born in The Hague on 4 May 1961. He is married and has two children. Marcel de Haas is officer in the Royal Netherlands Air Force. He completed his MA in Russian Studies at Leiden University (1987) on 'Soviet policy towards Southern Africa' and his PhD at Amsterdam University (2004) on 'Russian security policy and air power 1992–2000'.

He has taken courses on NATO's policies (NATO School, Oberammergau, Germany, 2003), Law of Armed Conflict (International Institute of Humanitarian Law, Italy, 2000), Didactics for College Education (VU University, Amsterdam, 1996–97), International Security (Clingendael Institute, The Hague, 1995), Political Journalism (Georgetown University, Washington DC, 1986), Modern Hebrew and Czech. He has published some 50 articles on international relations and on Soviet, CIS and Russian foreign and security developments, for example on the wars in Tajikistan and Chechenya. His articles were printed in the *Journal of Slavic Military Studies*, the *RAF Air Power Review*, the *Officer Magazine*, and for the Conflict Studies Research Centre of the British Defence Academy, as well as in a number of Dutch military-political journals.

From 2003 to 2004 Marcel de Haas was assigned to NATO School, Oberammergau, Germany, as Head of the Research Branch. From 1996 to 2003 he held the post of Lecturer in International Relations and International Law at the Royal Netherlands Military Academy. Before joining the RNLAF, from 1988 until 1998 he served as an officer in the Royal Netherlands Army, as a military-political analyst on the USSR, CIS, Russia, as well as on the former Yugoslavia. He started his military career in 1980 as an infantry conscript in the Dutch battalion of the United Nations Interim Force in Lebanon (UNIFIL). As an arms control inspector for the OSCE and for the CFE Treaty he has visited army and air force units of the Russian Federation and Belarus. He regularly presents lectures on international relations, international security and Russian studies at international conferences and for political, civic and military organizations.

GENERAL INDEX

AIR POWER INDEX